THE NOVEL
in
ENGLAND and GERMANY

A Comparative Study
by
H. R. KLIENEBERGER

OSWALD WOLFF
London

© 1981 Oswald Wolff (Publishers) Ltd. London

British Library Cataloguing in Publication Data

Klieneberger, H.R.
    The novel in England and Germany.
    1. English fiction – History and criticism
    2. German fiction – History and criticism
    I. Title
    823'.009   PR821

    ISBN 0-85496-079-1

Set by Robcroft Ltd. London
Printed by Billing & Sons Ltd. Guildford, Surrey

CONTENTS

ACKNOWLEDGEMENTS

I should like to thank the editors of *German Life and Letters*, *Oxford German Studies*, *Forum for Modern Language Studies*, *New German Studies* and the *Modern Language Review* for permission to reproduce material from articles of mine which first appeared in those periodicals, and University College Dublin for financial support.

Dublin, December 1980   H.R.K.

I

The Novel in the Age of Romanticism

1

There is no consensus as to what constitutes 'comparative literature'. For some critics it is primarily the study of the influence of one national literature on another or, more generally, the study of international literary relations. For other critics it is the study of themes, motifs and patterns common to several literatures, or the study of literary movements and of literary genres across boundaries of language and nationality. On occasions, the term 'comparative literature' has been stretched to include 'the comparison of literature with other spheres of human expression'.[1] What is attempted here is the study of national literatures as reflections of different political and economic environments, a type of comparative literature sometimes called 'comparative sociology of literature'. This term may not have been in use before Levin L. Schücking published *Die Soziologie der literarischen Geschmacksbildung* (The Sociology of the Formation of Literary Taste) in 1923, but the form of criticism it describes is very much older. As early as 1810, Mme de Staël practised comparative literature precisely in this sense when, in her book *De l'Allemagne*, she attributed the markedly individualistic tenor of German culture and the preponderance in it of metaphysics and lyrical poetry to the political disunity of Germany which had prevented the rise of a political and cultural élite, centred on a capital city, and had

7

produced instead a fragmented society where intellectuals lived and worked in relative isolation, without the opportunity of acquiring a wide experience of the world. Variants of Mme de Staël's diagnosis which we should now call sociological were advanced by German critics later in the nineteenth century to explain the absence, in Germany, of realistic fiction comparable to that produced in England, France, and Russia, and the growth, in place of it, of a prose-fiction exemplified by the 'Bildungsroman' (educational novel) which is concerned with the inner development of single individuals, and the 'Novelle' in which moral problems are frequently explored by means of allegory and symbolism in settings remote from contemporary social actualities. Otto Ludwig, for instance, pointed to the special contrast presented by the German tradition in prose fiction on the one hand, and the English tradition on the other. He admitted that he, like his German and unlike his English contemporaries, could depict with authority only a rural or small town milieu, but argued (as Mme de Staël had done) that German writers compensated for the lack of 'Extensität' (extensiveness) by greater 'Innerlichkeit' (inwardness).[2] And Wilhelm Dilthey argued, in an essay on Charles Dickens of 1877, that so detailed and extensive a grasp of empirical reality could have been acquired only by the citizen of a community with world-wide power and commitments, but he too echoed Mme de Staël in claiming that German writers compensated for the handicap of their provincial background and experience by greater 'Innerlichkeit'.[3]

The German social circumstances observed by Mme de Staël, which differed so greatly from those of England, had, of course, existed and been reflected in literature long before the age of Romanticism. Nor had Mme. de Staël been the first to perceive them. In 1764, Friedrich Gabriel Resewitz, the continuator of Lessing's *Briefe die neueste Litteratur betreffend* (Letters concerning the latest Literature), spoke of the helplessness of German writers who wished to depict the

German scene as English novelists had depicted that of England:

> Ohne Kenntniss der Welt, und ohne Kenntniss ihrer Nation, oft kaum mit ihrer kleinen Geburtsstadt recht bekannt, befinden sie sich gleich in einer dürren Wüste, sobald sie auch nur die Anlage zur Geschichte eines Romans machen sollen. Der Herr Schriftsteller hat ausser seines Vaters Hause eine Universität gesehen, ein paar Schulfreunde gekannt, ein paar Professoren in ihrer akademischen Würde von Ferne erblickt; und nun will er Sitten mahlen, und Charaktere schildern. Wo soll er sie hernehmen?[4]

> Without a knowledge of the world and without a knowledge of their nation, often barely familiar with the small town in which they were born, they find themselves in an arid desert as soon as they are to draw up a mere sketch for the story of a novel. Apart from his father's house, the author has seen a university, has known a few school-friends, has set eyes from afar on a few professors in their academic dignity, and now he wants to depict manners and portray characters. Where is he to take them from?

If Resewitz lacked the terminology of the twentieth century sociologist, he was yet able to see and explain why there had been no German Defoe and why the novel in the modern sense, which owes nothing to mythology and history, but seeks to render the daily lives of average comtemporary individuals, should have been pioneered in London: at that time, London was the largest and economically and politically most advanced city in the world, and Defoe had taken an active part, as a shopkeeper and manufacturer, a pamphleteer and journalist, in its expansion after the democratic revolution of 1688.

Although the German middle-classes could not have produced a Defoe, their enthusiastic response to *Robinson Crusoe* when, in 1720, it appeared in German translation, indicates that, however different their political situation, they shared the interests and aspirations of their English counterparts, as well as a Protestant ethos in process of secularization. The courtly romances and post-Baroque picaresque fictions which had dominated the German novel-market in the first two decades of the eighteenth century, now yielded to German imitations of the fictitious autobiography of Robinson, the individualist who believes that God's blessing is on those who seek to improve themselves by their own efforts. Some twenty German Crusoe-imitations appeared between 1720 and 1730, and several more in the following decades.[5] None of them achieved Defoe's grasp of the empirical, and it is revealing that the only German 'Robinson' which is credited with some distinction, J.G. Schnabel's *Wunderliche Fata einiger See-Fahrer* (Strange Fates of some Seafarers) 1731-43, re-published by Ludwig Tieck in 1828 as *Insel Felsenburg*, represents shipwreck on a desert island not as a peril to be resisted with courageous resourcefulness until deliverance arrives, but as an opportunity to establish an ideal community on what is presented as an idyllic refuge from a wicked world. The originality of the novel consists in its rendering of a Utopian vision, and in this respect it points forward to a tradition of German fiction to which Goethe, Stifter, and Raabe were to contribute.

The Robinson-vogue receded in the middle decades of the eighteenth century as Richardson began to make his impact on the German reading public. Defoe's particularity of portrayal was extended by Richardson from the sphere of the external circumstances of fictitious characters to that of their inner lives. *Pamela* appeared in German translation in 1742, *Clarissa* in 1748, and because of their high moral tone, these novels were acceptable to many who had previously regarded the reading of fiction with suspicion. The self-awareness in isolation of Richardson's heroines, their selectiveness in personal relationships, reflect a social process which had gone far only in London: the break-up of the traditional integrated community and the patriarchal family-system consequent on industrialization and the division of labour.

But Richardson's novels, being woman-centred and presenting the class-conflict of the age in terms of moral conflict between virtuous lower or middle-class heroines and vicious aristocrats, appealed to a predominantly feminine and bourgeois readership in every part of Europe, and the plots, revolving around courtship leading to marriage, set a pattern for a hundred and fifty years of European fiction.

It is noteworthy that the one novel which is represented in literary histories as standing out from a mass of German Richardson-imitations of poor quality, Ch. F. Gellert's *Das Leben der schwedischen Gräfin G.* (1747-8), should share with Schnabel's *Insel Felsenburg* a Utopian intention. The form of *Pamela* in which letters alternate with diary entries and other documentation, is copied by Gellert; but in contrast with Richardson's subtlety in the rendering of psychological processes, especially of the ambivalence in the lovers' feelings for each other, the characterization in Gellert's short novel is somewhat crude, and the plot is constructed with the ingredients of picaresque fiction: intrigue, adventure in distant places, and the return home from imprisonment of a character believed dead. But Gellert's primary interest is in tracing the emergence, from a series of interlocking love-relationships, of a community of superior spirits who renounce all passion in favour of Platonic friendship when blood-relationships, bigamous connections and other unlikely impediments come to light – an élite not unlike those which later practitioners of the German novel were to portray.

However, the principal eighteenth century initiator of a German tradition in fiction is not Gellert, but a rather more gifted prose-writer, Ch. M. Wieland who established the genre of the 'Bildungsroman', the educational novel. His *Die Geschichte des Agathon* (1766-7) is placed in ancient Greece, and its hero emerges, inexperienced and uncompromisingly idealistic, from the seclusion of a religious sanctuary, to discover that in the wider world priests are often hypocritical and politicians selfish and fraudulent. Agathon

11

comes to doubt the validity of his principles when he betrays the romantic love of his youth by lapsing into erotic adventures, and temporarily succumbs to the moral relativism propounded by Hippias. But after a period of near despair which is presented as a necessary stage in his growth towards maturity, Agathon adopts the synthesis of worldly wisdom and virtue, exemplified by the Socratic Archytas. The novel abounds in general reflections on religion and morality, and in dialogues between representatives of opposing philosophical view-points. It is, in a way, surprising to find that Wieland should claim in the preface to his novel that Fielding's *Tom Jones* served him as a model. Elsewhere he tells us that it was as the creator of mixed characters who found an absolute standard of moral purity to be unrealizable that Fielding appealed to him:

> Fielding belehrt uns, dass nicht alles lauter Gold sey, was gleisst, dass Engelreinigkeit von Sterblichen nicht gefordert werden sollte, dass man um einzelner Handlungen willen niemanden ganz verdammen müsse.[6]

> Fielding teaches us that not everything that glitters is pure gold, that angelic purity must not be demanded of mortals, that one must not condemn anyone totally because of single actions.

Wieland also follows Fielding's practice of distancing fictional characters by direct authorial comment. But, in fact, *Agathon* lacks the peculiar strengths of Fielding's fiction: the panoramic evocation of eighteenth century society, the zest for the actualities of its life. *Agathon* calls to mind, among English literary parallels, not Fielding but such unrepresentative fictions as W.S. Landor's *Imaginary Conversations* or Walter Pater's *Marius the Epicurean*. It is noteworthy that Lessing who praised *Agathon* highly, wondered whether it could be called a novel at all:

> Es ist der erste und einzige Roman für den denkenden Kopf, von klassischem Geschmack: Roman? Wir wollen ihm

diesen Titel nur geben; vielleicht dass es einige Leser mehr dadurch bekommt.[7]

It is the first and only novel for heads that think, of classical taste: a novel? Let us give it that title, perhaps it will get a few more readers because of it.

The book was to share the fate of many outstanding contributions to German fiction: it was acclaimed by creative writers and critics, but not widely read. Its place in the context of eighteenth century German literature is, however, secure; in presenting a young man's search, through trial and error, and without reference to convention, for a valid way of life, it provided a model for Goethe's *Wilhelm Meister*.

2

In the Richardsonian novel the registering of emotional nuances subserved a moral purpose; but in the later novel of sensibility the cultivation of feeling became an end in itself. In England, as in Germany, fictions became fashionable which were little more than imaginative self-projections of their authors; and, creating in this subjective genre, the isolated German man-of-letters was no longer at a disadvantage in comparison with his English counterpart; on the contrary. Resewitz argued that the very inability of the would-be German novelist to portray the external world made him take eagerly, by way of compensation, to the novel of sensibility as then practised:

Ein Roman geht gut ab; der Verleger nimmt ihn gern; solch ein *Thomas Jones* ist doch ein drollichtes Ding, das sich bey müssigen Stunden bald hinschreiben lässt. Die Feder wird angesetzt; das kleine Schulleben, auf dessen Schwänke man noch mit so vielem Wohlwollen zurückblickt, wird beschrieben; der Held geht auf die Universität, verliebt sich der Himmel weiss, in wen, und nun – ja nun, geräth die Arbeit ins Stecken! Der arme Schriftsteller martert sich. Was sollen nun

13

für Begebenheiten folgen? In welche Situationen soll er seinen Helden setzen? Wie die Geschichte verwickeln und den Leser interessieren? Er martert sich vergebens. Endlich wirft er aus Verzweiflung die Feder hin, ergreift, mit zer-knirschtem Geiste über die misslungene Arbeit, Youngs *Nachtgedanken*, wird wehmütig, vermuthlich über den fehl-gebohrnen Roman? Nicht doch; es sind moralische Empfin-dungen, hohe Begeisterungen! . . . Die Feder wird ergriffen; und die missgebohrnen Wesen, die den Kopf verwirrten und das Herz abdrücken wollten, fliessen stromweise in die Feder.[8]

There is a demand for fiction; the publisher will gladly take it; a *Tom Jones* is a comical thing that is soon written down in leisure hours. Pen is put to paper; one's petty school-life, those pranks one looks back on so indulgently, are described; the hero goes on to university, falls in love with Heaven knows whom, and then – well, then the work begins to flag. The poor author racks his brains. What incidents are to follow? In what situations is he to place his hero? How is the story to be elaborated and to arouse the reader's interest? He racks his brains in vain. At last he throws down his pen in despair, takes up, in a spirit of contrition because the novel has failed, Young's *Night Thoughts*, grows melancholy – presumably because of the abortive novel? Not at all, these are moral sentiments, exalted enthusiasms . . . The pen is taken up again; and the abortive creatures which confused his head and oppressed his heart, flow in torrents into his pen . . .

The best known English presentation of the lonely man who obeys the voice of his heart, speaking and acting spontaneously, in tragic defiance of a corrupt, dissembling society, Henry Mackenzie's *The Man of Feeling* (1771), could not compete with the German equivalent, Goethe's *Die Leiden des jungen Werther* (1774) (The Sorrows of Young Werther). The literary fashion of the seventeen-seventies favoured the German writer and his penchant; and Goethe's story, translated into the language of every literate country, achieved an international success, unequalled by any German novel before or since.

The unhappy love-affair of Werther, culminating in suicide, is set in a wide frame of philosophical reference. In his epistolary effusions, Werther reiterates that it is Lotte's naturalness which has charmed him, and he contrasts her simplicity, and also the simplicity of country-people, of children, with the soulless artificialities of bourgeois and aristocratic society. His passion for Lotte is doomed to frustration because it is in conflict with social convention which binds her to a good-natured but philistine bourgeois. In the spirit of Rousseau, the exaltation of natural man goes with the exaltation of nature as revealed in landscape. Central themes of Romantic and nineteenth-century German fiction are pioneered in the novel. The princely court with its pettiness and malignancy where Werther's frustration in his relationship with Lotte acquires a political dimension, was to be a recurrent feature of subsequent German fiction, as was the conflict of art and life, of the man of genius with philistinism. But if in Germany the issues raised in *Werther* were to remain topical for many decades, the impact of the book on the English public proved ephemeral. It is significant that Jane Austen whose work marks the transition from the eighteenth-century novel of manners to the social realism of the nineteenth century, should have started her career as a novelist, in the seventeen nineties, by satirizing *Werther* and the novel of sensibility, as well as the related genre of the Gothic novel in which German writers had also excelled. Admittedly, there was a reaction against the ethos of *Werther* in Germany also, not least in the later work of Goethe, but it took a different form. Inability to compromise, or accept limits, self-abandonment to the sphere of subjective feeling, of imagination as in *Werther*, was subsequently referred to by Goethe as diastole, the expanding movement of the heart which was of necessity succeeded by systole, the contracting movement.[9] The recoil from diastole, in the metaphorical sense, into systolic submission to society and the limitations it imposes, is the theme of *Wilhelm Meister* as of much subsequent German fiction.

In the first version, the fragmentary *Wilhelm Meisters theatralische Sendung* (1774-85), the hero deserts a commercial career to travel with a theatrical company, believing, with his contemporaries of the 'Sturm und Drang' (Storm and Stress) movement, that the poet, especially the dramatic poet, has a Messianic task, his mission being to create a national theatre. But on the other hand, in his situation between women who appeal to different facets of his personality, and in his generally passive rôle, he resembles Tom Jones and Agathon. In the fifth book of *Wilhelm Meister* where the differences between fiction and drama are discussed, Goethe appeals in this respect particularly to English precedents:

> Der Romanheld muss leidend, wenigstens nicht im hohen Grade wirkend sein; von dem dramatischen verlangt man Wirkung und Tat, Grandison, Clarisse, Pamela, der Landpriester von Wakefield, Tom Jones selbst sind,wo nicht leidende, doch retardierende Personen . . . [10]

> The hero of a novel must be passive or at least not in a high degree active, effectiveness and action are required of the hero of drama, but Grandison, Clarissa, Pamela, the Vicar of Wakefield, even Tom Jones, are, if not passive, at least characters who slow down the action . . .

Wilhelm Meisters theatralische Sendung has indeed a genuine affinity with *Tom Jones* in its lively characterization and rendering of contemporary social strata, but in the second version, *Wilhelm Meisters Lehrjahre* (1795-6) (Wilhelm Meister's Years of Apprenticeship), Goethe follows Wieland in constructing an allegory in which an exemplary educational process is traced. For in the intervening years, Goethe had entered his classical phase; he had abandoned his hopes for a cultural regeneration of German society, and now portrayed the cultivation of a timeless and cosmopolitan human ideal which isolated individuals, or perhaps an élite, might be inspired to emulate. In a conversation with Friedrich

16

von Müller in 1823, Goethe claimed that he was turning away, in his novel, from empirical reality to a Utopian vision because of the irremediable poverty of the material with which the German, as opposed to the English scene presented the novelist:

> Goethe bemerkte, dass er zu Marienbad und Karlsbad durchaus von keinem andern Autor als Byron und Scott habe sprechen hören. Aber Scotts Zauber ruhe auch auf der Herrlichkeit der drei britischen Königreiche und der unerschöpflichen Mannigfaltigkeit ihrer Geschichte, während in Deutschland sich nirgends . . . ein fruchtbares Feld für den Romanschreiber findet . . . [11]

> Goethe observed that at Marienbad and Karlsbad he had heard no authors other than Byron and Scott spoken of. But Scott's magic rested on the glory of the three British kingdoms and the inexhaustible diversity of their history, while in Germany a fruitful field for the novelist was nowhere to be found . . .

In the *Lehrjahre*, Wilhelm's involvement with the theatre is presented as a mistake, although, like his other mistakes, including successive love-relationships, an instructive one, in that it helps him to develop until he is ready to turn from diastole to systole, to engage in practical activity instead of aesthetic dilettantism, and so to become a 'Bürger' (bourgeois). The members of the 'Gesellschaft vom Turm' (Company of the Tower) not merely observe his progress but try to influence it in moments of crisis, not very effectively, however, so that in the end it appears that Wilhelm, making one mistake after another, has arrived spontaneously at the goal to which the members of the 'Gesellschaft' had sought to lead him. Nature and reason, we are given to understand, are not contradictory but complementary, and many of the aphorisms in which Goethe articulates his moods, which range from worldly shrewdness, cynicism even, to serene wisdom and, at times, to mystical faith, confirm this.

The first five books of the *Lehrjahre* contain, in a modified form, the bulk of the *Theatralische Sendung*; the last three books, which were written in the seventeen-nineties, are allegorical in character. In them, Mignon and the Harper, who appealed to Wilhelm as mysterious embodiments of an uncompromisingly poetic spirit, are explained away as pathological, and the three female figures who dominate the narrative, form a symmetrical pattern of ideal types: the 'schöne Seele' (beautiful soul) (Book 6) is presented as achieving inner harmony in a comtemplative and, therefore, one-sided mode; Therese achieves it too, but, by way of contrast, in a wholly practical life, while Nathalie as the perfect synthesis of the contemplative and the practical modes, becomes the wife of Wilhelm. In his *Life of Goethe*, G.H. Lewes writes to account for the fact 'that in England the novel is almost universally pronounced tedious':

> When we quit the parts which were written before the journey to Italy, and before the plan was altered – we arrive at characters such as Lothario, the Abbé, the Doctor, Teresa, and Natalie, and feel a totally new style is present. We have quitted the fresh air of Nature, and entered the philosopher's study; life is displaced by abstractions. Not only does the interest of the story seriously fall off, but the handling of the characters is entirely changed. The characters are described, they do not live. The incidents . . . have little vraisemblance and less interest . . . As the men and women are without passion, so is the style without colour . . . The mysterious Family in the Tower is an absurd mystification, without the redeeming interest which Mrs Radcliffe would have thrown into it.[12]

Lewes's strictures apply more forcibly still to the sequel, *Wilhelm Meisters Wanderjahre* (1821 and 1829) (Wilhelm Meister's Years of Travel) which is generally admitted to be a somewhat hurried collection of narrative pieces, of poems, and aphorisms, lacking coherence and consistency. The subordination of the individual to the community, proposed at the end of the *Lehrjahre*, is carried a stage further, and

Wilhelm becomes a doctor. There is a 'pädagogische Provinz', an elaborately hierarchical establishment, where boys are trained in 'Ehrfurcht' (reverence), an attitude, we are told, common to all the higher religions, but now threatened by political developments. However, the value of the educational methods described by Goethe are called in question when Felix, Wilhelm's son, representing the unpredictability of life, defies them. Finally, Wilhelm and the other members of the 'Gesellschaft vom Turm', now named 'die Entsagenden', the renunciants, prepare to emigrate to America where, in virgin territory, their projects would not meet opposition. The *Wanderjahre* include, however, two or three of the 'Novellen' which are perhaps Goethe's most distinguished contributions to prose-fiction.

The question as to whether the 'Novelle' constitutes a literary genre, distinct from that of the short story, has been discussed a good deal. Goethe's own definition of it as a 'sich ereignete unerhörte Begebenheit'[13] (an unheard of incident that has happened), clearly fits many prose-narratives that have never been called 'Novellen'; and other characteristics that have on various occasions been ascribed to the 'Novelle', the 'Rahmentechnik' (framework technique), the 'Wendepunkt' (turning-point), and the 'Dingsymbol' (an animal, such as the falcon of Paul Heyse's theory, or an inanimate object, functioning as a symbol), are not present in all German 'Novellen' and may be found in the *Arabian Nights* and elsewhere. But in so far as these terms, in combination, point to certain dramatic and poetic qualities, generally found in German 'Novellen', they may be of use. In any case, whether or not the 'Novelle' differs significantly from the short story, the fact is that many eminent German writers of prose-fiction eschewed the novel, or attempted it once or twice only, and turned instead to this shorter form where there is no scope for the rendering of a society, but where a poetic style and a metaphysical intention could help to compensate for an absence of empirical reality. The 'Novelle', like the 'Bildungs-

19

roman', constitutes therefore a characteristic German contribution to prose-fiction, and if Goethe did not initiate the tradition, he certainly helped to give it currency.

Renunciation of passion is a principal theme of the *Wanderjahre*, and of each of the 'Novellen' contained within the novel. In the most ambitious of them, *Der Mann von fünfzig Jahren*, the hero, as the title indicates, is a type rather than an individual, a middle-aged man who seeks to recover his youth through union with a young girl. She reciprocates his love, but the affair which ensues is presented as contrary to nature. After suffering considerably, she therefore learns to transfer her feelings from the father to the son. And the man of fifty, in turn, accepts his supposed biological limitations by forming a relationship with a woman of his own age. While Goethe makes some attempt to sketch in a contemporary social background of country-estates and minor nobility, the strength of the 'Novelle' lies in its lyrical evocation of feeling and a delicate poetic symbolism. As for its message, it suffices, perhaps, to bear in mind that in his own life, Goethe conspicuously refused to practise what he preaches here. Another late story, published separately, is actually entitled 'Novelle'. It was originally planned as an epic poem, and the completed prose-version retains a fairy-tale atmosphere and an allegorical structure. It possesses a 'Dingsymbol' in the lion: as Honorio, the principal character, gives way to his illicit passion for the princess, a fire breaks out in the market-place and a lion escapes from his cage. In the end a child, representing innocence and the arts, approaches the lion singing and playing a flute, and so subdues him, while Honorio overcomes his own violent inclinations. The story concludes with some rhyming stanzas in which the moral is pointed. It is evident, therefore, that after his early ventures into a contemporary mode (in *Werther* and the first version of *Wilhelm Meister*, the *Theatralische Sendung*), Goethe cultivated only non-realistic forms of prose-fiction, for reasons which he himself, as we saw, went to some length to justify. His 'Bildungsroman' and his 'Novellen' gave a strong impetus to Romantic and post-Romantic fiction in Germany, but found few readers in England, in spite of Thomas Carlyle's efforts on their behalf. Running counter to the prevailing trend in European fiction, they were denied the international recognition accorded to *Werther*.

3

In his *Life and Opinions of Tristram Shandy* (1760-67), Lawrence Sterne enriched the novel of sensibility with wit and humour without reducing its pathos, and the success of Sterne with the German reading public in the seventeen-seventies equalled that of earlier English novelists. Like Defoe and Fielding, Sterne excelled in the lifelike rendering of social milieux, and he surpassed Richardson in the recording of subtle shifts of feeling: his characters are comic and pathetic in turn as, with their obsessive idiosyncrasies and 'hobby-horses', they talk and live past each other. Sterne parodies the novel-form: the fictitious autobiography starts, not with the birth, but with the begetting of the hero, the accidents and coincidences which brought him into being and determined his subsequent development. The order of what is set out depends, not on chronological sequence but on the flux of ideas and feelings in the narrator's mind; and the pedantic zeal with which he pursues the associations and connections that occur to him, is the source of endless comic digressions. *Tristram Shandy* was a welcome model for many German writers, for it allowed them to depict the narrow circumstances with which they were familiar, to dispense with consecutive narrative and to communicate their own views and reflections when their creative impulse weakened. The best-known of the German imitators of Sterne, Theodor Gottlieb von Hippel, limits himself, in his *Lebensläufe in aufsteigender Linie* (1778-81) (Curricula Vitae in an ascending Line), to an account of his own childhood and youth, and to the portrayal of the lives of relatives and friends. Learned digressions and philosophical reflections abound in the book but are presented without Sterne's irony at the expense of his pedantic narrator. Like Sterne, Hippel introduces himself as a character into the novel and discusses its merits with real and imagined readers as he is writing it. Other English influences, especially those of Thomas Gray and Edward Young (*Night Thoughts*), are apparent in numerous graveyard scenes and lyrical passages on the subject of death. Hippel is important mainly because his example, along with that of Sterne, inspired Jean Paul to take up the writing of prose-fiction. Following them, Jean Paul includes narrators and readers, and himself, among the characters of his fiction and keeps them in dialogue with each other, with the purpose of breaking down the dividing line between fiction and reality. His digressions reveal a far wider range of knowledge and interests than Sterne's or even Hippel's, and he goes beyond his models in constantly tracing resemblances between disparate phenomena. Indeed, a confusing proliferation of metaphors, a vocabulary which is often abstruse, and an intransparent sentence-structure, make him difficult to read. In his *Vorschule der Ästhetik* (1804) (Primer of Aesthetics), Jean Paul claims a metaphysical purpose for his practices: the discovery of points of comparison between heterogeneous phenomena, he argues, is of the quintessence of wit and an assertion of mind over matter. (§ § 32, 42-55)'Der Humor . . . vernichtet . . . das Endliche durch den Kontrast mit der Idee' (§ 32) (Humour . . . destroys . . . the finite through contrast with the idea). The tendency of Jean Paul's wit to reduce, by paradoxical comparisons, the elements which differentiate phenomena from each other, is closely related to the experience which he attributes to his heroes and heroines in their moments of exaltation: that of everything finite and contingent in reality giving way to a mystical sense of infinity and universal oneness. This experience which is akin, of course, to the nature-pantheism in the work of Rousseau and in Goethe's *Werther*, is articulated in a metaphor-laden prose-style of such suggestiveness and intoxicating musicality that it prompted Stefan George, in the eighteen-nineties, to proclaim Jean Paul the precursor of European Symbolism.[14]

The central figures of Jean Paul, idealists, dreamers, enthusiasts, at loggerheads with prosaic reality and a philistine society, derive, not from Sterne, but from Rousseau and the 'Sturm und Drang' movement with its cult of genius. Jean Paul's men are, like Werther, artistically inclined and take their place in a long German tradition of writing which has the conflict of the artist and the bourgeois for its theme. That conflict as set out in Goethe's *Werther*, met with a temporary response in France and England, in the era of sensibility, but was to remain a central theme of German fiction throughout the nineteenth century. For in Germany, Hofmannsthal once wrote, the educated individual found himself 'vainly awakened to freedom' in the age of enlightenment, being denied outlets in active political life, available to his counterparts in England and, after the Revolution, in France. Jean Paul, in Hofmannsthal's words, gave expression to the

> Begierde, Sehnsucht und Verzweiflung, ja Raserei des Einzelnen, der sich von dem grellen Licht der allgemeinen Aufklärung zu einer vergeblichen Freiheit geweckt sieht – wie sie das eigentliche innere Erlebnis der Deutschen zu Ende des achtzehnten Jahrhunderts war, unabgeleitet durch Tatkraft, unbegleitet von dem Vermögen, an der Welt ringsum etwas zu verändern.[15]

> desire, longing and despair, indeed, the frenzy, of the individual who saw himself awakened by the dazzling light of the general Enlightenment to a vain freedom, not directed into action, and without the capacity to change anything in the surrounding world: this was the essential inner experience of Germans at the end of the eighteenth century.

The world of German princely courts, briefly introduced in Goethe's *Werther*, is the scene of Jean Paul's *Die unsichtbare*

Loge (1793), *Hesperus* (1795) and *Titan* (1800-03). Here the young idealist and man of genius is confronted with aristocratic opportunists and intriguers. In other novels, set in self-governing townships, the opposition to genius is bourgeois, and in depicting it, Jean Paul deploys an empirical realism of a kind that had eluded his German predecessors and contemporaries. However, Jean Paul chose not to develop his gift for realistic characterization and milieu-description but to exercize it marginally in his work; for, unlike the English novelists, he does not accept the empirical world on its own terms but presents it disparagingly as an obstacle in the path of his heroes who seek to transcend it. In *Siebenkäs* (1796-7), the petit-bourgeois world of Kuh-schnappel is the instrument of the hero's daily martyrdom, as is his marriage. Love, in Jean Paul's view, is based on a delusion of the imagination and cannot survive in the everyday world of married life. *Siebenkäs* was never completed, and it is hard to believe that Jean Paul could have convinced himself or any reader that his hero's desertion of the well-intentioned but uncomprehending Lenette for the exalted Natalie would result in happiness rather than a variant of the earlier misery. The sphere of imagination and that of empirical reality are incompatible in Jean Paul. While the whimsical characters of Sterne are reconciled to their circumstances, those of Jean Paul who are often said to derive from them, *Schulmeisterlein Wuz* (1793) and *Quintus Fixlein* (1796), achieve their satisfaction by imagining reality to be something other than it is. Jean Paul writes:

Ich konnte nie mehr als drei Wege, glücklicher (nicht glück-lich) zu werden, auskundschaften. Der erste, der in die Höhe geht, ist: so weit über das Gewölbe des Lebens hinauszu-dringen, dass man die ganze äussere Welt mit ihren Wolfs-gruben, Beinhäusern und Gewitterableitern von Weitem unter seinen Füssen nur wie ein eingeschrumpftes Kinder-gärtchen liegen sieht. – Der zweite ist: gerade herabzufallen ins Gärtchen und da sich so einheimisch in eine Furche

24

einzunisten, dass, wenn man aus seinem warmen Lerchennest hinaussieht, man ebenfalls keine Wolfsgruben, Beinhäuser und Stangen, sondern nur Ähren erblickt, deren jede für den Nestvogel ein Baum und ein Sonnen- und Regenschirm ist. – Der dritte endlich – den ich für den schwersten und klügsten halte – ist der: mit den beiden andern zu wechseln.[16]

I could never spy out more than three ways to become happier (not happy). The first, which leads upward, is: to push so far beyond the vault of life that one can see the entire external world with its wolf-traps, charnel-houses and lightning-conductors from far off, beneath one's feet, like the shrunken little garden of a child. – The second is: to fall straight down into the little garden and make oneself at home there in a furrow so that, when looking out of one's warm lark's nest one doesn't see wolf-traps, charnel-houses and stakes either, but only ears of corn, each of which is a tree and a screen from sun and rain for the bird in its nest. – And the third way – which I regard as the hardest and wisest – is to alternate between the other two ways.

The third way is taken by Walt in *Flegeljahre* (1804-05) (Years of Indiscretion). In that novel it becomes apparent that the way of the 'Käuze', the eccentrics, and the way of the 'hohe Charaktere', the idealistic enthusiasts, between which Walt alternates, have in common a hypertrophy of the imagination. For if the eccentrics are content because they live in a world of illusion, the enthusiasts undergo that enormous inner excitement which transports them above and beyond reality most often when they try to anticipate, in their imagination, the experience they yearn for. Admittedly, in *Titan* where Jean Paul flirts with the tradition of the 'Bildungsroman', the hero, Albano, finally comes to aspire to an involvement in the life of the world, but this is not described or enacted in the novel. A corresponding systole, following the powerfully rendered diastole, is promised but not realized in the case of Walt in *Flegeljahre*. Jean Paul is more plausible in the passages in which he expatiates on the inadequacy of finite reality and points to death as the only way out for his 'hohe Charaktere'. Jean Paul's ecstatic scenes in lyrical prose usually culminate in the formulation of a death-wish, even when the occasion is a lovers' tryst. For in Jean Paul, this is not as a rule an encounter between empirical individuals but a mystical union of two people with the divine in nature. In *Hesperus*, for instance, Viktor and Klothilde, having admitted their love for each other, are left

einsam in der ausgeleerten, dämmernden Unermesslichkeit, geblendet vom Thränenschimmer und vom Sonnenglanz, übertäubt vom Himmelsbrausen und vom Echo der Philomel, und erhalten von Gott im Ersterben aus Wonne.[17]

lonely in the emptied, twilit immensity, blinded by the gleam of tears and the sun's splendour, stunned by the roar of the sky and the echo of Philomel, and sustained by God in dying with bliss.

Hippel's eighteenth-century sentimentality about death and dying is carried by Jean Paul to orgiastic lengths; but it is characteristic of this highly intelligent writer that he should show himself aware of the questionable aspect of his tendency. Emanuel, the teacher of Viktor and Klotilde in *Hesperus*, who has worked up towards his death as to a consummation to be staged before an audience, is shown as suspecting, before he actually dies, that all his preparations had been 'bloss ein anderer, mit dem Zaubertrank der Phantasie vermischter Genuss des Lebens'[18] (only another way to relish life, by means of the magic potion of imagination).

Jean Paul's awareness of his own morbidity is evident also in the figure of Roquairol (*Titan*) who lives for the sake of experiencing sensations, using other people ruthlessly as means, acting out one adopted rôle after another until he kills himself while acting the part of a suicide on stage. Roquairol and Albano who love and hate each other are equally under the spell of their imaginations. And though Albano is endorsed because of his warm-heartedness and Roquairol is critically distanced because of his coldness, it is clear that the two characters represent different sides of Jean Paul's own divided personality. The warmth of Jean Paul is apparent not only in the sympathy he expresses in all the novels with the suffering of his characters, especially if this is due to social maladjustment, but also in frequent authorial asides to the reader who may have suffered similarly and who is offered consolation and encouragement. Jean Paul's coldness, on the other hand, is articulated by the so-called humorists who are associated as friends with the enthusiasts – Leibgeber with Siebenkäs (in *Siebenkäs*), Schoppe with Albano (in *Titan*) and Vult with Walt (in *Flegeljahre*). Where the enthusiasts, like the eccentrics, are sustained by illusion, the humorists who are presented as hypersensitive, seek to protect themselves against the shock of disappointment by renouncing the idealizing imagination and exposing satirically every human endeavour. Their alienation from reality involves self-alienation, and the problem of personal identity which troubled Tristram Shandy becomes in the case of Schoppe in *Titan* an existential terror which drives him insane.

If there is much in the novels that is original and of considerable psychological interest and value, Jean Paul is handicapped in communicating it by his incapacity for constructing plots. In *Die unsichtbare Loge*, *Hesperus* and *Titan*, we encounter identical constellations of characters, reflecting the contradictions in the author's personality, and to help along what little action there is, Jean Paul depends on the machinery of the popular fiction of his day. Goethe had drawn on the same sources for the conflagrations, robber-bands, kidnappings, and the pervasive manipulations of a mysterious secret society, in *Wilhelm Meister*. A secret society, with similar functions to that in *Wilhelm Meister*, figures in *Die unsichtbare Loge*; and in *Hesperus* and *Titan*, Jean Paul goes beyond Goethe and many a 'Gothic' tale of the period in puzzling and mystifying the reader by concealing until the end the relationships which exist between his characters. In *Titan*, moreover, there are unidentified agents who confuse and misdirect the hero from time to time with animated waxworks, disembodied voices and other auditory and visual phenomena, which are ostensibly of supernatural origin but turn out to be mechanically contrived. Jean Paul's talent for discursive prose, on the other hand, is evident in the many shrewd and illuminating reflections, often constituting entire essays, which are scattered through his fiction, and also in his theoretical works, especially the *Vorschule der Ästhetik* which marks an advance on the aesthetic writings of Lessing and Herder. The lyrical passages in his fiction which anticipate, with their fusion of musical effects and visual imagery, the 'poèmes en prose' of Baudelaire and the Symbolists, so impressed Stefan George and Karl Wolfskehl that when they brought out their three-volume anthology of German poetry (*Deutsche Dichtung*, 1901-03), they devoted an entire volume to extracts from Jean Paul. Expressionist and Surrealist poets have spoken of their indebtedness to his evocations of dreams. And yet the difficulties of his style and of his manner of presentation make his novels hard to read through. There is material in all of them, especially in *Siebenkäs*, which indicates that Jean Paul had the makings of a realistic novelist, yet he never became one. For his attitude to the empirical world is negative: everyday reality and ordinary humanity are presented satirically, and the principal characters are endorsed when they aspire beyond the finite to death and eternity. Jean Paul's influence on English writers has consequently been negligible, although Carlyle translated and publicized him, as he did Goethe. *Sartor Resartus* in which Carlyle echoed some themes and mannerisms of Jean Paul, is a dead end in English fiction. In Germany, however, where Jean Paul voiced the frustrations of middle-class intellectuals in the petty principalities which were to survive for many decades, his influence can be traced in the prose-fiction of the Romantics and of later writers.

While the greatest German novelist of the Romantic era, Jean Paul, made frequent use of motifs derived from Gothic terror-fiction and gave a fresh lease of life to the novel of sensibility, the major English novelist of the period, Jane Austen, burlesqued both genres in her earliest work. In *Love and Freindship*, an epistolary novel in which the lack of self-awareness in the heroines of romance, the cultivation of sentiment at the expense of reality and truth, are satirically exposed, one character remarks of another that he was 'sensible, well-informed, and agreeable'; however, 'we did not pretend to judge of such trifles, but as we were convinced he had no soul, that he had never read the Sorrows of Werther, and that his Hair bore not the least resemblance to auburn, we were certain that Janetta could feel no affection for him, or at least that she ought to feel none'.[19] The opening of *Love and Freindship* is reminiscent of the openings of *Hesperus* and *Titan*, where heroes and heroines of mysterious, exotic ancestry and antecedents in England, Spain and elsewhere, take up residence in a provincial corner of the reader's homeland on coming of age; but the tradition which was assimilated uncritically by Jean Paul, is ridiculed by Jane Austen whose heroine writes: 'My Father was a native of Ireland and an inhabitant of Wales; my Mother was the natural Daughter of a Scotch peer by an Italian Opera-girl – I was born in Spain and received my Education at a Convent in France. When I reached my eighteenth Year I was recalled by my Parents to my paternal roof in Wales'.[20] And as the title of Jane Austen's first novel indicates, its theme is that high-falutin' but egocentric cult of friendship, indulged in by men and women who regard themselves as 'great souls' – the 'hohe Charaktere' of Jean Paul.

In *Northanger Abbey* (written in 1798-9 and published posthumously in 1818), the principal character, Catherine Morland, is said to have had her imagination poisoned by

Gothic tales, some of which are of German origin or have German settings: Peter Teutold's *The Necromancer, or The Tale of the Black Forest*, Mrs Parson's *The Castle of Wolfenbach*, and Eleanor Sleuth's *The Orphan of the Rhine* are mentioned.[21] Jane Austen contrasts the women-characters of romance ironically with Catherine who captivates Henry Tilney, not with the usual 'kinship of soul', but with a naive pliability which appeals to his brand of schoolmaster's vanity. Henry's guidance, and a residue of good sense, enable Catherine eventually to see through the deceitful Isabella Thorne, and to realize that the people and circumstances at Northanger Abbey do not in fact resemble those in *The Mysteries of Udolpho*, that 'charming as were Mrs Radcliffe's works, and charming as were the works of all her imitators, it was not in them perhaps that human nature, at least in the midland counties of England, was to be looked for'.[22] The malignant intrigues of the Thorpes, mundane though they are, turn out, in the end, to be more spine-chilling than the 'alarms of romance',[23] and General Tilney hurts Catherine more deeply with his everyday mercenary schemes than he would have done in that rôle of Ogre of the Gothic Castle which she had at first ascribed to him.

Conflict between a tendency to give free rein to imagination, to spontaneous feeling (diastole) and a tendency to restrain both in the interest of social maturity (systole), figures as a central theme in all the literature of the later eighteenth century; it is as pervasive in the fiction of Jane Austen as it is in that of Goethe and Jean Paul. But in her treatment of the theme, Jane Austen had the advantage over her German contemporaries of being able to present and resolve it in terms of observed social reality. In the novel which was drafted in epistolary form as *Elinor and Marianne* in the seventeen-nineties and published in a revised version as *Sense and Sensibility* in 1811, Jane Austen shows up the limitations of either quality when cultivated in isolation. Marianne is led into grave errors of judgment by her insistence on intensity of feeling for poetry and landscape, on freedom and sincerity of expression, and learns that in Willoughby to whom she is attracted because he seems to excel in these qualities, an unrestrained indulgence of spontaneity has become the moral irresponsibility of the spoiled child: the devotee of sensibility is not the heroic idealist at war with mercenary utilitarianism which he imagines himself to be, but is dependent on money to sustain his life-style, and not scrupulous as to how he obtains it. While under his spell, Marianne is betrayed into self-contradiction too, learning to practise secrecy and dissimulation towards her own sister whom she had criticized for her lack of candour. Marianne discovers that she has become guilty not only of 'imprudence towards myself' but of 'want of kindness to others',[24] for she has tyrannically imposed her moods on them and treated them with contempt if they were unable to share her aesthetic tastes.

Elinor, on the other hand, who combines urbanity with self-control and is always considerate towards others, over-values rationality to the point where she fails to perceive the calculating ruthlessness in ostensibly prudent people like the Steeles and the Dashwoods. Both sisters misjudge Mrs Jennings: Marianne writes her off because of her ignorance of literature and the arts, her lack of refinement, and Elinor looks down on her as a vulgar chatter-box who wears her heart on her sleeve. Yet Mrs Jennings turns out to be both kind and shrewd, and it is due to her intervention that tragedy is averted. The sisters gravitate in the end towards a delicate equilibrium between urbanity and emotional sincerity, social poise and moral independence, which is not schematically posited by Jane Austen but worked out in a plausibly rendered milieu in which the fates of minor characters illuminate the central issues.

Where the religiosity of Goethe and Jean Paul tends towards a pantheistic mysticism and goes with a relative indifference towards the empirical life of ordinary people,

31

Jane Austen's is an Anglican Christianity, modified by the Evangelical movement of her time: it comes out in her keen attention to seemingly commonplace people in whom minute fluctuations of character, expressed in dialogue and action, are shown to have serious and far-reaching effects. Her very closeness to the observed particulars of daily life is, in fact, a condition of that subtlety and maturity of moral discernment in her fiction, which is without parallel in German literature contemporary with hers. What in *Mansfield Park* are called 'the less common acquirements of self-knowledge, generosity and humility',[25] have for her a supernatural sanction, and are always vindicated, but qualities other than the central Christian ones appear now in a favourable, now in an unfavourable light, for the context in which they figure is as variable in her novels as it is in life. Wit and charm, for instance, are endorsed in the case of Elizabeth Bennet in *Pride and Prejudice*, but viewed as meretricious in that of the worldly Mary Crawford in *Mansfield Park* who admits to Edmund and Fanny in a passing moment of self-criticism that 'you have all so much more *heart* among you than one finds in the world at large. You all give me a feeling of being able to trust and confide in you, which, in common intercourse, one knows nothing of'.[26] In *Sense and Sensibility*, vivacity goes with fecklessness in Willoughby, and integrity with a gauche manner in the inarticulate Edward Ferrars, but in *Persuasion*, Captain Wentworth combines moral worth with a good physical presence and a gift of repartee. In *Pride and Prejudice*, the critical disposition of the Bingley sisters is accompanied by conceit and snobbery, and is destructive, but Jane Bennet who in contrast with them is always charitable in her judgments, appears insensitive and, indeed, dull, because she fails to remark actual differences between other people. Vulgarity of manner is often indicted, but when it is linked with kind-heartedness, as in Mrs Jennings in *Sense and Sensibility* and Miss Bates in *Emma*, the contempt for it expressed by other characters in the novels appears odiously snobbish. The indulgence of love at the expense of prudence is frequently exposed as irresponsible, but of Anne Elliott, in *Persuasion*, we read: 'she had been forced into prudence in her youth, she learned romance as she grew older – the natural sequel of an unnatural beginning',[27] and Captain Wentworth has to learn to distinguish between the 'darings of heedlessness and the darings of a collected mind',[28] before he can appreciate Anne's past conduct. Jane Austen shows a particularly sympathetic insight into the anguish of those characters who are condemned to live in the shadow of aggressively self-confident relatives; Fanny Price in *Mansfield Park*, Anne Elliott in *Persuasion*, emerge Cinderella-like from obscurity, and are vindicated, as their persecutors fall victim to their own folly; and in *Emma*, the heroine abandons her egocentric belief in her own superiority on discovering that she has misjudged the feelings of others, and caused them serious harm by her interventions in their lives.

Jane Austen's novels could, indeed, be called educational novels though they bear little resemblance to the 'Bildungsromane' of Goethe or Jean Paul. For where the conversions of Marianne and Elinor, of Elizabeth Bennet, Darcy and Emma, take place in a vividly rendered social context, the ideal of harmony towards which Wilhelm Meister gropes his way, remains a shadowy abstraction as does the society which he enters, while the heroes and heroines of Jean Paul seek to transcend mystically a society which is never rendered objectively and in the round, but is only introduced intermittently for the purposes of satire and disparagement. In contrast with Goethe and Jean Paul, Jane Austen writes as a member of the society to which her readers and, indeed, her fictional characters belong, even if those who, like Fanny Price in *Mansfield Park*, have sufficient inner resources to be able to form independent opinions and to dispense with the constant companionship of others, are compared favourably with socialites, like Mary Crawford, who cannot do so. But in fragmented Germany there was no society which could accept itself as Jane Austen's closely knit families of landowners and naval officers, of clergymen and businessmen did, aware that they constituted the homogeneous élite of what was then the leading nation in the world. If the conflict between subjective aspirations and the claims of the external world forms the initial theme of all three writers, Jane Austen handled it with a psychological and social realism which was not available to her German contemporaries; she was therefore able not merely to state a theoretical resolution of the conflict as Goethe and Jean Paul did, but to let it be enacted by the characters of her novels.

5

Where Jane Austen was therefore able to provide models for the practitioners of social realism in the later nineteenth century, the influence of Goethe and Jean Paul was confined to the prose-writers of the German Romantic movement and their successors. But here it proved decisive. In each of the 'Bildungsromane' of the Romantics, just as in *Wilhelm Meister*, a young man sets out from a conventional and frustrating existence to travel in search of spiritual fulfilment; there is a similar constellation of representative characters surrounding the hero, including, as a rule, a variant of the Mignon-figure. Tieck, Novalis, Brentano, Arnim and Eichendorff follow Goethe's practice of interspersing prose-narratives with lyrical poems and discursive passages. In other respects they were the heirs of Jean Paul. What came to be known as 'Romantic irony' had been practised by those 'humorist' figures in the novels of Jean Paul who were the detached spectators not only of other people's lives but of their own. And the preoccupation of the Romantics with the sphere of dreams and with music as the pathway to mystical experience had been anticipated by Jean Paul. It was in 1797 that

Friedrich Schlegel defined 'romantische Poesie' (romantic poetry) as 'progressive Universalpoesie' (progressive universal poetry) in the second issue of *Athenäum* (Fragment 116). And though it could be argued that Jean Paul had already come nearer than anyone before or since to realizing Schlegel's programme of an art-form in which prose, poetry, music and criticism were to mingle in unending progression, the writers who now called themselves the Romantics, were determined to differentiate themselves from their predecessors. As Jean Paul – and, for that matter, Goethe, apart from his one venture into literature about 'knights in armour', the play *Götz von Berlichingen* of 1773 – had avoided the mediaevalizing of the popular Gothic fiction of the period while drawing many other motifs from it, the Romantics now made this peculiarly their own.

An 'altdeutsche Zeit' (German antiquity) was evoked in the *Herzensergiessungen eines kunstliebenden Klosterbruders* (Effusions from the Heart of an Art-loving Monk) by Wilhelm Heinrich Wackenroder which Ludwig Tieck published with additions of his own in the autumn of 1796, and in Tieck's *Franz Sternbald's Wanderungen* of 1798. In these two fictions, the age portrayed is that of Albrecht Dürer. In Novalis's *Heinrich von Ofterdingen*, published posthumously in 1802, references to castles and knights, to the crusades and to some historical figures, indicate that the period of the action is the thirteenth century. But the intention is clearly not to provide authentic period-flavour but to contrast an idealized past in which art and religion are believed to have flourished in mutual harmony, with a godless, rationalistic present.

The artist now figures once again, as he did in the 'Sturm und Drang' era, as the inspired prophet in whose work the divine essence of the world manifests itself. And if he fails to gain recognition on these terms, it is his environment that is assumed to be at fault. While the Romantics imitate the form of *Wilhelm Meister*, they reject its call for the submission of the artist to a society with predominantly practical interests; instead, they revert to the pattern of *Werther*: an inevitable conflict between the artist and his environment is postulated, as well as conflict within him, and extremes of suffering due to isolation and real and imagined persecution. The musician Berglinger, for instance, in the 'Novelle' included in Wackenroder's *Herzensergiessungen*, and Tieck's Sternbald, are afflicted with hypertrophy of the imagination and an excessive sensibility which leave them unfit for the requirements of daily life, and both artists regard their vocation ambivalently, as a curse and a blessing combined.

Where the plot of *Sternbald's Wanderungen* is concerned, Tieck, like Goethe and Jean Paul, operates with the familiar machinery of the popular Gothic novel; and his characters, too, are book-derived, except for the central figure, a self-portrait. However, the superiority of Sternbald, as of Berglinger, to those who are not committed to art, is presupposed; and so, for all their introspection, Wackenroder and Tieck fail to communicate any realistic insight into the psychological causality and significance of their contempt for and dissociation from ordinary life, the withdrawal into fantasy, which they describe. Similarly, their mystical conception of art prevents them from rationally elucidating the actual processes, within the individual and in society, which bring about the production of poems and paintings. Subjectivism, therefore, became dominant once again in German literature at the very time when Jane Austen was exposing the delusions on which it thrived; and it now received encouragement from concurrent developments in German philosophy. Fichte's message of the primacy of the human mind over the external world, Schelling's apotheosis of art, proved powerful intoxicants for authors, predisposed to compensate in the imagination for the frustrations of real life.

Novalis who, unlike Wackenroder and Tieck, had engaged in philosophical studies at university before taking up the writing of fiction, carried the subjectivism of the period to its furthest limits in his fragment *Heinrich von Ofterdingen*, a mixture of prose-narrative and lyrical poetry, of allegory and philosophical speculation. The first part of the novel presents a series of encounters between Heinrich, on his journey from Eisenach to Augsburg, and various symbolical figures who reveal to him one representative sphere of human experience after another, and thereby educate him for that poetic calling which had – it is suggested – been latent in him from the start. The merchants with whom he travels introduce him to the sphere of commercial life and at the same time give him a first inkling of the rôle of art by relating two tales about ancient poets with magic powers. While resting in a castle, Heinrich is informed by crusading knights about the sphere of heroic action; and the contrasting sphere of poetic suffering, symbolically associated with the Orient, is disclosed to him by a Mignon-figure, the captive Moorish girl Zulima. A miner, who is a mystical geologist, reveals to him the sphere of nature, and a hermit who has withdrawn from a successful worldly career into a cave, speaks to him of the mystery of human history. In Augsburg, at a festive banquet, Heinrich learns to appreciate the pleasures of conviviality as one of the formative human experiences. Klingsohr, the poet, makes him acquainted with the problems of poetic creativity, while Klingsohr's daughter, Mathilde, initiates him into sexual love as a quasi-religious experience. The programmatic character of the encounters is stressed by Klingsohr in his conversations with Heinrich:

> Das Land der Poesie, das romantische Morgenland, hat Euch mit seiner süssen Wehmut begrüsst, der Krieg hat Euch mit seiner wilden Herrlichkeit angeredet, und die Natur und die Geschichte sind Euch unter der Gestalt eines Bergmanns und eines Einsiedlers begegnet.[29]

> The land of poetry, the romantic Orient, has greeted you with its sweet sadness, war has spoken to you in its wild glory, and you have encountered nature and history in the guise of a miner and a hermit.

With reference to the union of Heinrich with Mathilde, and its significance, Klingsohr remarks: 'Liebe und Treue werden Euer Leben zur ewigen Poesie machen'[30] (Love and loyalty will turn your life into eternal poetry). The analogical correspondence between the contrasting spheres of experience to which Heinrich has been progressively exposed, is made explicit on other occasions. The hermit, for instance, traces a parallel between the disposition of the minerals in the ground and that of the stars in the sky, as the two spheres revealing to geologists and astrologers respectively the past and the future of the world: 'Jenen ist der Himmel das Buch der Zukunft, während euch die Erde Denkmale der Urwelt zeigt'[31] (To them the sky is the book of the future, while to you the earth shows monuments of the original world). The discoveries of Galvani which suggested to Novalis and some of his contemporaries that electricity and magnetism were non-material phenomena affecting matter, are invoked repeatedly in support of the mystical view that everything in the universe is animated and intimately related to man.

Novalis seeks to make plausible his vision of a world-unity, transcending all appearance of diversity, the concept that the external world is contained within the self and that the human self is omnipresent in the external world, by presenting Heinrich's discovery of the different spheres of human experience as a form of self-discovery: the journey outward becomes a journey home – 'nach Hause'[32] – by means of a peculiar narrative device: that of the premonitory dream which anticipates each crucial new experience of Heinrich so that what actually happens in his waking life is a repetition, and stirs up memories in him.

It is Novalis's ambition that the story of Heinrich's development into a poet should convey not only the ultimate meaning of existence but the history of humanity, past, present and to come, as the youth in the second of the merchants' tales sums it up when he sings

38

von dem Ursprunge der Welt, von der Entstehung der Gestirne, der Pflanzen, Tiere und Menschen, von der allmächtigen Sympathie der Natur, von der uralten goldenen Zeit und ihren Beherrscherinnen, der Liebe und Poesie, von der Erscheinung des Hasses und der Barbarei und ihren Kämpfen mit jenen wohltätigen Göttinnen, und endlich von dem zukünftigen Triumph der letztern, dem Ende der Trübsale, der Verjüngung der Natur und der Wiederkehr eines ewigen goldenen Zeitalters.[33]

of the origin of the world, of the genesis of the stars, of the plants, of animals and men, of the all-powerful sympathy of nature, of the ancient golden age and its mistresses, love and poetry, of the appearance of hate and barbarism and their conflicts with those beneficent goddesses, and finally of the future triumph of the goddesses, the end of dejection, the rejuvenation of nature and the return of an eternal golden age.

The history of humanity is narrated at some length in Klingsohr's 'Märchen' (fairy-tale): rationalist enlightenment is shown to profit from the strife which dispels original harmony as wisdom is separated from love, each of these qualities being embodied in an allegorical figure. Poetry, in the end, overthrows rationalism and under her aegis a new golden age begins.

In the second part of the novel, Heinrich finally matures into a poet through his discovery of the unreality of separateness and death when the deceased Mathilde appears to him. In the uncompleted portion, he was, after participating in the world of action, to have found the blue flower of poetry which he had set out to seek and which is identical with Mathilde; he was then to have inaugurated the new golden age in which the distinction between this world and the next, the finite and the infinite, material and spiritual reality, should have ceased to be. The ultimate state of harmony towards which mankind, supposedly, tends, had already been evoked earlier by Novalis in terms of a permanent combination of religious and sexual ecstasy, as in Heinrich's words to Mathilde:

Was ist Religion, als ein unendliches Einverständnis, eine ewige Vereinigung liebender Herzen? Wo zwei versammelt sind, ist er ja unter ihnen. Ich habe ewig an dir zu atmen; meine Brust wird nie aufhören, dich in sich zu ziehen. Du bist die göttliche Herrlichkeit, das ewige Leben in der lieblichsten Hülle.[34]

What is religion but an infinite mutual understanding, an eternal union of loving hearts? Where two are gathered together, He is amongst them. I must breathe with you eternally; my breast shall never cease to draw you in. You are divine glory, eternal life in the loveliest guise.

Novalis was, of course, writing in an era in which writers, from Rousseau and Herder down to the philosophers of German idealism and Karl Marx, conceived of human history as a process in which an original state of innocence and happiness had suffered disruption, but was due to be restored again on a superior level. Novalis presents variants of this pattern in a somewhat confusing fashion. At times, in *Heinrich von Ofterdingen* and in his essay *Die Christenheit oder Europa* (Christendom or Europe), he talks as if the golden age of the past had existed in mediaeval Europe, and that of the future were to be established here and now. At other times – for instance in the tales which the merchants relate to Heinrich –the golden past is identified with some early, primitive, phase of human history, and the golden future is posited in a transcendent dimension.

Although Novalis's novel is constructed with an exuberant ingenuity which seems playful at times, it deserves to be taken seriously as the culmination of Romantic diastole in what is in effect a fantasy of the poet's omniscience and omnipotence. In the work of Goethe, the diastole expressed in *Werther* and 'Sturm und Drang' poetry led to a systolic recoil which is apparent in the discipline and restraint of Weimar classicism; a similar rhythm is present in Romantic literature. The Romantic artist, in abandoning himself to the sphere of imagination, experienced for a while an intoxicating sense of freedom and self-sufficiency, but then was seized with the fear of losing himself in a vacuum; repenting of what now seemed to him the artist's hybris, he sought to recover a social context. Novalis himself did not live to voice disillusionment with an art that had been deified; but the younger Romantic writers who came together in Heidelberg in the middle eighteen hundreds explicitly rejected individualistic aestheticism in favour of commitment to a historical community. This found expression in a concern with the culture of the common people, with folk-beliefs, with the folk-songs and folk-tales which were collected and studied. Achim von Arnim, Clemens Brentano and Joseph von Eichendorff championed simultaneously German patriotism – it was the era of resistance to Napoleon – and the Christian faith, not as mystical philosophers but as active members of their respective churches. In prose and poetry they articulated a conflict, inconceivable to Novalis, between the claims of art and of Christian morality. For instance, in his novel *Ahnung und Gegenwart* (1815) (Foreboding and Presence), Eichendorff presents true spirituality as threatened by bourgeois philistinism on the one side and by aesthetic irresponsibility on the other. The characters, however, in whom he embodies these contrasting qualities, are lifeless shadows, and the creaking plot of *Ahnung und Gegenwart* follows the pattern of *Wilhelm Meister*, for all the differences in the philosophical messages in Goethe's and Eichendorff's novels. *Ahnung und Gegenwart* remains readable only because of some fifty haunting lyrical poems scattered through the text, and some landscape descriptions of great atmospheric density in a highly musical prose. Eichendorff was a lyrical poet, not a novelist, and far more successful when he expressed his dualistic vision in 'Novellen' such as *Aus dem Leben eines Taugenichts* (From the Life of a Good-for-nothing) and *Das Marmorbild* (The Marble Statue), allegorical prose-poems in which there is little attempt at rendering empirical reality.

In the former story, the spirit of the poet, spontaneous,

41

free, and open to life, is threatened by a utilitarian environment which would stifle his creativity by imposing on him the servitude of a soulless career and bourgeois family-life. The avenue of escape is into 'Wanderleben' (a life of travel, of wandering), which Eichendorff endows with considerable glamour. But 'Wanderleben' in turn poses a threat to the poet, that of the loss of self, inner disintegration, through unrestrained abandonment to ever new experiences. Eichendorff's 'Taugenichts' is protected in the end by a nostalgic attachment to home and native land, which is supposedly poetic, not philistine, but forms a counterpoise to his 'Wanderlust'. In *Das Marmorbild*, the artist is tempted to immerse himself in an unbridled eroticism, precluding the achievement of an adult love-relationship that could issue in marriage. Eichendorff uses legendary material according to which the pagan goddess of love, displaced from Heaven by the advent of Christ, periodically reappears to men on earth in order to lure them into the service of Satan. More clearly than in *Aus dem Leben eines Taugenichts*, Eichendorff here formulates a synthesis in which the poet's Christian belief enables him to resist bourgeois materialism and preserve the emotional spontaneity and inner freedom which he needs in order to remain creative, but to combine these qualities with moral restraint and modesty which the Romantic aestheticists lacked. *Das Marmorbild* is far from being merely didactic; for the symbolism of the story points to a conflict, familiar from psychoanalytic literature, within the subconscious mind of the poet, who has to choose between infantile regression and the claims of maturity.

Clemens Brentano wrote his one and only novel, *Godwi* (1801), during the first phase of the Romantic movement, prior to his friendship with Arnim at Heidelberg and to his religious conversion. In the spirit of early Romanticism, the novel portrays abandonment to the senses, to the present moment, aesthetic enjoyment, of oneself and of others, as the way to self-fulfilment; for Godwi, however, the goal proves elusive, and he is left in the end with a feeling that everything in his life, including art, has only been a game, and consequently with a sense of emptiness, of waste and, indeed, of moral guilt. The complicated plot, involving stock characters and situations, and many echoes of Goethe, Jean Paul, Tieck and others, is not set out in chronological sequence. This is meant to create an impression of chaos: the novel is sub-titled 'ein verwilderter Roman' (a novel run wild), and Brentano has thrown into it a random collection of dramatic interludes and satirical sketches, as well as many fine lyrical poems. The confessional element is to the fore, however; and the hero possesses characteristics which are peculiarly Brentano's, and which make the novel, like Eichendorff's 'Novellen', of interest to the student of psycho analysis. In particular, the early mother-fixation of Godwi, his vain searches, later on, for a mother-substitute in every erotic encounter, going with an incapacity for sustained personal relationships, are credibly rendered, as well as the ambivalence which shows itself in a continual conflict within him between emotional enthusiasm and destructive wit. The book ends on a near-nihilistic note; and if Godwi is more plausible as a self-projection of the author than the corresponding figures in earlier Romantic literature, Brentano fails in his attempts to portray subsidiary characters and their relationships. Like Eichendorff, he is more successful in the limited sphere of the 'Novelle'. In *Die Geschichte vom braven Kasperl und dem schönen Annerl* (1817) (The Story of brave Kasperl and fair Annerl), he is able to articulate his characteristically ambivalent oscillation between a desire to identify with the inspired naivety of simple people, as evidenced in folk-literature, and the need to express his highly complex sensibility in an elaborate and sophisticated art-form. The confrontation in the story between the narrator – clearly Brentano himself – and the old peasant-woman who with her visionary insight establishes a moral ascendancy over everyone with whom she comes into contact, leads to a highly critical description of the rôle of the professional writer which is at the furthest remove from the idolization of art and the artist in early Romanticism. And for all the magical and psychic material included, village-life is presented here by Brentano with an empirical realism, unprecedented in the writings of the earlier Romantics.

A growing concern with the empirical world is apparent also in the 'Novellen' produced by two writers, Heinrich von Kleist and E.T.A. Hoffmann, who were contemporary with, but detached from, the group of Romantics which had gathered at Heidelberg. But the art of neither author tends towards social realism. Kleist was primarily a playwright, and his eight 'Novellen' present extreme occurrences and isolated and exposed individuals who, after a period of moral confusion, come to terms with a tragic fate. No full-length novel by him has survived. E.T.A. Hoffmann, however, left two novels as well as several volumes of 'Novellen'. His first novel, *Die Elixiere des Teufels* (1815-16), treats of a theme which is found in ancient Greek tragedy and was revived by the Romantics, that of the curse which is passed on from an ancestor to his descendants in such a way that the same crimes of murder and incest are reenacted in every generation until expiation is achieved. In the second novel, *Kater Murr* (1820-22) (Murr, the Tom Cat), the cult of art and in particular of music, characteristic of the early Romantics, which had been called into question by Eichendorff and Brentano, is reasserted once more. Hoffmann's Kreisler finds it as hard as Wackenroder's Berglinger had done, to reconcile the rival claims of life and art, and is just as resentful as Berglinger of a society, which fails to respond to transcendent reality as revealed in his music. And just as in the fiction of Jean Paul, the irony of the hero is directed not only at his environment but at himself, to the point where he fears for his sanity. While avoiding the scholarly allusions and digressions which make Jean Paul hard to read, E.T.A. Hoffmann rivals his model's scurrilous humour in *Kater*

Murr, where pages from the life of Kreisler alternate with pages from the supposed confessions of a tom-cat. The cat is Kreisler's anti-type, a social conformist and opportunist; he voices the tenets of Weimar classicism as clichés, conducive to the mental comfort and self-satisfaction of an educated but philistine public.

E.T.A. Hoffmann owed his great popularity not to his novels but to his 'Novellen' in which an empirical contemporary world interacts with every kind of preternatural phenomenon known in folk-literature. The serious subjects of his two novels – the artist's predicament in a philistine society, the psychology of mental derangement – frequently figure in the 'Novellen' also. But it was the extreme sensationalism of many of Hoffmann's stories which appealed to a readership, reared on Gothic fiction; and so it came about that for the first time since the publication of Goethe's *Werther* a German author was translated and widely read in every country of Europe; and a minor tradition of nineteenth century fiction, represented by Edgar Allan Poe and the early detective novel, has in fact come out of Hoffmann.

The only German writer who attempted to give expression in a novel to that growing interest in the empirical world which is apparent in the 'Novellen' of the later Romantic period, was Achim von Arnim. His *Armut, Reichtum, Schuld und Busse der Gräfin Dolores* (1810) (Poverty, Riches, Guilt and Expiation of Countess Dolores), depicts the Germany of his own time. The unhappy marriage of a self-centred and pleasure-seeking woman with an earnest and idealistic nobleman whom she cannot appreciate, reflects the conflict between a decadent eighteenth century feudalism and the new ethos of the Prussian reform-movement of Stein and Hardenberg, which sought to extend not only the privileges but the chivalrous values of the older aristocracy to the middle-classes. It is the reiterated intention of Count Karl, the hero of the novel, to pass on to other classes the spiritual legacy of feudalism, and in the process to 'ennoble

45

all the world'. In depicting the wreck of the marriage, the adultery of the wife, the attempted suicide of the husband, and their subsequent remorse and atonement, Arnim stays fairly close to observed and experienced actualities. But he is also under the spell of *Wilhelm Meister* and the Romantic 'Bildungsroman', and therefore introduces numerous songs and longer poems into the text of his narrative, although his talent for writing verse is not comparable with that of Goethe, of Novalis, Brentano and Eichendorff. And the dreams, visions and miraculous occurrences which Arnim allows to proliferate in tenuously linked sub-plots, in deference to Romantic fashion, run counter to the realistic tenor of the central plot.

A similar lack of balance and harmony characterizes Arnim's historical novel, *Die Kronenwächter* (1817). In its preface, Arnim dissociates himself from the vague mediaevalizing of earlier Romantics; he emphasizes that he has studied chronicles and other sources of the period in which the novel is set, and promises to present a faithful portrait of sixteenth century small-town life. But at the same time its philosophical message makes the novel anachronistic in that it projects into the past Arnim's belief, formed in the aftermath of the Napoleonic period, that an ethical and cultural reformation of Germany must precede any attempt to restore a German empire. Arnim's novel is therefore far removed from the reconstructions of the past in which Sir Walter Scott was engaging at just that time. For all the historical scholarship that has gone into it, *Die Kronenwächter* is ultimately a Romantic allegory, while Scott's fiction explores the conflict of individuals, formed by the differing attitudes and interests of the historical communities into which they are born, and so inaugurates the social realism of the nineteenth century.

6

While Scott was the acknowledged master of Balzac in France, of Tolstoy in Russia, of George Eliot in England, and of Fontane in Germany, his work was in its turn indebted not only to the eighteenth century novel of manners, but to the tradition of Gothic fiction. Scott not only shared the interest in the past, particularly the mediaeval past, characteristic of the tradition, but cultivated various motifs associated with the Gothic romance. There is the theme of the missing heir, for instance in the novel *Guy Mannering* (1815), in which the son of the Laird of Ellangowan is irresistibly drawn to the place of his origins where his true identity comes gradually to light, and there is the mysterious Lovell in *The Antiquary* who turns out in the end to be the long lost heir of the Earl of Glenallan. And like Byron whose fame was at its height when the Waverley novels began to appear, Scott cherishes the sombre heroes of Gothic fiction, the men 'of loneliness and mystery, Scarce seen to smile and seldom heard to sigh',[35] who exercise a fatal fascination on the women they encounter. There is Staunton in *The Heart of Midlothian* (1816) who accuses himself of having been 'the destruction of the mother that bore me – of the friend that loved me – of the woman that trusted me – of the innocent child that was born to me',[36] and the Master of Ravenswood in *The Bride of Lammermoor*, for whom 'some secret sorrow, or the brooding spirit of some moody passion had quenched the light and ingenuous vivacity of youth in a countenance singularly fitted to display both'.[37]

Along with these outlaw figures, familiar from Gothic fiction, but realized with a vitality and psychological plausibility unequalled by earlier novelists, Scott creates vagrants and gypsies who resist the levelling forces of modern civilization. Meg Merrilies in *Guy Mannering*, Eddie Ochiltree in *The Antiquary*, and Madge Wildfire in *The Heart of Midlothian*, intervene forcefully in the lives of the heroes and

47

heroines, and become vehicles by which Scott transmits his wide knowledge of Scottish folklore. Gothic motifs and a pervasive interest in folklore are, of course, shared by Scott with the German Romantics, but his attitude to the preternatural is quite different from theirs. Where the German Romantics present folk-beliefs as literally true, Scott allows for natural explanations. In his *Journal* he writes, with reference to *Woodstock*: 'my object is not to excite fear of supernatural things in my reader, but to show the effect of such fear upon the agents in the story'.[38] Indeed, he explicitly censures the German Romantics for believing, or pretending to believe, in the popular superstitions which they write about. In his essay of 1827 'On the Supernatural in Fictitious Composition: and particularly in the Works of Ernest Theodore William Hoffmann',[39] Scott presents it as a weakness, as evidence of Hoffmann's morbid sensibility, that he should have made 'the fantastic or supernatural grotesque in his compositions' so life-like as to give the reader the impression that he, the author, was 'afraid of the beings his own fancy had created'.[40] He concludes that Hoffmann 'would have distinguished himself as a painter of human nature, of which in its realities, he was an observer and an admirer', if he had not strayed 'too much beyond the circle not only of probability but even of possibility'.[41] In his portrait of the German adventurer Dousterswivel in *The Antiquary*, Scott presents the irrationalism of German Romanticism as an aberration. While the sceptical Oldbuck polemicizes against Dousterswivel's message of 'sympathies and antipathies – of the cabala – of the divining rod – and all the trumpery with which the Rosicrucians cheated a darker age, and which to our eternal disgrace, has in some degree revived in our own',[42] Dousterswivel insists that his tale of the 'Brockengespenst' – it reads like a parody of a Romantic 'Novelle' – has actually occurred, and half believes his own claim that the spirits he tries to call up, would lead him to a spot where a lost treasure lay buried. In this case as in that of

48

the 'Bodach glas' which appears to Fergus Mac-Ivor in *Waverley* (1814) to warn him of his impending death, or of the seemingly effective charms and incantations of Meg Merrilies in *Guy Mannering*, of the astrology in that novel, or of the mediaeval folklore of Scott's later fiction, a natural explanation is always hinted at. And in *The Bride of Lammermoor* (1819), in which omens and prophecies, apparitions and witchcraft figure, Scott explains: 'We are bound to tell the tale as we received it; and considering the distance of the time, and propensity of those through whose mouths it has passed to the marvellous, this could not be called a Scottish story, unless it manifested a tinge of Scottish superstition'.[43]

The Bride of Lammermoor is, in fact, a characteristic product of Scott's mature social realism; for it presents the conflict of Whig and Tory, Presbyterian and Episcopalian in early eighteenth-century Scotland as the type of group-conflict by which historical change is accomplished. The invoking of sinister omens and prophecies is shown to be the peasant's way of articulating his intuitive perception of the doom of the Master of Ravenswood, the hopelessness of the efforts made by this representative of a lost cause, to placate his hereditary enemies and to marry into the upstart Whig family which has usurped the Ravenswood estate. The sorcery of Alice serves a similar purpose: that of bringing home to Edgar, the Master of Ravenswood, the contradiction between his inherited duty to restore the fortunes of the Ravenswoods and resist the Ashtons, and his courting of their daughter, and of warning him against the imprudence of proposing marriage to the girl; for under the circumstances, it can and does only strengthen her mother's resolve to complete his ruin. The destructive violence which is unleashed by Edgar's 'impious' attempt at a match with Lucy Ashton is regarded by the onlookers as a daemonic phenomenon but not so by Scott who writes: 'The peasant who shows the ruins of the tower, which still crown the beetling cliff and behold the war of the waves, though no more tenanted save by the sea-mew and cormorant, even yet affirms, that on this fatal night the Master of Ravenswood, by the bitter exclamations of his despair, evoked some evil fiend, under whose malignant influence, the future tissue of incidents was woven. Alas! what fiend can suggest more desperate counsels, than those adopted under the guidance of our own violent and unresisted passions?'[44]

It is the rendering of the network of political intrigues which, during the Tory ascendancy under Queen Anne, makes the achievement of Edgar's ambition seem temporarily feasible, and the setting of the intrigues in a Scottish scene in which all classes, from the peasantry to the higher aristocracy, are seen to be involved in the party-struggle, that shows up Scott as primarily a realist in *The Bride of Lammermoor*, one who is sociologically more aware even than Jane Austen while in psychological subtlety he is at times her equal. For instance, he is able to present a conflict of unconscious impulses with conscious motives in Edgar, his seemingly accidental death by drowning, for the villagers the fulfilment of a prophecy, being shown up as the result of a suicidal tendency of which Edgar is unaware himself. Again, the mutual attraction of Edgar and of Lucy, who has been reared in a passive rôle by domineering, battling relatives, is well-motivated as is her mental breakdown when the rival pressures on her of her possessive lover and her possessive mother come to a head. 'It usually happens,' says Scott, with reference to the appeal she has for Edgar, in one of many shrewd asides, 'that such a compliant and easy disposition, which resigns itself without murmur to the guidance of others, becomes the darling of those to whose inclinations its own seem to be offered, in ungrudging sacrifice.'[45] In Edgar, the survivor from a feudal past, selfishness does not exclude a chivalrous ethos which goes with a certain blindness to mundane realities; it contrasts with the hard-headed utilitarianism of the Whig usurpers. But Scott does not simplify here either; in Sir William Ashton, dedication to the cause of his party is modified by a tendency to take the line of least resistance, while the implacable Lady Ashton is in the last resort prepared to sacrifice even self-interest to the cause of party and family as she conceives it. As always, Scott is scrupulously fair to both sides. The ingratitude of the villagers to the Ravenswoods is commented on, but we are made to realize that they have gained more than they have lost by the shedding of feudal bonds. And the loyalty of Caleb to his master is not wholly disinterested, for he looks back nostalgically to the power and status he and his like had enjoyed in feudal times; this does not, however, lessen the dignity of his lonely defiance which resembles his master's. And the folkloristic figure here, old Alice, sides with Caleb and the old family against the new, in the same way as Meg Merrilies in *Guy Mannering* sides, from motives of genuine piety, with the Bertram family against the usurper of the Ellangowan estate. Moreover Alice, like Caleb, is aware that the Ravenswoods have suffered injustice, that they have succumbed to a combination of force and trickery, and that their destruction involves the destruction of real values.

In this great novel, Scott's power of evoking folk-tradition, his power of presenting a panoramic picture of a society in process of change, and his power of creating characters who are representative products of strata in that society, yet at the same time unique individuals, are in equilibrium; and a note of doom is pervasive, and is rendered with the lyrical and dramatic intensity of a Border Ballad. In *Waverley* (1814) and many subsequent works, the hero occupies a half-way position between the conflicting parties, and has a foot in each camp. Waverley, a young English officer who changes sides, but in the end recovers his original allegiance, is a mediator between, on the one hand, Jacobitism and the vanishing way of life of the Scottish Highlands, which its characteristic virtues and traditions – the 'old Scottish faith, hospitality, worth, and honour' of which Scott writes in the

'Postscript'[46] – and the progressive, but by comparison drab, Hanoverian cause. He has witnessed integrity of character, as well as the lack of it, on each side and has seen how those wholly committed to one side are blinded by prejudice to the merits of their opponents. This novel is, like some of Jane Austen's, a true 'Erziehungsroman', an educational novel; for Waverley's transition from youth to maturity is skilfully traced to the point where he realizes 'though perhaps with a sigh, that the romance of his life was ended, and that its real history had now commenced'.[47] Even in novels like *Waverley* where the advocates of moderation survive, we encounter the elegiac, not to say tragic, note which has led Georg Lukács to invoke the Roman poet Lucan with reference to Scott: 'Victrix causa diis placuit, sed victa Catoni' (The victorious cause pleased the gods, but the vanquished cause pleased Cato).[48]

Also in *Old Mortality* (1816), a study of the transformation of seventeenth century Scotland by the struggle of Covenanters with Episcopalians, the hero, Morton, is pulled in two directions and attempts, vainly, to mediate between the opposing sides. Scott again shows that degrees of moral worth are to be found among the representatives of both camps, irrespective of the specific opinions on religious and political matters to which they subscribe and which must seem equally misguided to the modern reader. Morton's warm sympathy goes out to the Covenanters who are oppressed for conscience' sake, but he comes to realize that 'these people, rendered wild by persecution, would, in the hour of victory, be as cruel and as intolerant as those by whom they are now hunted down'.[49] Scott's account of a situation in which people are forced into opting for one party or the other by the total polarization of political life which prevails, rings as true to human experience in the twentieth century, with its rival dictatorships and murderous ideological wars, as it does to that of seventeenth century Scotland.

In *Waverley*, *Guy Mannering* and *The Antiquary*, lower

class characters, speaking in vigorous Scots, mixed on terms of easy familiarity with high-born characters, and were portrayed with the greatest respect and sympathy by Scott, a new phenomenon in European fiction. *Old Mortality* is the first of Scott's novels in which representatives of the Lowland peasantry have a major rôle to play. And in *The Heart of Midlothian* (1818), the principal character is drawn from this class, Jeanie Deans, who rises to a stature where she holds her own with the Duke of Argyle. Scott does not present her as altogether exceptional but traces with characteristic shrewdness how her childhood conditioning as the manager of her widowed father's household and of a younger sister, 'tended greatly to establish this fortitude, simplicity, and decision of character',[50] which enabled her to confront Queen Caroline in London. Heinrich Heine emphasized the combination of democratic with aristocratic elements in Scott's fiction, and contrasted it specifically with the practice of the German Romantics 'die das demokratische Element in ihren Romanen gänzlich verleugneten und wieder in das aberwitzige Gleise des Ritterromans, der vor Cervantes blühte, zurückkehrten'[51] (who wholly disowned the democratic element in their novels and returned to the crazy tracks of the romances of chivalry which flourished before Cervantes).

It has generally been held that Scott is at his best in the novels set in the relatively recent Scottish past, or in those which, like *Old Mortality*, deal with causes which are still alive for the near-contemporary narrator, Pattieson. The mediaeval novels, however, often deal with broadly analogous issues, and occasionally open even wider vistas than the Scottish novels. *The Talisman*, for instance, unfolds in the Christian-Islamic contest of crusading times a historical dialectic, similar to that of the novel set in seventeenth century Scotland. And the sympathetic portrayal of Catholicism, on the defensive against the incipient Protestantism of Reformation times, in *The Monastery* and *The Abbott*, created a climate of opinion in Anglican circles which, according to Cardinal Newman, made the Oxford Movement of the eighteen-thirties and forties possible.[52] Perhaps most modern readers find that there is too much fictionalized reconstruction of past manners and customs, too much pageantry, in a novel like *Ivanhoe* (1820); but if the Saxon-Norman conflict corresponds to the Tory-Whig conflict in the Scottish novels, its very remoteness in time makes it easier for Scott to bring out the universal implications. And the Jewish theme adds a new dimension. The Saxons, suffering, like the Highlanders of the eighteenth century, at the hands of ruthless, if more progressive, conquerors, are not idealized, and the schemes of Cedric and Athelstane for overthrowing the Normans and restoring Saxon rule are shown to be no more feasible or desirable than is the restoration of the Stuarts in *Redgauntlet*. Urfried, the maltreated Saxon woman, clings to an irretrievable past with atavistic fanaticism, while Ivanhoe points the way to the future as one of reconciliation though, like Morton in *Old Mortality*, he does not live to see it fully realized. The Jewish people, as represented by Isaac of York, are no more idealized than are Saxons or Normans, but, Scott shows, with considerable irony, how the supposed rapacity and other unamiable qualities of the Jews are induced by the very persecution for which they serve as a pretext. And Isaac becomes the touch-stone by which those who come into contact with him, are judged: for he brings out arrogant contempt, cruelty and cynical exploitation in some, and fairness and compassion in other people, while his daughter Rebecca is shown to profit from her suffering until she rises superior to the passions and prejudices of those around her, and changes for the better those who are open to her influence. But this novel, too, ends on an elegiac note; for Rebecca and her father leave England: 'Not in a land of war and blood, surrounded by hostile neighbours, and distracted by internal factions, can Israel hope to rest during her wanderings'.[53] *Ivanhoe*, too, is a novel remarkable for its truth to twentieth century experience: the present writer remembers how a courageous and enlightened teacher introduced it to a class of German school-boys in 1937, and the searching discussions it provoked. For the portraits of the Knight Templar, a pre-Nietzschean superman, aspiring to world-power, of the Grand Master of the Templars, originally an upright man, but blinded and hardened by his dedication to a misguided cause, and of the opportunists, manoeuvring alongside them, seemed reflections of German types of the period, while the exposure by Scott of anti-Jewish prejudice, his depiction of the terror and helplessness of the persecuted, seemed equally topical. Scott's illusionless portrayal of man's folly and malice, of human history progressing through deadly conflict between rival cultures and ideological systems, is balanced by his belief that integrity, justice and humanity can and must be asserted across the dividing lines, even though this does not bring temporal rewards. To readers who would have preferred *Ivanhoe* to issue in a match between Rebecca and the hero, Scott replied: 'a glance on the great picture of life will show, that the duties of self-denial, and the sacrifices of passion to principle, are seldom thus remunerated, and that the internal consciousness of their high-minded discharge of duty, produces on their own reflections a more adequate recompense, in the form of that peace which the world cannot give or take away.'[54]

Because of his combination of sociological insight and power of characterization with moral vision, Scott was generally honoured in the nineteenth century as the greatest writer since Shakespeare. Goethe frequently expressed his admiration for Scott, referring to the advantages which a British context gave – though he showed no awareness of the fact that it was the peculiarly Scottish experience of the loss of political independence and the consequent erosion of Scotland's national identity, which enabled Scott to write perceptively about this process, and about analogous processes in other times and places and – by portraying social conflicts as ubiquitous agents of historical change, destructive of values but creative also – to inaugurate the sociological novel of the nineteenth century. It was the Bloomsbury movement, with its exclusive interest in the psychology of personal relationships, E.M. Forster's *Aspects of the Novel* and Virginia Woolf's disparaging references to Scott, which broke the spell, at least in England, which he had exercized for so long. And by the nineteen-forties, F.R. Leavis was able to dismiss Scott as at best 'a kind of inspired folk-lorist . . . not having the creative writer's interest in literature'.[55] However, more recent critical studies have gone some way towards re-establishing Scott's former reputation, and his novels figure again on the curricula of English schools and universities.

7

We saw that with the early triumph, in England, of a middle-class which had pioneered the parliamentary system, the industrial revolution, and world-wide trade, centred on the metropolis of London, there appeared a fiction which owed little to literary precedent and classical aesthetics but sought to reflect contemporary reality. At that time, the growing German middle-class, frustrated in a politically fragmented and socially and economically backward environment, took avidly to German translations of the English novelists; and there were unsuccessful German imitations of them. But we saw that in the course of the eighteenth century there emerged a strain of prose-fiction in which the Germans could hold their own: in the novel of sensibility, failure plausibly to describe social milieux, could be counterbalanced by imaginative evocations of spheres of withdrawal and by the portrayal of the sensibility of isolated intellectuals and artists, in conflict with society.

During the decades when the novel of sensibility was in

fashion, the outstanding German contribution to it, Goethe's *Werther*, became an international best-seller. But in the eighteen-nineties, Jane Austen opposed to the subjectivism of this genre the claims of an external world, enacted with the resources of a new psychological and social realism, while Goethe turned the 'Bildungsroman', as developed by Wieland, into an increasingly allegorical medium in which the individualism of the hero is corrected not, as in Jane Austen, by a realistically rendered, integrative society – there was, Goethe argued, no such society to be found in the Germany of his time – but by constructions of a utopian nature.

In the same decade, Jean Paul and the early German Romantics reasserted a radical subjectivism in fictions in which the aesthete mystically transcended a finite reality which was disparaged as philistine. We saw, however, that the later Romantics followed Goethe in writing 'Bildungsromane' which voiced disillusionment with the cult of the artist. In the fictions of Arnim and of Eichendorff, the antidote to the 'diastole' which is rejected, is an orthodox Christianity, a German patriotism and an ethical commitment, abstractly stated, however, rather than realized in character and action. Like Goethe, the Romantics were more successful in the shorter narrative form, the 'Novelle', where there is little scope for depicting a society but where metaphysical themes could be treated in a poetic prose-style. Through E.T.A. Hoffman who combined the themes of Gothic terror-fiction, in particular its occultism, with satirical and grotesque elements, the German 'Novelle' obtained for a time international recognition. The Mediaevalism of Gothic fiction was cultivated by other German Romantic writers, but the reconstructions of the past in Tieck, Novalis, and Brentano, are vague and idealizing, and even the historical fictions of Arnim who had studied chronicles and other source-material, are primarily Romantic allegories. We saw that it was left to Sir Walter Scott who was heir to the tradition of British realism and to a specifically Scottish experience of the clash of rival cultures and ideologies, to transform the historicizing popular fiction of the period into the sociological novel of the nineteenth century.

Much German fiction of the Romantic era is therefore curiously hybrid: an attempt is made, in what are often stereotyped and cliché-ridden plots and character-patterns, to portray a social scene, although the author is only capable of projecting himself and his problems, and his ostensible interest may be to communicate some philosophic message of doubtful validity. However, we saw that in parts, at least, of some novels, and in many 'Novellen' in which lyricism is given free rein, genuine insights are transmitted, if in an allegorical form – into the sphere of the unconscious mind, the vagaries of the artistic temperament, and various aspects of morbid psychology which had never before been treated by creative writers. There is continuity between German literature of the Romantic era and some German prose-fiction of the mid-nineteenth century, but there is no continuity between it and the mainstream of nineteenth century European fiction which Jane Austen and Sir Walter Scott had initiated. But in the twentieth century when the era of social realism had come to an end, German authors who were experimenting with non-realistic modes of prose-fiction looked for precedents in German literature of the Romantic and post-Romantic periods. One of these authors, Kafka, met with a world-wide response, and as a consequence some German prose of the late eighteenth and early nineteenth centuries came into vogue again and was found to have contemporary interest and relevance. And if we call the exploration in depth of the subjective experience of problematic characters 'inwardness', it is arguable that by cultivating it German writers of the age of Romanticism do manage to compensate for the empirical 'extensiveness' which they lack.

II

Adalbert Stifter and the Reception of his Work

The so-called Wars of Liberation of 1813-1815 did not lead to German unification and constitutional government as many had hoped, but to fresh fragmentation and the restoration of princely absolutism. The frustration of German middle-class intellectuals is reflected in the pessimism, the 'Welt-schmerz' (world sorrow), which distinguished many poems and poetic plays of the eighteen-twenties from those of the Romantic era. It is less evident in the sphere of prose-fiction where Eichendorff continued to publish in his earlier mode and Tieck, ever responsive to new influences, now modelled himself on Scott. Of a mass of other German Scott-imitators of the decade only Wilhelm Hauff (with *Lichtenstein* in 1826) and Willibald Alexis (with *Schloss Avalon* in 1827) still earn a mention in literary histories. The decade was characterized by swift economic progress; industrialization was under way in several German provinces, but it failed to precipitate political reform. The revolutionary outbreaks of 1830, in the wake of the July Revolution in Paris, proved abortive; and the repression of the liberal intelligentsia of Prussia was intensified at the very time when the English middle-classes achieved full access to political power with the passing of the Great Reform Bill.

While the self-confidence, the released energies of the English middle-classes, found expression in the new realistic movement in prose-fiction, pioneered by Dickens and Thackeray in the eighteen-thirties, the outstanding German novelist of that decade, Karl Lebrecht Immermann, saw himself as the impotent heir of the era of Weimar classicism, of idealist philosophy and German Romanticism, as the title of his first major novel, *Die Epigonen* (1836), indicates. In style and form and in its stereotyped characterization, *Die Epigonen* is indebted to Jean Paul, to Goethe and the novel of Romanticism; but Immermann is more concerned than his predecessors were, to record contemporary phenomena. He writes of his own involvement with the post-Napoleonic student movement, and of the problem presented by the conflict between an aristocracy in decline, a rising bourgeois plutocracy, and a professional middle-class, excluded from wealth and power, and trapped in the culture it has inherited. The Meister-like principal character, Hermann, is shown groping his way through a series of milieux and representative experiences, with the Utopian intention of achieving a synthesis between the three warring factions of society. Immermann's most important novel, *Münchhausen* (1838-39), while it is also concerned to analyse contemporary social issues, is nevertheless rooted in the same Romantic tradition. We have jeux d'esprit in the manner of Sterne and Jean Paul with the supposed binder of the novel who places the eleventh chapter in front of chapters one to ten, and later explains his reasons for doing so to the author who is introduced as Immermann into the narrative. Not only is the main action continually interrupted by short stories, anecdotes, poetic fairy-tales and long discursive sections, but, as in E.T.A.Hoffmann's *Kater Murr*, two autonomous fictions intersect and illuminate each other by a contrast of perspectives. The sphere of the isolated, maladjusted, but inspired artist and the sphere of the socially integrated but smug philistine in Hoffmann, are replaced in Immermann's novel by the sphere of the 'Lügenbaron', the liar-baron Münchhausen, who represents an era of disintegration in which binding social norms, shared beliefs and consequently integrity of mind and character are said to have vanished, and, in opposition to it, the sphere of the Oberhof-peasantry, disciplined by arduous work in close communion with nature, and therefore able to preserve health of mind and body, a timeless normality. In his apotheosis of village-life, of an incorruptible common people, Immermann follows a Rousseauistic trend in German Romanticism. The juxtaposition of the peasant's inner soundness with the corrupt sophistication of the educated had been anticipated by Brentano in his *Geschichte vom braven Kasperl und dem schönen Annerl*. On the other hand, the peasant-realism which is to be found in *Münchhausen*, led in turn to those portraits of rural life with which Berthold Auerbach and the Swiss Jeremias Gotthelf tried to give a realistic dimension, if of a parochial and limited kind, to German literature in the eighteen-forties. In other respects, too, *Münchhausen* proved a link between Romanticism and German prose-fiction of the forties. The exhaustive discussions, in Immermann's novel, of the literary, religious, social and political issues of the day recommended it to advocates of a politically topical literature: the journalists of the liberal 'Young Germany' movement, some of whom – among them Heinrich Laube and Karl Gutzkow – tried their hand at writing didactic novels. But many critics and readers to-day would hold that the outstanding German prose of the eighteen-forties was contributed not by the practitioners of peasant-realism nor by the politically committed writers of the 'Young Germany' movement, but by an isolated outsider, the Austrian Adalbert Stifter.

There are few, if any, writers whose reputation has fluctuated as widely, who have been the subject of as much controversy among critics and literary historians as Stifter has. For there is a radical ambiguity about him which has fascinated and repelled one generation of readers after another. His work exemplifies in a particularly acute form the problems raised by the German contribution to prose-fiction: the critical response to Stifter's fiction illustrates the difficulties which critics and the reading-public had in

61

coming to terms with a characteristic product of a German narrative tradition. A close look at it is therefore called for in the context of this study.

Stifter's situation was that of many a German writer before and since: a conviction that he had an artist's temperament and vocation preceded first attempts on his part to prove this to the world by creative work with which he hoped to emulate the success and the fame of predecessors whom he admired. So being by no means a 'born writer' or a natural story-teller, he found he had the utmost difficulty in translating his literary ambition into actual productions and was therefore greatly dependent on his models. Stifter's first 'Novellen', published in magazines and then re-written for publication in book-form as *Studien*, were well received by critics and reviewers in the early and middle eighteen-forties, and this in part because they were not marked by originality of a kind which would have offered a challenge to contemporary taste. For Stifter was indebted for his style and his plots to Jean Paul, who was still in vogue with the reading-public. He was indebted also to fashionable contemporaries: the presence of Fenimore Cooper in *Der Hochwald* has long been recognized as has the connection between those stories in which the principal character is a traveller – *Brigitta*, *Der Hagestolz* (The Bachelor), *Zwei Schwestern* (Two Sisters) and, for that matter, the later *Nachsommer* (Indian Summer) – with the travel-fiction of Tieck and Heinrich Laube. Stifter's first Austrian reviewer, J.G. Seidl, praised the early *Studien* in the *Wiener Zeitung* (24. Dec. 1844); the notices that appeared in *Wiener Zuschauer*, *Österreichisches Morgenblatt* and *Österreichische Blätter für Literatur* followed the lead given by Seidl. The first German response, by Levin Schücking, was favourable too, though with some significant reservations: Schücking argues that Stifter is better at describing landscapes than people (*Allgemeine Zeitung*, 10. Jan. 1845). Joseph von Eichendorff, on the other hand, was wholly positive in the article on Stifter which he contributed to the *Historisch-politische Blätter* of 1846, and so was the anonymous reviewer of volumes 3-4 of *Studien* in *Gegenwart* (1. June 1847). The early reviewers did not note the surface derivativeness of Stifter's *Studien*, but neither were they sensitive to the fact that, through borrowed character-sketches and plots, Stifter was articulating some highly personal anxieties and concerns.

The tide of critical opinion turned against Stifter in the later forties. By this time the German reading-public had developed a taste for the new realism of Thackeray, of Dickens, and, to a lesser extent, of French contemporaries. A first German translation of *Pickwick Papers* ran into three editions in four years, and two further translations appeared; and subsequently, German translations of Dickens's novels appeared invariably within a year of their publication in England and sold more widely than any German fiction of the period.[1] In 1859, Robert Prutz characterized the development which had taken place, as follows:

Unser Publikum liest die Dickens und Thackeray, die Sue und Dumas nicht deshalb, weil sie Engländer und Franzosen sind, noch lässt es die deutschen Romane ungelesen, weil sie deutsche; sondern es liest die einen, weil sie unterhaltend sind, weil es das Leben der Wirklichkeit darin abgespiegelt findet, weil interessante Charaktere, mächtige Leidenschaften, spannende Verwicklungen ihm daraus entgegentreten – und wirft die andern beiseite weil sie langweilig sind oder doch wenigstens eine Sprache reden und von Dingen handeln, die das Publikum im Grossen entweder nicht versteht, oder für die es sich nicht interessiert.[2]

Our public reads the novels of Dickens and Thackeray, of Sue and Dumas not because they are Englishmen and Frenchmen, nor does it leave the German novels unread because they are German; but rather, it reads the former because they are entertaining, because it finds real life reflected in them, because it encounters in them interesting characters, powerful passions, thrilling plots, and it throws the others aside because they are boring or, at least, speak a language and deal with matters which the public, by and large, doesn't understand or doesn't find interesting.

Prutz intends, perhaps, some criticism here of the public for its inability or unwillingness to respond to the scholarly subtleties of German fiction, rather as Lessing had done (see pp. 12-13 above). But most leading critics saw it differently. Julian Schmidt, who became co-editor, with Gustav Freytag, of the influential *Grenzboten* in 1848, now wrote some articles on Dickens – they appeared in book-form in 1852 – in which he opposed contemporary English fiction to the 'ungesunden Richtungen, welche durch die jungdeutsche Abhängigkeit von französischer Bildung und durch die Willkür der alten Romantik in die Seele der Deutschen gekommen war'[3] (unhealthy tendencies which had entered the souls of Germans because of the dependence of Young Germany on French culture, and because of the licence of the old Romantics). If Julian Schmidt's review of Stifter's early *Studien* had been sympathetic, his references to Stifter after 1848 were predominantly disparaging. Stifter responded by developing his own style and ethos in conscious defiance of the change in literary fashion. Indeed, ever since he had begun to prepare his early stories for publication in book-form, he had sought to eliminate from them the lyrical effusiveness and the colourful metaphors derived from Jean Paul, and the later *Studien* are characterized from the start by a paucity of striking incidents and actions, and a reticence in the expression of emotion while the external settings – landscapes, gardens, houses with their furniture and fittings – are evoked at ever greater length and with loving attention to minute particulars. Levin Schücking, in a second article on Stifter (*Allgemeine Zeitung*, 23. June 1847), reversed his former favourable estimate and pointed to Stifter's preoccupation with themes from the sphere of home and family and to the increasing prominence given to the extra-human element, to nature and the world of 'Dinge' (things), as disabling weaknesses in his fiction. Schücking was reacting here against Eichendorff's

64

attempt in the previous year to set off Stifter on moral and metaphysical grounds from the new social realism favoured by the politically committed. Stifter, however, followed Eichendorff's lead and now castigated the prevailing literary fashion, extolling his own works for being diametrically opposed to it. He now took the late Goethe instead of Jean Paul for his model, and as the human figures receded into the background of his fiction, their changing fortunes being deprived, relatively, of all urgency and importance, the stories became remarkable for a lack of tension and suspense. This went with Stifter's ever more emphatic stigmatization of passion as a destructive force in the life of the individual and, after the Revolution of 1848 which he had at first cautiously welcomed but then experienced as a nightmare, in world-history. In his work, from the early *Studien* to *Der Nachsommer*, it is, paradoxically, passionate feeling which not only fails to unite, but actually separates lovers; only when they have been purged of passion, years later as a rule, do they become ready for union. For passion, in Stifter's view, is inseparable from egotism, subjectivity and moral blindness. Stifter points explicitly now to a moral law that he believes to be operative in human life and in nature, superseding the conflicts and passions of individual people which are dwarfed into insignificance by it – a law that, almost masochistically, he likes to trace in wild and barren landscapes, in deserts, heaths, steppes, the immense forests of his homeland, and mountains covered in ice and snow which in *Die Mappe meines Urgrossvaters, Bergkristall* and *Der Nachsommer* are described in a revealingly ambivalent manner, as at once terrifying and breathtakingly beautiful. It is in resignation to and cooperation with this law which is present even in natural calamities – in the lightning which heals and destroys in *Abdias*, the flood in *Kalkstein*, the snowfall in *Bergkristall*, the hail-storm in *Katzensilber* – that the characters of the tales rise to that objectivity and serenity which Stifter values so highly.

Stifter himself argued that his new manner marked a development from a subjective to an objective, an epic prose-style – as for instance in *Der beschriebene Tännling* where the growth of jealousy and murderous hate in the wood-cutter's heart and his ultimate renunciation of violence, are never directly expressed but left to be inferred from his actions which are described in a calm and matter-of-fact tone. Stifter realized that many of his readers were now bored by him but attributed this to a defect in them, not in his fiction; for he believed that by his indirectness in the treatment of emotion, his elimination of subjective sentiment, of psychological analysis and suspense he was reverting to the naivety and innocence of the true epic genre as found in the Bible and Homer, and saw himself as alone among his contemporaries contributing to this, the highest form of literature.[4]

His pervasive Utopianism, however, placed Stifter in the German tradition to which Schnabel, Wieland and the Goethe of *Wilhelm Meisters Wanderjahre* had contributed. The construction of a world apart, an idyllic refuge, is a central motif in practically every one of Stifter's stories, from his first, *Feldblumen*, to his last, *Der Kuss von Sentze*. If in the earlier stories, particularly in *Der Hochwald* and *Die Narrenburg*, untamed nature figures in Rousseauistic fashion as the setting of island-like spheres of withdrawal which contrast with the corrupt world of civilization, in the later work, i.e. in *Die Mappe meines Urgrossvaters, Abdias, Brigitta, Zwei Schwestern, Der Nachsommer*, nature is integrated into the Utopian oasis by means of agriculture, pursued with the same perfectionist zeal as are the tasks of house-building and furnishing. In all these stories Stifter emphasized the classical, Arcadian character of his idylls:

Die Einsamkeit und Kraft dieser Beschäftigungen erinnerte mich häufig an die alten starken Römer, die den Landbau auch so sehr geliebt hatten, und die wenigstens in ihrer früheren Zeit auch gerne einsam und kräftig waren. 'Wie schön und ursprünglich', dachte ich, 'ist die Bestimmung des

Landmannes, wenn er sie versteht und veredelt. In ihrer Einfalt und Mannigfaltigkeit, in dem ersten Zusammenleben mit der Natur, die leidenschaftslos ist, grenzt sie zunächst an die Sage von dem Paradiese.'[5]

The loneliness and strength of these occupations reminded me frequently of the old, strong Romans who had also loved agriculture so much, and who at least in their earlier time had also liked to be lonely and vigorous. 'How beautiful and original', I thought, 'is the vocation of the countryman when he understands and ennobles it. In its simplicity and diversity, in that first living together with nature which is passionless, it borders most closely on the legend of paradise.'

'Einsamkeit' (loneliness) is a key-word in Stifter's fiction, and his attitude to it, as to the long line of his 'Sonderlinge' (eccentrics), is ambivalent. Where an eccentric character cuts himself off from humanity, in hate and defiance, like Abdias and the 'Hagestolz', he is condemned, but not ambiguously, for both Abdias and the old bachelor are credited with a strength and integrity lacking in the people from whom they have detached themselves.

The central figures of *Die Narrenburg, Die Mappe meines Urgrossvaters, Der Waldsteig*, are cured of their misanthropic tendencies and become involved socially in what is, however, a very constricted rural milieu. And they remain men apart, 'einsam und kräftig' (lonely and vigorous) like Brigitta. The wise doctor who sets Tiburius in *Der Waldsteig* on the road to recovery, is very much an individualist and, like many of the characters who enjoy Stifter's approval, e.g. Angela in *Feldblumen*, and Brigitta, he is regarded as an eccentric, if not a madman, by the people around him, the implication being that it is the isolated individual who lives in harmony with reason and nature, rather than the people who constitute society. There is a touch of eccentricity about Risach in *Der Nachsommer*. When Heinrich Drendorf first visits him, he finds his manner of dressing quaint and old-fashioned but as his education progresses, Heinrich comes to the conclusion that Risach's dress is in fact singularly appropriate to his way of life and evidence of his superiority to the follies of fashion. The isolation of Heinrich and Gustav in youth is presented as protective, and the hermit's life which Franz Rikar in *Zwei Schwestern* leads, is explicitly endorsed as is that of the priest in *Kalkstein* who is not defiant and misanthropic like Abdias but resigned, humble and charitable in his solitude. In *Der Waldgänger*, the lonely Corona is recommended to the reader's sympathy, not society which has persecuted her. Few of Stifter's 'Sonderlinge', however, are individualized to the extent of becoming living presences for the reader, and the same may be said of that long series of youths in Stifter's work, all of them described as noble, beautiful and innocent, but not endowed with any more concrete qualities.

The basic theme of *Der Nachsommer* (1857), that of the lovers separated in youth by wrong-headed passion and reconciled in maturity and that of the idealistic young man who enters into a Platonic relationship with an older, wiser man, to be educated by him, had figured in several of Stifter's 'Novellen'. In two of the *Studien*, *Brigitta* and *Der Hagestolz*, both themes had actually been treated in conjunction as they are in *Der Nachsommer*. The third theme, that of the idyllic refuge, carefully cultivated and protected, had occurred in *Brigitta* and a number of other stories. But in *Der Nachsommer* all psychological analysis and all elements of conflict, present in the earlier works, have been eliminated. It could, of course, be argued that Stifter did well to abandon psychological analysis as he had shown no aptitude for it. In *Brigitta*, for instance, we have an introductory paragraph on the mysteries of the human heart to prepare us for the fable of the plain girl who withdraws from social life, being sensitive and proud, and yet wins the admiration of the handsome and popular Stephan Murai; the ambivalent love-hate relationship which ensues is, however, of a kind familiar in Romantic and post-Romantic literature; it remains literary cliché in Stifter's story and neither Brigitta nor Stephan are convincingly realized fictional characters. But *Der Nachsommer* differs from the 'Novellen' in which the same themes are treated, not only because conflict and psychology are eliminated, but because it is a full-length 'Bildungsroman', modelled on *Wilhelm Meister*. The characters, their relationships with each other, their social context, are not rendered more fully than they had been in the 'Novellen'; the great length of *Der Nachsommer* is due to the didactic passages which interrupt the narrative. They range over a host of subjects, from geology to aesthetics. The art-theories of *Der Nachsommer* are put into the mouths of characters who talk in the same literary idiom as the author even when, like Heinrich and Natalie, they break off their scientific discussions in order to declare their love for each other. Stifter's intention here too, as in the 'Novellen', is to deflate human subjectivity by emphasizing impersonal considerations. Heinrich keeps the reader informed of the progress of his geological studies throughout *Der Nachsommer* and remarks:

> Wenn eine Geschichte des Nachdenkens und Forschens wert ist, so ist es die Geschichte der Erde, die ahnungsreichste, die reizendste, die es gibt, eine Geschichte, in welcher die des Menschen nur ein Einschiebsel ist, und wer weiss es, welch ein kleines . . . [6]

> If there is a history worth reflecting on and researching into, it is the history of the earth, the most suggestive and appealing there is, a history in which that of man is a mere interpolation, who knows how small a one . . .

There is something paradoxical about a novelist who glories in nature and the natural sciences because they reveal the relative insignificances of human life. It was to this paradox that Hebbel pointed when he published his review of *Der Nachsommer*:

> . . . dem Manne der ewigen Studien, dem behäbigen Adalbert Stifter, war es vorbehalten, den Menschen ganz aus dem

Auge zu verlieren.[7]

... it was reserved for the man of the eternal Studies, comfort-loving Adalbert Stifter, to lose sight of man altogether.

Other reviews, that by Hieronymous Lorm,[8] by von Schmidt-Weissenfels[9] and by the anonymous critic in the 1858 volume of the periodical *Europa*, were negative too. Julian Schmidt finds some merit in the work and calls Stifter a 'seelenvolle und bedeutende Natur' (a spiritual and impressive personality), but he censures Stifter's long-windedness and, incidentally, his glorification of the aristocracy; he remarks:

> Die Genauigkeit in der Ausmalung ist zwar sehr instruktiv, aber nicht eigentlich dichterisch. Der Ernst, mit dem diese Dinge behandelt werden, macht in den meisten Fällen einen unfreiwillig komischen Eindruck.[10]

> The precision of his descriptions is indeed highly informative, but not really poetic. The seriousness with which these matters are treated, gives in most instances an involuntarily comic impression.

Only the undiminished admiration of Heckenast, his publisher, continued to compensate Stifter for the indifference of the public and the hostility of the critics. But even Heckenast deferred to the taste of the public by making many cuts in *Der Nachsommer* when he brought out a new edition of it (3. Auflage, 1877); and the '4. Auflage' of 1897, by Amelang of Leipzig who had inherited Heckenast's stock, is much shorter still. It wasn't until 1919 that the complete text of *Der Nachsommer* was made available again.[11]

Witiko (1865-7) fared no better at the hands of critics who found it laborious and arid. Stifter's intention, as expressed in a letter to Heckenast, was to make broad historical movements, illustrative of a law operative in history, central and the individual characters marginal. This is, of course, as paradoxical as the stress on extra-human factors at the expense of the human in earlier stories:

> Es erscheint mir ... in historischen Romanen die Geschichte

die Hauptsache und die einzelnen Menschen die Nebensache,
sie werden von dem grossen Strome getragen und helfen den
grossen Strom bilden.[12]

History seems to me the main issue in historical novels, and
individual people a side-issue, they are carried along by the
great stream and help to form the stream.

For all Stifter's emphasis on historical objectivity in *Witiko*,
there is evidence of close personal involvement in the fact
that, contrary to historical actuality, he made his native
Oberplan the centre of the military campaign by which the
legitimate king of Bohemia, a loyal vassal of the Holy Roman
Emperor, is reimposed upon the Czech nobles who are
presented as self-willed in their recalcitrance. The triumph of
an authoritative tradition over rebellion – the novel culminates
in the overthrow of republican Milan by the Emperor –
mirrors Stifter's endorsement of the Habsburg restoration
after the revolution of 1848. The formality which governs
social intercourse in *Witiko* and imparts a ritual flavour even
to relationships between friends and relatives in that novel, is
the dominant motif in Stifter's last stories, *Der Kuss von
Sentze* and *Der fromme Spruch*. Stifter had difficulty in
getting them published, so decisively had fashion turned
against him.

The view of the critics hostile to Stifter, the argument of
Hebbel that Stifter showed no aptitude for or interest in the
creation of real characters in real situations, but instead
allowed description to proliferate which, according to Lessing's canon, was incompatible with the epic genre,[13] prevailed
in the later nineteenth century; and those who opposed the
Stifter revival of the twentieth century did little more than
elaborate on it. It is, perhaps, equally true to say that the
defence of Stifter's work, has also, frequently, tended to echo
that first put forward in the eighteen-forties and fifties – by
Stifter himself, in fact. Stifter had only a limited insight into
the nature and sources of his creative achievement: there is a
contradiction between the pervasive Utopianism of his work,

occasionally admitted by himself, and his claims elsewhere to objectivity and realism. In a letter to his publisher Heckenast he writes of *Der Nachsommer*: 'Ich habe ein tieferes und reicheres Leben, als es gewöhnlich vorkömmt, in dem Werke zeichnen wollen und zwar in seiner Vollendung'[14] (I wanted to draw a deeper and richer life in this work than is normally found, and that in its perfection). But in another letter he claims that his aim as a novelist is 'das Vorhandene auszuplaudern'[15] (to divulge what exists), and in the story *Nachkommenschaften* he recommends an uncompromising realism in art.[16] He follows his own advice in so far as he always aims at visually precise descriptions of landscapes and objects but he shies away increasingly from empirical realities, preferring Utopian constructions, free of passion and conflict.

In the prefaces to his earlier works, Stifter adopts a self-deprecating tone in striking contrast with his later apologias; in the 1843 'Vorrede' (Preface), for instance, he refers to the earlier *Studien* as 'lose Blätter'[17] (loose sheets). The use of the term 'Studien', signifying, by analogy with painting, sketches as opposed to fully finished compositions, is in itself evidence of a tendency to self-belittlement. He writes that he isn't sure whether the stories which he had tried hard to improve since their first publication, were worth bringing out in book-form at all; as their author he was in no position to judge, 'da er aus seinen Arbeiten zuletzt doch immer nur das Gewollte herauslieset, nicht das Gewirkte'[18] (since his own reading of his works always reveals to him only what he intended, not what he achieved). In the preface to the second edition of 1846 he states that volumes one and two of *Studien* were 'mit mehr Anteil aufgenommen . . . als sie verdienten'[19] (received with more interest . . . than they deserved). But after reading Levin Schücking's adverse criticism, he expresses extreme indignation and even hints at possible legal action against the editor of the *Allgemeine Zeitung* unless he agreed to appoint a more sympathetic reviewer for subsequent

Studien volumes.[20] By 1850 when the consensus of critical opinion had turned against him, he argues that his works are morally superior to those of his more fashionable contemporaries: 'Meine Bücher sind nicht Dichtungen allein (als solche mögen sie von sehr vorübergehendem Werte sein), sondern als sittliche Offenbarungen, als mit strengem Ernste bewahrte menschliche Würde haben sie einen Wert, der bei unserer elenden frivolen Litteratur länger bleiben wird als der poetische'.[21] (My books are not only works of poetic art (as such they may be of very transient value), but as moral revelations, as human dignity preserved with strict seriousness, they have a value which, with our wretched, frivolous literature, will last longer than their poetic value.) Stifter's peculiar ambivalence, his tendency to be modest and boastful in turn, is apparent in the 'Vorrede' (preface) to *Bunte Steine* (Coloured Stones) of 1852 where he calls these stories 'allerlei Spielereien für junge Herzen' (various playthings for young hearts) and claims that 'ich meine Schriften nie für Dichtungen gehalten habe noch mich je vermessen würde, sie für Dichtungen zu halten'[22] (I have never regarded my writings as works of poetic art nor would I ever regard them as such), but then goes on to defend his work against Hebbel's disparaging references to it. In his famous epigram 'Die alten Naturdichter und die neuen'[23] (The old nature-poets and the new ones), Hebbel had accused Stifter of ignoring the central issues of human life in an escapist preoccupation with petty domesticity and the idyllic aspects of nature. Stifter now goes on to contrast his own concern for the truly significant, the 'sanfte Gesetz' (gentle law), the 'Kräfte, die nach dem Bestehen der gesamten Menschheit hinwirken, die durch die Einzelkräfte nicht beschränkt werden dürfen, ja im Gegenteile beschränkend auf sie selber einwirken'[24] (forces which promote the continuance of the whole human race, which may not be limited by the force of individuals but must, on the contrary, have a limiting effect on these), a law revealed in the 'gewöhnlichen, alltäglichen, in Unzahl wiederkehrenden Handlungen der Menschen'[25] (ordinary everyday actions of men which are repeated over and over again), with the supposedly immoral 'Einseitigkeit' (one-sidedness) of currently fashionable literature which describes 'das nur von einem Standpunkte Gültige, dann das Zerfahrene, Unstimmende, Abenteuerliche, endlich das Sinnenreizende, Aufregende und zuletzt die Unsitte und das Laster'[26] (what is only valid from one point of view, then, what is disordered, incoherent, adventurous, what stimulates and excites the senses and, finally, the immoral and vicious). As time goes on and Stifter feels himself increasingly isolated and ignored, he comes to claim not only moral, but also aesthetic value for his work as in a letter to his publisher of 16 March 1865, in which he writes of *Der Nachsommer*:

> es hat eine Zukunft, weil es für das gegenwärtige Geschlecht zu tief ist, und erst reifen muss, es hat gewisser eine Zukunft als alles, was ich früher geschrieben habe. Ich erlabe mich jetzt an dem Reinen, das in ihm ist.[27]

> it has a future because it is too deep for the present generation and has yet to mature, it is more certain of a future than everything I have written before. I now relish the purity that is in it.

Confusion, due to vacillation between ethical and aesthetic criteria, has remained characteristic of Stifter apologias since, just as a common assumption underlies the adverse criticism directed at his work, from that of Schücking in the eighteen-forties to that of Glaser in the nineteen-sixties:[28] that great novelists are interesting to read, not because they deal in those subjective sentiments and the artificial suspense which Stifter eschewed, but because they enter with emotional intensity into the crucial situations, the issues, conflicts and dilemmas, of their time, and render these by the methods of social realism – as Stifter did not. Stifter's claim to epic objectivity could be, and was, challenged on the grounds that the style of the Bible and Homer which he claimed to be restoring, was natural and inevitable for the writers of antiquity but not for the modern novelist, and also on the testimony of the autobiographical element in his fiction; the fact, for instance, that the early career of Risach in *Der Nachsommer* resembles Stifter's own so closely as to suggest an idealized self-portrait, his Indian summer with Mathilde being the fulfilment Stifter wished for but failed to achieve with Fanni Greipl, and the fact that even in *Witiko* where he claimed to be faithful to his sources, he defied them by making his birth-place and native region the centre of the action.

That Stifter's reputation had reached a nadir in the later nineteenth century, is apparent from the literary histories of the period. Herbert Koenig devotes eight lines in 671 pages of his *Deutsche Literaturgeschichte* (8th edition, 1880) to Stifter, noting as an anomaly his 'vorübergehend grossen Erfolg' (great, but short-lived success) in the forties.[29] G. Brugier dismisses Stifter as a 'Maler mit der Feder' (painter with the pen) in his *Geschichte der deutschen National-Litteratur* (8th edition, 1888), a work of 592 pages where a mere fourteen lines are assigned to Stifter.[30] Other literary historians, Hermann Kluge[31] and Otto von Leixner,[32] are as negative. The point of departure for the Stifter-revival of the twentieth century was the well-known paragraph in *Menschliches Allzumenschliches* (1878) (Human All-too-Human) in which Nietzsche listed *Der Nachsommer* with Lichtenberg's *Aphorismen*, Jung-Stilling's *Lebensgeschichte* (Story of My Life), Keller's *Die Leute von Seldwyla* (The People of Seldwyla) and Eckermann's *Gespräche mit Goethe* (Conversations with Goethe) as the only German books that deserved 'wieder und wieder gelesen zu werden' (to be read again and again).[33] Nietzsche did not account for his choice, but it seems likely that the aristocratic, Utopian element in the novel was congenial to him, and it is evident from the context, a polemical one, that *Der Nachsommer* and the other books were invoked because they exhibit the classical virtues of restraint, sobriety and serenity which Nietzsche was just then opposing to the turbulent pathos of Wagner's art. It was not until the turn of the century that Nietzsche's championship of Stifter received critical endorsement, and this from adherents of the Aestheticist movement who were in rebellion against the tendencies of their time, represented by Naturalism, Socialism and the cult of Progress. They now hailed Stifter as their precursor who had espoused 'eternal values' against the transient aberrations of the 'Young Germany' movement. The foremost of Stifter's new champions, Hugo von Hofmannsthal[34] and Hermann Bahr, were Austrians, and in Austria and Bohemia Stifter had in any case continued to be read as a local writer and patriot. It was at Prague that A.R. Hein brought out the first full-length biography of Stifter in 1904 and that the first complete edition of Stifter's works now began to be published. Another apostle of Stifter came from the George-circle: Ernst Bertram's *Studien zu Adalbert Stifters Novellentechnik* (Studies of Adalbert Stifter's Technique of the 'Novelle') appeared in 1907 and in his *Nietzsche: Versuch einer Mythologie* (Nietzsche: attempt at a Mythology) a whole chapter is devoted to the supposed kinship between Stifter and Nietzsche. It is of some interest that after the turn of the century when Nietzsche was at the height of his reputation, literary historians invariably referred to the aphorism in *Menschliches Allzumenschliches* when they discussed Stifter – even if, like Eduard Engel, they considered it an incomprehensible aberration on Nietzsche's part.[35] It was not until the nineteen-twenties that the positive estimate of Stifter, as formulated by Hofmannsthal, Bahr and Bertram, found its way into the literary histories, e.g. the later editions of Alfred Biese's *Deutsche Literaturgeschichte* and Josef Nadler's *Literaturgeschichte der deutschen Stämme und Landschaften.*

The difficulties which academic critics had even now to agree as to the actual significance of Stifter's prose is illustrated in particular by the controversy which has raged for fifty years over the most ambitious of his tales, *Abdias*. The story opens with some generalizing statements about fate in the spirit of the Enlightenment, and the Jew Abdias is then introduced as someone 'an dem sich manches davon darstellte, und von dem es ungewiss ist, ob sein Schicksal ein seltsameres Ding sei, oder sein Herz'[36] (in whom various aspects of this were manifested, and of whom it is uncertain whether his fate or his heart were a stranger thing). Some earlier critics, among them Josef Bindtner,[37] Albert Gerhard Müller,[38] and Anneliese Märkisch[39] tried to trace a complete correspondence between the character and the tragic fate of Abdias, explaining away the apparent contradictions in the work, while later commentators, including W. Silz,[40] Urban Roedl,[41] Erik Lunding,[42] F.W. Wodtke[43] and K. Spalding[44] found a discrepancy between the optimism of the philosophical statement, with which the story opens and the pessimism of the narrative which follows. As against these critics who believed that Stifter was unconscious of the ambiguities in his tale, Benno von Wiese argued that these were deliberate,[45] pointing to an ultimate mystery. The debate seemed deadlocked, but progress was made when critics came to pay attention to certain symbolical features in the narrative. The significance of Stifter's choice of a Jew as the protagonist of his story was gradually adverted to. There is a New Testament allusion in *Abdias* – to the XIth chapter of the Epistle to the Romans in which St. Paul speaks of the call to the Jews, and the failure of many of them to perceive it, in terms of a spiritual blindness that 'is happened to Israel', under Providence. Stifter's reference to a spiritual blindness of which Abdias is healed when his daughter Ditha is born who represents the 'Heil' (salvation) he has vainly groped for – 'es fiel ihm von den Augen herunter, wie dichte Schuppendecken, die darüber gelegen waren . . . so wurde ihm in seinem Herzen, als fühle er drinnen bereits den Anfang des Heiles, das nie gekommen war und von dem er nie gewusst hatte, wo er es denn suchen sollte . . . '[46] (there fell from his eyes thick scales, as it were, which had covered them . . . it was as if in his heart he felt already the beginning of that salvation which had never come and of which he had never known where he was to seek it) – echoes the terms in which St. Paul speaks of Israel: 'Israel hath not obtained that which he seeketh for; but the election hath obtained it, and the rest were blinded. According as it is written, God hath given them the spirit of slumber, eyes that they should not see . . . ' (Romans XI, 7-8); and in the subsequent verses St. Paul prophesies the ultimate removal of this blindness from the whole Jewish people whose special vocation remains: 'for the gifts and the calling of God are without repentance' (Romans XI, 29). St. Paul concludes with a declaration of faith in Providence whose intentions can occasionally be glimpsed though they are, as yet, largely intransparent, a paradox resembling that stated by Stifter at the opening of his story – with this difference, that for Stifter, the heir of the Enlightenment, the state of perfect knowledge is to be attained in the course of the future history of the human race here on earth, not, as in St. Paul, in a transcendent sphere, after death.

That the vocation of the Jew who renounces God's call stands symbolically, in this story, for that of the artist who betrays his art, was first suggested by Urban Roedl: 'Der Berufene, der sich seinem höheren Auftrag entzieht, vergeht sich am Geist und verstrickt sich in Schuld. Es ist ein Leitgedanke der Stifterschen Anfänge, eine Rechtfertigung seiner Entscheidung zum Künstlertum'[47] (He who has received a call but evades his higher vocation, offends against the spirit and becomes entangled in guilt. This is a leading thought in Stifter's early work and a justification of his decision to become an artist). Urban Roedl's suggestion was subsequently developed by Paul Requadt into the theory that Abdias and Ditha represent the artist and his art,[48] and two recent critics, Friedrich Wilhelm Korff[49] and Kurt Mautz[50] have made it the basis of their respective interpretations of *Abdias*. That lightning, with its dual impact, stands symbolically for the role of fate in the story, had already been recognized by W. Silz.[51] Requadt, Korff and Mautz relate it more specifically to the mythological tradition according to which lightning derives directly from God or the gods and represents poetic inspiration. Mautz alludes to precedents in German literature, Goethe's poem 'Grenzen der Menschheit', with its 'segnenden Blitze' (flashes of lightning which bring blessings), and Hölderlin's poem 'Wie wenn am Feierabend' where Semele who gives birth to Dionysus when Zeus appears to her in the form of lightning, and dies[52] is representative of the poet. An even closer parallel, not alluded to by Mautz, occurs in Hölderlin's poem 'Der blinde Sänger' where a thunderstorm restores the eyesight along with the poetic inspiration of the stricken poet.

The critic who approaches Stifter's fictions as allegory is, of course, also up against the author's pervasive ambiguity. Not everything that Stifter writes is allegorical; after all, he claimed to be reviving the true epic genre, particularly in his novels, and he incorporates autobiographical elements into almost all his fictions. To reduce Ditha to a mere symbol of art is surely to over-simplify. Admittedly, her blindness has a symbolical significance; that it should not be discovered until she is four years old, that she is unable to talk at that age although she is said to be highly sensitive and responsive to sound and music, all this distracts from her plausibility as a living individual. Her aetherial nature is indicated by the blue of her eyes, and the special attraction which the blue of the sky and of flowering flax have for her. The symbolism of blue in an existence in which the dreams of night and the wakefulness of day are said to merge, is stressed by Stifter himself:

> So lebte sie eine Welt aus Sehen und Blindheit, und so war ja auch das Blau ihrer Augen, so wie das unsers Himmels, aus Licht und Nacht gewoben.[53]

So she lived (in) a world of sight and blindness, and so the

79

blue of her eyes, like that of the sky, was woven from light and night.

Her death, which occurs when she is drawn irresistibly, although a thunderstorm threatens, to a field of flax which has burst into blossom overnight, suggests a willing return to heaven when in her state of perfection the burden of earthly existence has come to afflict her with a 'Spannung' (tension) as of 'süssen Leidens' (sweet suffering).[54] But her affinity to electricity, symbol of heavenly inspiration, is shared, to a lesser extent, by Abdias; and no-one has yet ascribed a purely symbolical rôle to him. It is worth remembering that those other figures whom the same critics have reduced to symbols of the poetic, the mysterious, wild girls in *Turmalin*, *Katzensilber* and *Der Waldbrunnen*, derive not merely from Stifter's struggle with his art, and from Goethe's Mignon, but from his unhappy experiences with his adoptive daughter Julie.

The fact remains, however, that the preoccupation of earlier criticism with externals of plot and characterization in *Abdias* has proved less rewarding than the tendency of more recent criticism to focus on allegorical and metaphysical elements in the narrative. Reference has been made to the ambivalence of Stifter's evocation of extreme landscapes, regions of ice and snow, of barrenness and desolation as both terrifying and beautiful, and natural calamities which are blessings also. The possibility that nature which is seemingly indifferent to man, which now destroys and now creates, can be an instrument of Providence, has been ruled out by Mautz as well as by Walter Benjamin whom he invokes. Benjamin has written:

> was (Stifter) höchst unsicher kennt und mit schwächlicher Hand zeichnet ist die Grenze zwischen Natur und Schicksal, wie es sich zum Beispiel geradezu peinlich am Schluss des *Abdias* findet.[55]

Stifter has a highly uncertain knowledge of the borderline

between nature and fate and draws it with a weak hand – as appears for instance, embarrassingly so, at the end of *Abdias*.

F.W. Korff, on the other hand, draws on the terminology of religious experience, evolved by Rudolf Otto in his book *Das Heilige* (2. edition, 1918) (The Holy), to elucidate the ambivalence of nature in Stifter.[56] For the concept that God speaks to man through the phenomena of nature, not in a rationally intelligible fashion, but in 'judgments' that are 'past finding out' (Romans XI, 33), is at least as old as the Bible, and is frequently encountered in Christian mystical and devotional literature. The English-speaking reader will call to mind a poem which is concerned with the search for a providential design in a seemingly arbitrary and destructive act of nature: for in 'The Wreck of the Deutschland', Gerard Manley Hopkins uses not only the image of lightning which has figured symbolically in Greco-Roman literature and since, but that of a snow-storm, so pervasive in Stifter's fiction, to point to a double-effect in God's dealings with man which can be accpeted as meaningful, in a spirit of faith, though it remains paradoxical. Referring to his own experience in prayer, Hopkins writes:

> I did say yes
> O at lightning and lashed rod;
> Thou heardst me truer than tongue confess
> Thy terror, O Christ, O God.[57]

and again:

> Beyond saying sweet, past telling of tongue,
> Thou art lightning and love, I found it, a winter and warm;
> Father and fondler of heart thou hast wrung:
> Hast thy dark descending and most art merciful then[58]

Hopkins proceeds to describe the snow-storm in the Thames estuary in which a quarter of those on board the 'Deutschland', including five Franciscan nuns expelled from Germany, were washed overboard and drowned, and hints that, amidst

terror and destruction, God may have been merciful not only
to the nuns who were ripe for death but to those who died with
them, comforted by the faith and hope to which the nuns bore
witness during the storm:

> Loathed for a love men knew in them,
> Banned by the land of their birth,
> Rhine refused them. Thames would ruin them;
> Surf, snow, river and earth
> Gnashed: but thou art above, thou Orion of light;
> Thy unchancelling poising palms were weighing the worth,
> Thou martyr-master: in thy sight
> Storm flakes were scroll-leaved flowers, lily showers – sweet
> heaven was astrew in them.[59]

When due allowance has been made for Stifter's secularization, here as elsewhere, of orthodox Christian motifs, the
psychological ambivalence evident in the last line of Hopkins
can be seen to correspond to the 'Gewitter, welches dem
Kinde mit seiner weichen Flamme das Leben von dem
Haupte geküsst hatte'[60] (thunderstorm which, with its soft
flame, had kissed away life from the head of the child), the
Bohemian valley in which Abdias settles because of its
'Ähnlichkeit mit der Lieblichkeit der Wüste'[61] (similarity
with the loveliness of the desert), shunned as frightening and
barren by the local people, and yet successfully cultivated by
Abdias, also the desolate landscape of *Kalkstein* which yet
seems beautiful to the priest who has settled in it, and the
glaciers of *Bergkristall* which holds no terror for the trusting
children who have lost their way in the mountains and see
'den heiligen Christ'[62] (the holy Christ) in the Northern
Lights above them.

The children in *Bergkristall*, like the country-priest in
Kalkstein, manifest what Stifter terms serene innocence in
cooperating with a forbidding nature which seems to dwarf
human beings into insignificance. Abdias, too, in his fortitude,
patience and resilience under the blows of fate, his forebear-

ance towards Deborah when she turns against him, at times measures up to the calm grandeur of nature as Stifter depicts it; and it, in turn, has its counterpart in the prose-style which remains unruffled and matter-of-fact when acts of violence and natural disasters are recounted. This is a phenomenon to which metaphysical significance has been ascribed by recent critics. J.P. Stern, for instance, in 'Adalbert Stifters ontologischer Stil'[63] (The ontological Style of Adalbert Stifter), argues that Stifter, in reducing the human interest of specific manifestations of being, in individual characters and situations, focuses attention on being as such, thereby anticipating the existentialist ideal, advocated for fiction by Roquentin in Sartre's *La Nausée*. And Peter Küpper approaches the same phenomenon from another angle when he writes of understatement and concealment as narrative devices in *Bergkristall*:[64] the reader is gradually alerted to the fact that essential information is being withheld from him when the statements of this or that figure in the story, the reassurances given to the children by their grandparents and later by Konrad to his little sister, turn out to be misleading or false while the author yet continues to endorse the unquestioning trust with which they are received. By these means that tension of ambiguity is built up which Thomas Mann has referred to as a 'Sensationellwerden der Langenweile'[65] (boredom becoming sensational) in Stifter's fiction.

The reader who takes a superficial look at the mass of secondary literature on *Abdias* might well form the impression that the critical endeavours of Germanists are liable to be erratic. On closer scrutiny, however, a progressive pattern may be discerned in them. The earlier critics, it is true, were at cross-purposes. Some of them tried to prove that the correspondence between the character and the fate of Abdias was total, disregarding Stifter's hints to the contrary; others emphasized the incommensurability of character and fate, attributing this to a failure on Stifter's part to realize the intention with which he had set out, or else to his deliberate cultivation of ambiguity. Subsequent discussion, however, came to focus on the Biblical echoes in the story, the Jewish theme, and the correspondence now traced was that between a character possessed of great virtues but also of great failings, who is called to a spirituality which he realizes only in part and intermittently, and a fate in which strokes of good luck alternate with disasters. Nature is the instrument of fate: a thunderstorm takes Ditha's life but proves a blessing for the parched countryside. Lightning has a special significance in relation to the vocation of Abdias which has come to be interpreted as symbolizing that of the artist. The rainbows which mark the conclusion of the two storms, intimate an ultimate harmony in apparent contradiction which dispose the reader to accept as plausible the statement with which the story opens: that human fates might appear just and appropriate to us if our vision were less limited than it is at present. Stifter's ambivalence, therefore, takes its place in a literary tradition which includes the Bible, and European poetry from Homer to Hopkins. To read *Abdias* purely as an allegory as some have done, is to over-simplify. But many of the apparent contradictions in the story which have troubled critics admit of resolution, if they are viewed in the perspective of the metaphysical experience which Stifter evokes.

What has been argued with reference to the secondary literature on *Abdias*, that after much confusion a process of elucidation has set in, holds true of Stifter criticism in general. Not that there is now a consensus or anything like it, among Stifter interpreters. The contradictions and ambiguities in his work continue to lead his readers to opposite conclusions. Even within a single volume, the centenary essays edited by Lothar Stiehm in 1968, irreconcilable differences emerge. While, for instance, Kurt Mautz, in 'Das antagonistische Naturbild in Stifters Studien' (The antagonistic image of nature in Stifter's Studien), ascribes a wholly symbolical function to Stifter's nature descriptions,[66] Roy Pascal, in 'Die Landschaftsschilderung im *Hochwald*' (Landscape description in *Hochwald*), claims that Stifter's primary concern is with visual accuracy and scientific truth.[67] And where Requadt argues that Stifter goes beyond Goethe in his 'Naturalisierung des Christentums'[68] (naturalization of Christianity) – the revelation of God to the children on the mountain is more direct than that to the villagers in church – Hermann Kunisch insists that the traditional Catholic concept of hierarchical world-order is central in *Witiko*.[69] But there has been real progress, in so far as there are critics writing now who admit what had previously only been proclaimed by critics hostile to Stifter – his derivativeness, the lack of convincing characterization in much of his fiction, its unreality by the standards of the mid-nineteenth century – and who yet believe that his work has great value. J.P. Stern, as we saw, attributes an ontological purpose to Stifter's deliberate 'distancing' of his characters and their fates.[70] And it is the merit of F.W. Korff's study to have emphasized a connection between the artist-theme in Stifter's work and the metaphysical element in it.[71]

Recent interpretations have the merit of placing Stifter's fiction in a context other than that of realism. For Stifter's own claims to be a realistic writer, restoring epic objectivity to fiction, are hardly acceptable at their face-value, any more than his endeavours to justify his own work as vindicating a timeless ideal of classical harmony and beauty, of moral and aesthetic purity, in opposition to what, he alleges, is the depravity of contemporary literature. If his fictions still command interest it is not because of their characters and plots which are often book-derived, but because of what is expressed by means of them, the dilemma of the artist confronted by the conflicting claims of art and life, a dilemma projected into natural phenomena which inspire exaltation and terror in the onlooker, and communicate experiences of a metaphysical kind in allegorical form. Stifter exemplifies preeminently the recurrent predicament of the German artist in whom the will to excel in art and to emulate the achievements of the past precedes any artistic endeavours on his own part. In the absence of spontaneous creativeness, Stifter's actual productions were bound to show traces of the contrived and imitative; the authentic vision which shines through them, often went unrecognized. For his expressed intentions are frequently at loggerheads with the deeper, not fully conscious, concerns and anxieties that inform his writings. To contemporary critics who had accepted Dickens and Thackeray as the representative novelists of the era, his work was bound to appear anachronistic; the contradictions in it could not but cause confusion, and it was with some reluctance, and only intermittently, that Stifter was accepted as the leading German prose-writer of the eighteen-forties. He never reached a wide reading-public, but should now seem at least assured of recognition as a key-figure in German literary history because his work manifests most conspicuously the peculiarly problematic character, the limitations and the genius, of the German contribution to prose-fiction.

III

George Eliot and Gottfried Keller

The impact of the new English realism and especially of Dickens on the German reading-public of the later eighteen-forties and of the eighteen-fifties is reflected not only in the enthusiastic tone of most German reviews of Dickens's novels, the translations and re-translations that flooded the market, but by a number of German imitations of, in particular, the *Pickwick Papers*.[1] Most of the imitators were dismissed as hack-writers in contemporary reviews, but two novelists, Gustav Freytag and Otto Ludwig, were acclaimed for a time as successful practitioners in a Dickensian mode. Both had committed themselves in theory to the new English realism before they had tried their hands at fiction of their own.[2] German critics spoke of Gustav Freytag's *Soll und Haben* (1855) (Debit and Credit) as a German *David Copperfield*, and lauded Ludwig's *Zwischen Himmel und Erde* (1856) (Between Heaven and Earth) in similarly extravagant terms. The English reaction, when it came, was rather different.

In 1858, G.H. Lewes studied both novels and compared them unfavourably with the work of Gottfried Keller, a Swiss contemporary who continued to cultivate the 'Bildungs-roman' and the 'Novelle' though he introduced a far greater degree of empirical reality into these genres than his predecessors had done. There are, in fact, certain points of contact between the companion of Lewes in these years, George Eliot, and Gottfried Keller, although the two novelists contributed to two different literary traditions. In July 1854, George Eliot had gone to Germany with G.H. Lewes who was collecting material for his *Life of Goethe*. During the winter months which she spent in Berlin, George Eliot frequented the same salons as Gottfried Keller did, and the same names figure in their correspondence: especially Varnhagen von Ense, and Fanny Lewald whose liaison with Adolf Stahr aroused George Eliot's keen interest and sympathy as it reminded her of her own and G.H. Lewes's defiance of convention. There is no evidence that George Eliot and Gottfried Keller, who was in Berlin until the end of 1855, met face to face. But when she and G.H. Lewes returned to Germany, in April 1858, they read together the first volume of *Die Leute von Seldwyla* (1856). It is discussed by Lewes in his article 'Realism in Art: Modern German Fiction'[3] along with Freytag's *Soll und Haben*, Otto Ludwig's *Zwischen Himmel und Erde*, two novels by Theodor Mügge, and two volumes of 'Novellen' by Paul Heyse. While George Eliot writes that her 'only contribution to' the article 'was reading the novels aloud after dinner',[4] Lewes's view of realism is similar to that expressed by her elsewhere. Lewes praises the German contribution to philosophy, scholarship and poetry, but finds that 'the novels of Germany are singularly inferior to those of France or England; indeed, graceful as are many of the German legends and fairy-tales, fiction seems but little suited to the German genius, and novels of real life almost altogether beyond its range'.[5] Freytag's book 'which produced so profound a sensation in Germany, produced none at all in England . . . We should scarcely suppose that even German critics would place *Soll und Haben* beside Balzac or George Sand, Thackeray or Dickens; while English critics assuredly would place it below the works of very inferior writers.'[6] *Zwischen Himmel und Erde* he dismisses as inadequately realized: 'a mawkish, ineffective, wearisome story . . . It is possibly "the meaning" which charms (Ludwig's) admirers, who take the will for the deed, they see what the author intended to execute, and give him the credit for the execution'.[7] Mügge is, in Lewes's view, even less successful than Freytag and Ludwig in achieving the social realism he aspires to. 'We have no belief in any of the characters; they do not affect us as real beings.'[8] Keller's achievement, on the other hand, convinced Lewes that the miniature art of the 'Novelle', with its fairy-tale elements, was better suited to the 'German genius' than the novel, and was at its most impressive when, as in Keller's *Romeo und Julia auf dem Dorfe* (A Village Romeo and Juliet), 'a free poetic fancy in the conception' was in fruitful tension with 'a thorough realism presiding over the execution'.[9]

However, there was a more important link between George Eliot and Gottfried Keller than that exemplified by their common attendance at certain literary salons in the Berlin of the eighteen-fifties. Some years earlier, during formative periods of their lives, both authors had been exposed to similar intellectual influences, in particular those of David Friedrich Strauss and Ludwig Feuerbach. In 1839, when Strauss, the modernist author of *Das Leben Jesu* (The Life of Jesus), was called as professor of theology to Zürich's new university, and 5,000 peasants, led by a pastor, marched on Zürich to overthrow the Liberal régime, Keller was a passionate partisan of the 'Strausse'; and he abandoned his belief in God and immortality in the winter of 1848-9 under the personal influence of Feuerbach at Heidelberg. It is to the 'Feuerbach-experience' that Keller's turning to prose-fiction and his 'Diesseitsgläubigkeit' (faith in this world) are usually attributed. Keller himself claimed that this experience made everything in the world 'glühender und sinnlicher' (more glowing and sensual) for him and strengthened his sense of responsibility for his own life and the lives of others.[10] George Eliot's break with the Christian practice of her environment was precipitated by her acquaintance with Charles Bray at Coventry in 1841. Charles Bray was an admirer of Strauss; and it was to oblige him and his relatives, the Hennels, that George Eliot completed the translation into English of Strauss's *Leben Jesu*, begun by Rufa (Brabant) Hennell. The task occupied her from 1844 to 1846. Her translation of Feuerbach was commissioned work also; she undertook it in the early eighteen-fifties for John Chapman whom she assisted in editing the *Westminster Review*. At that time she wrote to Sarah Hennell: 'With the ideas of Feuerbach I everywhere agree, but, of course, I should, myself, alter the phraseology considerably.'[11]

One would have expected a Feuerbachian rejection of all transcendentalism to manifest itself in a particular way in the fictions of the two authors: in a hostile portrayal of the rôle of the churches and of religious believers. But, in fact, while Christianity and its representatives, especially clergymen, are presented in a negative light in the work of Gottfried Keller, the reverse is usually the case in that of George Eliot. The publisher Blackwood to whom Lewes had sent the manuscript of *Scenes of Clerical Life*, was convinced that the author was a clergyman, because it was so familiar with and sympathetic towards the world of Midland Anglicanism. She writes of Evangelicalism in *Scenes of Clerical Life* that it

> brought into palpable existence in Milby society that idea of duty, that recognition of something to be lived for beyond the mere satisfaction of self, which is to the moral life what the addition of a great central ganglion is to animal life. No man can begin to mould himself on a faith or an idea without rising to a higher order of experience: a principle of subordination, of self-mastery, has been introduced into his nature; he is no longer a mere bundle of impressions, desires and impulses . . . The first condition of human goodness is something to love; the second something to reverence. And this latter precious gift was brought to Milby by Mr Tryan and Evangelicalism.[12]

In *Felix Holt the Radical* and *Middlemarch* idealism takes a more secular form and in *Daniel Deronda* it is embodied in Jewish figures. The cause which Daniel Deronda serves is not really that of the Jewish religion but that of Zionism, and if it lacks the compelling merit in some readers' eyes which George Eliot evidently attributes to it, it serves the purpose of showing up the limitations of those characters to whom disinterested concerns of any kind are incomprehensible.

Keller's portrayal of religion, on the other hand, is consistently hostile. In *Der grüne Heinrich*, Heinrich Lee is in conflict with the Christianity of his environment from the start. His reluctance to join in family prayers prompts the insertion of the story of Meretlein, the girl who was hounded to death in his father's village, a hundred years earlier, for her inability to pronounce the name of the Trinity. The growing boy is sensitive to the discrepancy between the practice and the professed beliefs of Christians in the case of Frau Margret and her husband. When he stays in his father's village after his expulsion from school, he avoids the church, and the Christian doctrines proposed to him in the confirmation class, are rejected as irrational and absurd (Book II, Chapter 11). Elsewhere in the novel, Wurmlinger who advocates a religious revival in opposition to the scientific spirit of the age, is presented as a fraud and a pervert. Christian ethics are repeatedly criticized, especially the cult of resignation. Dortchen, the Count, and Heinrich himself, are favourably contrasted, as active and balanced humanists, with the theistic chaplain on the one hand and the doctrinaire atheist, Peter Gilgus, on the other. Keller's clergymen, unlike George Eliot's, are invariably base and fraudulent. The 'Stadtpfarrer' in *Die missbrauchten Liebesbriefe*, the minister of Schwanau in *Das verlorene Lachen*, the preacher who seduces Aglaja in *Der Landvogt von Greifensee*, and the Redemptorist who practises similar deception of the youthful Lucia in *Das Sinngedicht*, the Jesuits in *Don Correa*, the clergyman who marries the Salander daughters to the Weidelich twins in *Martin Salander*, spring to mind. Louis Wohlwend in the same novel, who poses as the prophet of a 'Gottesstaat der Neuzeit'[13] (City of God of modern times) is guilty of advocating the same fraudulent concoction of

Christian orthodoxy and free thought as the clergyman in *Das verlorene Lachen*. In *Ursula*, Zwingli is presented as a progressive figure, 'soweit das Zeitalter es erlaubte'[14] (in so far as the age permitted it), a humanist and secularizer, caught between the opposing forces of millenarian fanaticism, a destructive epidemic to which even good people, like Ursula, succumb, and what is called the 'Priesterheidentum'[15] (priestly paganism) of the Roman Catholics. Ursula is eventually liberated from the powers of superstition and restored to sanity and reason by Hanslic, as Justine is by Jukundus in *Das verlorene Lachen*. The two sectarian women, Ursula and Agathchen, are indeed charitable and serene. But where George Eliot presents such qualities as the fruit of faith, Keller differentiates between the women's moral goodness and their deluded beliefs.

Throughout his work, therefore, Keller portrays Christianity, especially in its clerical representatives, as inimical to truth and progress; George Eliot, on the other hand, presents religion as an instrument of social cohesion and, positively, as an ego-transcending force in the lives of many of her characters, whether or not the dogmas in which it is formulated – Evangelical in *Scenes of Clerical Life*, Methodist in *Adam Bede*, Catholic in *Romola*, and Jewish in *Daniel Deronda* – can be rationally sustained. The fact that the two authors contributed to different traditions of fiction is of greater consequence here than their common adherence to the views of Feuerbach. Ideological tendentiousness is in keeping with the procedure in Keller's chosen genres, 'Bildungsroman' and 'Novelle', where human life had often been presented in a schematically simplified form, for the purpose of communicating a metaphysical insight or a system of psychological categories and moral values. George Eliot, however, began as the pupil of Sir Walter Scott and adopted his sociological approach in the presentation of different religions as providing discipline, meaning and purpose in the cultures of particular historical communities.

In a letter to Harriet Beecher Stowe, George Eliot writes: 'I think your way of presenting the religious convictions which are not our own, except by indirect fellowship, is a triumph of insight and true tolerance. A thorough comprehension of the mixed moral influence shed on society by dogmatic systems is rare.'[16] This thorough comprehension is in evidence in all the fiction of George Eliot.

That George Eliot and Gottfried Keller, for all their shared convictions, operate in different narrative traditions, shows in other ways. George Eliot, after all, has behind her not only the work of Sir Walter Scott but Jane Austen's novels of society, and Charlotte Brontë who had broken new ground in fiction by articulating the consciousness of girls making their way independently in the world as Maggie Tulliver, Romola, Dorothea and Gwendolen were to do. The social and political analysis in *Felix Holt*, *Middlemarch* and *Daniel Deronda*, the presentation, in these novels, of the clash of classes, the rising proletariat, the new industrialists and the landed gentry, Radicalism and Toryism, is in a tradition which includes Disraeli's *Coningsby* and *Sybil*, Mrs Gaskell's *Mary Barton* and Dickens's *Bleak House*: all of them novels where social conflict is depicted, as it is by George Eliot, in terms of Parliamentary electioneering. In her realistic medium, George Eliot uses conscious analysis in support of an intuitive rendering of the inner lives of her characters in all their subtle fluctuations, and to trace moral growth and decay in detail, and unconscious promptings, at variance, often, with conscious motives, and all this against the background of the social and political life of a community. Even in *The Mill on the Floss* which could conceivably be regarded as an autobiographical 'Bildungsroman' like *Der grüne Heinrich*, George Eliot, unlike Keller, is as interested in evoking a complex social scene, the conservative rural society of the Midlands in the eighteen-thirties which is unsuccessfully resisting the encroachments of commerce and industry, as she is in tracing the development of Maggie Tulliver who is, like Keller's Heinrich, a self-projection. George Eliot believed that a full presentation of an individual character and his fate required the rendering of the life of an entire society: 'These social changes in Treby parish', she writes in *Felix Holt*, 'are comparatively public matters, and this history is chiefly concerned with the private life of a few men and women; but there is no private life which has not been determined by a wider public life, from the time when the primeval milkmaid had to wander with the wanderings of her clan, because the cow she milked was one of a herd which had made the pastures bare . . . If the mixed political conditions of Treby Magna had not been acted on by the passing of the Reform Bill, Mr Harold Transome would not have presented himself as a candidate for North Loamshire, Treby would not have been a polling-place, Mr Matthew Jermyn would not have been on affable terms with a Dissenting preacher and his flock, and the venerable town would not have been placarded with handbills, more or less complimentary and retrospective . . . '[17] If in the genre of the 'Novelle' to which the bulk of Keller's fiction belongs, there is no room for the full evocation of a social environment, there is none either for character studies in depth such as George Eliot's. In Keller's 'Novellen', psychological types are often defined with remarkable shrewdness, but not fully realized in dialogue and action; the transformations which many of them undergo, are often described in a few sentences, but they are not fully enacted, as in George Eliot's work, by slow stages over a long period of time. Where Keller 'überliefert', as Fontane put it,[18] 'die ganze . . . Welt seinem Keller-Ton' (makes the whole . . . world speak in his, Keller's, tone of voice), in George Eliot's fiction, characters reveal themselves as individuals and members of a collective by their speech which may be that of a region like the racy Midland idiom of Mrs Poyser in *Adam Bede*, of the Dodson sisters in *The Mill on the Floss*, or that of a class as in the case of Grandcourt in *Daniel Deronda* with his languid and monosyllabic style, redolent of aristocratic refinement and hauteur. The realism that Lewes admired in *Die Leute von Seldwyla* as modifying the 'poetic fancy of the conception'[19] is found in the rendering of domestic interiors and of the trades and occupations of a pre-industrial society, but the plots are undisguisedly fables in which representative types, universally recognizable if previously unrecorded in fiction – the sulking Pankraz, Frau Amrain who seeks in her boy compensation for the inadequacies of her husband – are subjected to a series of tests and exposed in a denouement where the author points the moral; in his chosen genre Keller is free to indulge his penchant for the fantastic, his caricaturing bent. Even in the treatment of the marriage-theme, the moral factors involved in the choosing of prospective partners in marriage, pervasive in the work of both writers, Keller's approach is characteristically schematic, with those 'Liebesproben' (love-tests) which predominate in *Der Landvogt von Greifensee* and *Das Sinngedicht*, and occur even in earlier stories such as Spiegel's tale in *Spiegel das Kätzchen* and in *Die missbrauchten Liebesbriefe*. In some of the later works, for instance in *Sieben Legenden* (1872), Keller's playfulness is as exuberant as ever, but in other 'Novellen' in which the vigour of the original Seldwyla tales is not maintained, we get a formal elaboration and a pointing of themes by obtrusive symbolism – in *Das Sinngedicht* (1881), for instance, the story of Reinart's quest for a partner, for a relationship that should harmonize freedom, pleasure, sensuality, with moral responsibility, as prescribed in Logau's poem with the same title, and in *Das verlorene Lachen* where the match of Jukundus and Justine, as their names indicate, represents a similar reconciliation between 'vital' and moral values.

George Eliot, on the other hand, has scope, in her long novels, to explore marriage in tracing the interaction of her heroines with their partners from early courtship through many years of marriage to widowhood. Wrong choices are made by many of George Eliot's heroines, from Caterina in the second of the *Scenes of Clerical Life* who passes over the Rev. Gilfil for Captain Wybrow because her values are external ones, and Hetty who similarly rejects Adam Bede in favour of Captain Donnithorne, to Gwendolen Harleth in *Daniel Deronda*. Unhappy marriages figure in *Scenes of Clerical Life* (*Janet's Repentance*), in *Romola*, *Felix Holt*, *Middlemarch* and *Daniel Deronda*. If Romola is largely the innocent victim of Tito's deception, Mrs Transome in *Felix Holt* is herself responsible for her marriage tragedy, and Dorothea Brooke in *Middlemarch* is impelled, in accepting Casaubon, by a mixture of motives: admiration for learning, but also a somewhat priggish contempt for her more ordinary suitors, and her attitude to her partner is an egocentric one. Only by slow degrees is it borne in on her 'that he had an equivalent centre of self, whence the lights and shadows must always fall with a certain difference.'[20] Lydgate, in the same novel, is betrayed into his disastrous marriage with Rosamond by an equally egocentric preconception of woman, and her rôle in marriage as a subordinate and decorative one. Gwendolen Harleth's acceptance of Grandcourt is not merely an error of judgment due to inexperience, it is presented as morally reprehensible. If Romola, Dorothea and Gwendolen suffer extremes of misery in their marriages, their husbands do not go unscathed: 'Tito felt that Romola was a more unforgiving woman than he had imagined; her love was not that sweet clinging instinct, stronger than all judgments, which, he began to see now, made the great charm of a wife.'[21] Tito's disappointment is paralleled by that of Casaubon in *Middlemarch* and of Grandcourt in *Daniel Deronda*. Rosamond who, with her hard and petty egotism has thwarted all her husband's noble aspirations, feels cheated herself and indulges in day-dreams of a match with Will Ladislaw: 'He would have made, she thought, a much more suitable husband for her than she found in Lydgate. No notion could have been falser than this, for Rosamond's discontent in her marriage was due to the conditions of marriage itself, to its demands for self-suppression and tolerance, and not to the nature of her husband.'[22]

Where Keller is concerned to present typical patterns, George Eliot regards it as her duty to try and render the exact truth of observation and experience however difficult this might prove. 'Examine your words well', she writes, 'and you will find that even when you have no motive to be false, it is a very hard thing to say the exact truth, even about your own immediate feelings – much harder than to say something fine about them which is *not* the exact truth.'[23] Keller, on the other hand, defended his contrivances, the spurning of all probability in the pursuit of symmetrical plots, as the time-honoured privilege of the creator of 'Bildungsroman' and 'Novelle':

> Die Unwahrscheinlichkeit betreffend . . . Auch die Geschichte mit dem Logauschen Sinngedicht, die Ausfahrt Reinharts auf die Kussproben kommt ja nicht vor; niemand unternimmt dergleichen, und doch spielt sie durch mehrere Kapitel. Im Stillen nenne ich dergleichen die Reichsunmittelbarkeit der Poesie, d.h. das Recht, zu jeder Zeit, auch im Zeitalter des Fracks und der Eisenbahnen, an das Parabelhafte, das Fabelmässige ohne weiteres anzuknüpfen, ein Recht, das man sich nach meiner Meinung durch keine Kulturwandlungen nehmen lassen soll.[24]

> Concerning the implausibility . . . The story with Logau's 'Sinngedicht', the journey of Reinhart in pursuit of kissing-tests, such things don't happen, no-one embarks on an action of that kind, and yet it runs through several chapters. Privately, I call that the autonomy of poetic creation, i.e. the right in every age, even in that of the tail-coat and of railways, to continue the tradition of parable and fable, a right which, in my opinion, one must not let oneself be deprived of by any cultural changes.

Even Keller's one attempt at a novel of social realism, *Martin Salander* (1886), is too schematic to bear comparison with the work of his English contemporaries. Its main character, the idealistic and gullible Salander and the malignant and parasitical Wohlwend, do not, it is generally agreed, spring to life and the symmetries of plot – that Wohlwend should deceive and nearly ruin Salander twice over, and the Weidelich heirs enter as twins, in token of their lack of individuality, and come, independently of each other, to an identical bad end, – is evidence of an artificiality foreign to this genre.

In the tradition stemming from Sir Walter Scott, veracity implied a duty to understand and therefore to sympathize with the characters portrayed. There is no scope for satire which, on the other hand, could and did flourish in the German 'Novelle'. It is clear that in this respect George Eliot and Gottfried Keller were by temperament well suited to contribute to these two genres. Keller's was the 'herbe Gemütsart'[25] (harsh temperament) which he attributes to *Pankraz der Schmoller*; it goes with the sardonic tone in much of his fiction, and the irritable, suspicious and scathing utterances to be found so often in his correspondence, and with his difficulties in personal relationships. By contrast, George Eliot seems well adjusted, and capable of striking up good relationships with everyone she encounters. Her sense of human community is too insistent for feelings of loneliness, so pervasive in the biographies of German writers, to arise even when she suffers ostracism on her return to England with G.H. Lewes. Bessie Parkes recorded that the qualities which distinguish George Eliot's fiction, were apparent also in her conversation: 'The odd mixture of truth and fondness in Marian is so great. She never spares, but expresses every opinion, good and bad, with the most unflinching plainness, and yet she seems able to see faults without losing tenderness'.[26]

It was not only sociological awareness of the role of religion in history, but human sympathy with individual believers, that made it impossible for her to translate Feuerbachian theory into fiction in as simplistic a fashion as Keller did. Charges of intellectual inconsistency did not trouble her. When in 1859 her identity as the authoress of

Scenes of Clerical Life and *Adam Bede* became known, friends who had met her ten years earlier, expressed surprise. To one of these, François D'Albert-Durade with whom she had stayed in Geneva in 1850, she wrote:

> I can understand that there are many pages in *Adam Bede* in which you do not recognize the 'Marian' or 'Minie' of old Geneva days. We knew each other too short a time, and I was under too partial and transient a phase of my mental history, for me to pour out to you much of my earlier experience. I think I hardly ever spoke to you of the strong hold Evangelical Christianity had on me from the age of fifteen to two and twenty and of the abundant intercourse I had had with earnest people of various religious sects. When I was at Geneva, I had not yet lost the attitude of antagonism which belongs to the renunciation of *any* belief . . . Ten years of experience have wrought great changes in that inward self: I have no longer any antagonism towards any faith in which human sorrow and human longing for purity have expressed themselves; on the contrary, I have a sympathy with it that predominates over all argumentative tendencies.[27]

It was to the world of ordinary people, of 'mixed' character, around her that she wanted to reconcile her readers: 'It is these more or less ugly, stupid, inconsistent people, whose movements of goodness you should be able to admire – for whom you should cherish all possible hopes, all possible patience'.[28] We have the paradox that George Eliot who, on the one hand, sets higher standards for her characters than Keller does, is, on the other, less censorious than he is. While she, as has been noted, attaches the highest value to lives that are dedicated to the service of religious causes and of other people, to the point of self-sacrifice, Keller tends to favour a combination of humane qualities with enlightened self-interest, on the grounds which the 'Statthalter' in *Der grüne Heinrich* formulates:

> Wer seinen Vorteil nicht mit unverhohlener Hand zu erringen und zu wahren versteht, der wird auch nie imstande sein,

seinem nächsten aus freier Tat einen Vorteil zu verschaffen.[29]

He who does not know how to gain and maintain his advantage open-handed, will never be in a position to obtain an advantage for his neighbour by free action.

Those who suffer defeat as a consequence of their weaknesses or misdeeds retain the reader's sympathy and respect in the work of George Eliot while they forfeit it, as a rule, in that of Keller. In *Der grüne Heinrich*, the narrator's account of his own failures and humiliations is for the most part coolly detached, and where he describes the downfall of other people, that of the teacher at the 'Realschule', or the painter Römer, he dwells with equal coldness on the most embarrassing phases of their histories even though he expresses remorse for his contribution to their downfall. It is interesting to find in Ermatinger's study of the sources of the novel[30], that Keller's models in real life, the teacher Egli in the Zürich 'Industrie-schule' and the artist Meyer, were by no means as cruelly exposed and wretched as their counterparts in the novel. While Keller applauds the humanity of a Judith, of a Marie Salander, or the kindness which is shown to Zambo, the 'arme Baronin', and to Regine, in *Das Sinngedicht*, cruel humiliation is invariably the lot of those characters whose adjustment to reality is defective. They may be capable of reform, like Strapinski in *Kleider machen Leute*, or Wilhelm in *Die missbrauchten Liebesbriefe*; but where – as in the case of Manz and Marti in *Romeo und Julia auf dem Dorfe*, of *Die drei gerechten Kammacher*, and many others – rehabilitation is not feasible, Keller's description is characterized by a total withdrawal of sympathy so that the final degradation they suffer, appears merely grotesque, and not tragic. Martini has spoken of the 'typisierend Schwankhafte' (type-casting farcical) in Keller's work, 'das die "verkehrten Menschen" in das Marionettenhafte verändert'[31] (that turns the 'wrong-headed people' into puppet-like creatures).

There is nothing comparable in George Eliot's work. Reference has been made to the fact that the Berlin authors,

Adolf Stahr and Fanny Lewald, who are supposed to have provided the models for Viggi Störteler and Kätter Ambach in *Die missbrauchten Liebesbriefe*, were personally known to George Eliot also. While Keller expressed detestation of them, George Eliot, characteristically, spoke of them with respect[32]. George Eliot would, of course, never have ridiculed a 'blue-stocking' as Keller does in *Die missbrauchten Liebesbriefe* and in *Die drei gerechten Kammacher*. Her characterizations are by no means free from irony but she is totally averse to caricaturing simplification. The Dodson sisters in *The Mill on the Floss* expose themselves, whenever they speak, in all their pettiness, their money- and status-conscious rigidity, but their positive qualities, their integrity and family-loyalty, are in evidence at the same time. Silas Marner, in the opening chapter of the novel, resembles Jobst in *Die drei gerechten Kammacher* in his single-minded preoccupation with his work and his hoard of gold, but George Eliot shows how the life-thwarting constriction that characterizes him originated in early experiences, so that we follow the gradual restoration of his sense of community with eager sympathy. Her analyses may expose a character's weaknesses and failings, but not without establishing that the qualities deplored are shared in varying degrees by many people, that even the seemingly depraved are capable of suffering, that tragedy can reach them. There is no condescension in George Eliot's compassion, even where a woman apparently as hard, mean and snobbish as Mrs Transome in *Felix Holt* is concerned:

> If she had only been more haggard and less majestic, those who had glimpses of her outward life might have said she was a tyrannical, griping harridan, with a tongue like a razor. No one said exactly that; but they never said anything like the full truth about her, or divined what was hidden under that outward life – a woman's keen sensibility and dread, which lay screened behind all her petty habits and narrow actions, as some quivering thing with eyes and throbbing heart may lie crouching behind withered rubbish.[33]

The unflinching seriousness and truthfulness in the delineation of character to which George Eliot is committed makes her present even a self-centred and, apparently, brainless and heartless beauty like Hetty in *Adam Bede* or Rosamond in *Middlemarch* as more complex than Keller's corresponding figures, Lydia in *Pankraz der Schmoller* and some of the girls who let down Landolt in *Der Landvogt von Greifensee*: there is the temporary breakthrough of generosity in Rosamond after her disillusionment with Ladislaw, for instance, which prompts her to mediate between him and Dorothea, and Hetty's growth to tragic stature in Book Fifth of *Adam Bede*. Dr. Casaubon in *Middlemarch* seems, as a literary figure, as pretentious and hollow, at first, as Viggi Störteler in *Die missbrauchten Liebesbriefe*. But George Eliot warns the reader against a contemptuous dismissal of him:

> Doubtless his lot is important in his own eyes; and the chief reason that we think he asks too large a place in our consideration must be our want of room for him, since we refer him to the Divine regard with perfect confidence; nay, it is even held sublime for our neighbour to expect the utmost there, however little he may have got from us. Mr Casaubon, too, was the centre of his own world; if he was liable to think that others were providentially made for him . . . this trait is not quite alien to us, and, like the other mendicant hopes of mortals, claims some of our pity. Certainly this affair of his marriage with Miss Brooke touched him more nearly than it did any one of the persons who have hitherto shown their disapproval of it.[34]

The figure of the artist is marginal in the fiction of George Eliot but as pervasive in the work of Keller as in the fiction of Goethe and the Romantics. In George Eliot's *Romola*, there is a hostile confrontation between Tito, the aesthete, and Fra Luca, the ascetic, all the credit going to the latter. In *Middlemarch*, Dorothea reacts with distaste to the proliferation of artistic monuments in Rome, as she does to the objets d'art in her uncle's house:

> That is one reason why I did not like the pictures here, dear uncle – which you think me stupid about. I used to come to the village with all that dirt and coarse ugliness like a pain within me, and the simpering pictures in the drawing-room seemed to me like a wicked attempt to find delight in what is false.[35]

In *The Mill on the Floss*, Philip Wakem's love of etching is indicative of feminine sensibility and weakness, the painters in *Middlemarch* (Naumann) and *Daniel Deronda* (Hans Meyrick) are presented as high-spirited, amiable but light-weight. George Eliot did care for music, however, and the figure of Klesmer, the pianist and composer in *Daniel Deronda*, is used by her to place the insularity of English county society. As for the theatre, Daniel Deronda's mother is considered to have betrayed her family and nation when she became an operatic star while Mirah is complimented on having resisted her father's attempt to train her for a stage-career which is associated with lax morals.

If in George Eliot's case it is clearly a residue of her Evangelical heritage, which is reflected in her suspicion of art and the portrayal of artists as inclined to hedonism and moral irresponsibility, in Keller's fiction, as in that of his German predecessors, it is the recoil from aesthetic diastole into systolic commitment to society which informs the presentation of the artist and his problems. In *Der grüne Heinrich*, the hero's attainment of maturity involves the renunciation of art, a choice which is anticipated by Lys and Erikson. Dilettantism characterizes the activities of the literary couple in *Die missbrauchten Liebesbriefe*, and of Jacques in the *Züricher Novellen*, and the artists subsequently introduced into that cycle, Buz Falätscher and Hadlaub, are human failures while in the case of Landolt, in *Der Landvogt von Greifensee*, it is stressed that his mature involvement in social and political life presupposed the abandonment of the artistic preoccupations of his youth. In the 'Novellen' of

Keller, as in those of Stifter, there are characters who may not be described as artists but who sustain the same conflict between claims of the imagination and the claims of empirical reality, and who find spiritual health in renouncing fantasy and adjusting to practical life, or who fail to do so and go under. And Keller reveals an ambivalence similar to Stifter's in his portrayal of the conflict. In the preface to the second volume of *Die Leute von Seldwyla* (1874), Keller admits that he reverts to the inhabitants of the older Seldwyla because, with their fancies and foibles, they provide more interesting narrative material than their sober and business-like descendants.

The two authors, however, share a strong normative impulse, which shows in their preoccupation with the theme of guilt and retribution to which reference has been made earlier. In Keller's work this is frequently formulated in terms of artist's problems while George Eliot registers a rather wider spectrum of moral vicissitudes. Both writers are given to commenting on the actions they relate, and often draw similar conclusions. Both, for instance, observe with some dismay that misfortune is not always, or inevitably, the consequence of wrong-doing. Mr Jermyn in *Felix Holt* learns 'in anger, in exasperation' that he is threatened with exposure and regards this as 'bad luck, not justice; for is there any justice when ninety-nine men out of a hundred escape?'[36] And in *Romeo und Julia auf dem Dorfe*, Keller remarks that misdeeds like those of Manz and Marti do not normally have such grim consequences for their perpetrators, but 'zuweilen stellt das Schicksal ein Exempel auf'[37] (but at times, fate makes an example of someone), and in *Kleider machen Leute*, he admits that the punishment of fraud, in Strapinski's case, is exceptional, that often the fraudulent, particularly if highly placed, survive and prosper[38]. Both authors record suffering that is unmerited and observe that some of those who bring suffering on themselves, profit from it while others do not. In *Das verlorene Lachen*, Keller writes that an individual's recovery from misfortune – as in the case of Jukundus – is not necessarily due to his own merit: 'das Finden seiner selbst in dunkeln Tagen ist meist mehr Glücksache als die Menschen eingestehen wollen'[39] (finding one's way in dark days is often more a matter of luck than most people are normally prepared to admit).

Both authors, however, show a distinct preference for situations where, in Keller's words, 'das Schicksal ein Exempel aufstellt'[40] (fate makes an example of someone) and this, paradoxically, leads them at times close to a providentialism which, as L. Wiesmann has put it 'in einer Feuerbachschen Weltsicht eigentlich nichts zu suchen hat'[41] (is really out of place in a Feuerbachian view of the world). We have, for instance, the dismemberment of the doll by the infant Sali at the opening of *Romeo und Julia auf den Dorfe* which foreshadows his subsequent mutilation of Vrenchen's father, forebodings and premonitions in this and other stories, and the simultaneous arrival of Justine and Jukundus at the cottage of Agathchen in *Das verlorene Lachen* – clearly more than a coincidence – which leads to their reconciliation. On the other hand, Heinrich Lee's tendency to see the hand of Providence in the events of his life, as in the case of what he calls the 'Flötenwunder' (miracle of the flute) (Book IV, chapter 4), is exposed as a dangerous superstition, for it weakens his resolve to help himself, and he is cured of it only by his Feuerbach-experience in the Count's castle. When Heinrich sees the poem on hope which Dortchen had given him, inscribed on the window of the inn where he and Judith go to eat, he finds this 'Aufdringlichkeit des Zufalls . . . eher ängstlich und beklemmend als freudig'[42] (importunity of chance . . . really frightening and oppressive rather than joyful), fearing that this coincidence might tempt him to relapse into his former fatalism. George Eliot was a keen student of Aeschylus and Sophocles and frequently quotes passages from their plays in which the Eumenides are acclaimed as the powers which bring to light hidden truths, and guide the guilty to judgment. She seems to allow for such a guiding fate behind some, at least, of the coincidences in the lives of her characters, particularly in *Silas Marner* and in the later novels, from *Romola* where Tito is again and again brought face to face with Baldassare whom he flees, and *Felix Holt* where the guilt of Mr Jermyn and Mrs Transome is exposed by their son Harold as the unwitting agent of Nemesis, to *Daniel Deronda*: Daniel's seemingly accidental encounters, first with Mirah, then with her lost brother Ezra, and with his own mother in the very hotel in Genoa in which Gwendolen and her husband come to stay, lead him step by step to the discovery of his Jewish origins and the acceptance of his prophetic vocation.

However, even a common preoccupation with Nemesis in the fictions of George Eliot and Gottfried Keller fails to result in any significant degree of resemblance. Whereas George Eliot had passed from a provincial to a cosmopolitan world before she started to write fiction, Keller was confined for most of his life in a Swiss regional milieu; the novel of social realism was not, therefore, within his scope, any more than it had been within that of his German predecessors. G.H. Lewes who admired the German contribution to lyrical poetry and the fairy-tale, recognized that Keller, in accepting his limitations, was more successful than German writers who tried to imitate the social realism of their English contemporaries without having any comparable experience to draw on. Keller worked in a German tradition, infusing new life into the 'Novelle' by extending its empirical range; but at the same time he retained the schematically simplifying patterns characteristic of this genre, providing brief, if shrewd and vivid, sketches of representative characters and problems which are exposed in parable-like narratives. The 'free poetic fancy' which so charmed Lewes – and many readers since – is evidence of some compensatory 'inwardness' in Keller also. George Eliot, on the other hand, was concerned to record truthfully and sympathetically slow processes of interaction between complex individuals in the context of fully rendered historical societies. That their respective fictions should, therefore, appear so very different, in spite of the fact that both authors had come under the same philosophical influences and faced many similar issues, is testimony to the strength and homogeneity of the contrasting literary traditions to which they chose to contribute.

IV

Charles Dickens and Wilhelm Raabe

While the claim that the achievement of Gustav Freytag and Otto Ludwig was comparable to that of the English realists, was not long sustained, a German novelist who produced some forty novels in as many years in the second half of the nineteenth century, Wilhelm Raabe, continued to be referred to as 'the German Dickens' until the nineteen thirties.[1] It is true that the themes and methods of Raabe are not primarily those of social realism; but then Dickens has not always been regarded by English-speaking critics as a realist writer either. Lionel Trilling, for instance, states with reference to *Little Dorrit*, that a novel 'in which a house falls physically to ruins from the moral collapse of its inhabitants, in which the heavens open over London to show a crown of thorns, in which there are characters named nothing else than Bar, Bishop, Physician . . . is only incidentally realistic, its finest power of imagination appears in the general images whose abstractness is their actuality, like Mr Merdle's dinner-parties, or the Circumlocution Office itself . . . '[2] Other critics have pointed to the improbable coincidences on which so many of Dicken's plots hinge, the forced pathos and contrived melodrama here and there in his novels, the element of exaggeration and caricature in his characterization. As for Raabe, it has been argued by Walther Killy that his most significant contributions to fiction wholly transcend the conventions of realism[3]. But before discounting the realistic character of Dickens's fiction, one might do well to recall that the names of many Dickensian characters – and the nouns and adjectived derived from them: Bumbledom, Pecksniffian, Micawberish, etc. – have entered the language as terms descriptive of identifiable types of temperament and behaviour; and, as G.K. Chesterton reminds us[4], the most 'improbable' incidents in *David Copperfield* have a factual basis in Dickens's own life. More recent critics have indeed conceded the reality of many Dickensian figures, but, at the same time, claimed that their – supposedly – 'larger-than-life' impact expresses a child's experience of the adult world. But this limiting judgment is also open to question, in the words of Santayana: 'When people say that Dickens exaggerates it seems to me that they can have no eyes and no ears. They probably only have *notions* of what things and people are; they accept them conventionally, at their diplomatic value.'[5]

Whatever the reality of Raabe's evocations of the social world of his time, it is indisputable that Dickens always manages to inject vivid particulars of an accurately observed environment into his novels, even where the general outlines of the plot are contrived and implausible. Indeed, if we look at the reception of Dickens's work in mid-nineteenth-century Germany, we find that it was precisely its realism, the depth of his penetration of the contemporary social world that most impressed Wilhelm Raabe and his fellow-countrymen. In the essay on Dickens referred to earlier, Wilhelm Dilthey emphasizes the German public's shock of recognition on reading the English novelist. Of Mrs Nickleby, Dilthey says: 'Jedermann hat eine Person dieser Art gesehen, und niemand hätte geglaubt, dass es möglich sei, sie in einem Roman auftreten zu lassen, ohne dass jeder Leser verzweifelt das Buch weglegt.'[6] (Everyone has seen a person of this kind, and no-one would have believed it possible that she could have appeared in a novel without making every reader put down the book in despair.) Dilthey dwells on the extent of Dickens's knowledge of private and public life; he acknowledges the comprehensiveness of Dickens's presentation of social classes, of English institutions, of a variety of psychological types who are yet individualized so compellingly that they seem unique. Dilthey traces the characteristics of Dickens's fiction back to the wide scope of his personal experience: to his early plumbing of the lower depths, followed by his years of apprenticeship in lawyers' offices and as the parliamentary reporter of national newspapers, and all this before he was out of his teens. The fact, Dilthey argues, that German intellectuals and authors had to spend their youth and early manhood invariably in provincial, academic surroundings accounts for the absence in Germany of any comparable fiction. Berthold Auerbach echoes this view:

> Dickens . . . hatte das Glück, ein Engländer zu sein. Was sind wir? Immer und immer Provinzialmenschen. Wir haben kein Zentrum, das jeder kennt, wir haben keine Nationaltypen . . . Was hat Freytag, und was habe ich gemacht? Doch nur provinziales Leben.[7]

> Dickens had the good fortune to be an Englishman. What are we? Ever and always provincial people. We have no centre that everyone knows, we have no national types . . . What has Freytag, and what have I done? Only provincial life.

However, it was Wilhelm Raabe who was now held to rival Dickens, and there are a number of reasons why Raabe should from the start have challenged comparison specifically with Dickens. He had been strongly influenced by Dickens, particularly in his earlier work, and had himself been the first to acknowledge this. Apart from the direct influence which can be traced there are certain characteristics of style and theme common to both authors, as well as the obvious differences – the much wider social range of the Englishman and more explicit metaphysical concerns of the German.

The instances where Raabe has borrowed characters and situations from Dickens are easily identified, particularly as Raabe, with his characteristic honesty, often acknowledges Dickens on these occasions. For instance, in *Die Chronik der Sperlingsgasse*, the chronicler Wachholder introduces the Christmas scenes which vividly recall Dickens by saying: 'Die Geister, die den alten Scrooge des Meisters Boz über die Weihnachtswelt führten, hätten mich nicht besser leiten können, als Herr Ulrich Strobel!'[8] (The spirits which led old Scrooge of Master Boz across the Christmas world, could not have guided me better than Herr Ulrich Strobel!) In *Die Leute aus dem Walde*, Friedrich Wolf's journey through the United States is expressly paralleled with that of Martin Chuzzlewit on which it is obviously modelled. That *Der Hungerpastor* was inspired by Raabe's reading of *David Copperfield* is evident not only from the resemblance between the characters and fates of the heroes; Raabe lifted whole sub-plots from the book which made so great an impact on him and rearranged them to fit into the fabric of *Der Hungerpastor*. For instance, in *David Copperfield* it is Steerforth whose boat is wrecked in a storm outside the village where Emily, the woman he has seduced and deserted, used to live; in *Der Hungerpastor*, Kleophea, seduced and deserted by Moses Freudenstein, suffers shipwreck and is washed up on the beach of the fishing-village where the 'Hungerpastor' has found refuge. Among the echoes of Dickens in Raabe's later work, perhaps the most obvious are in *Drei Federn*, in which the characters of the lawyer Hahnenberg and his secretary Pinnemann recall those of Wickfield and Uriah Heap in *David Copperfield*; and in *Fabian und Sebastian*, where Raabe has reassembled the pattern of characters and relationships of *Dombey and Son*. The young hero of *Prinzessin Fisch*, in his ingratitude to his benefactors, his pursuit of false values, and his subsequent remorse, appears to be modelled on Pip of *Great Expectations*. E. Doernenburg and W. Fehse, who have listed many of Raabe's borrowings from Dickens, conclude that Raabe's literary talent was not originally 'epic' in character, that he lacked the imaginative inventiveness of the born story-teller, and therefore needed to take over the plots and situations as material for his great lyrical and reflective powers.[9]

Quite apart from the kind of derivativeness referred to, there are a number of less tangible resemblances between general themes and attitudes in the work of the two authors. These are not necessarily due to any influence of Dickens on Raabe, but rather to some degree of kinship between them and the similarity of taste of the public for which they wrote. (There can, of course, be no suggestion of any influence in the reverse direction: Raabe was twenty years younger than Dickens and only started to publish in the mid-eighteen-fifties; Dickens's novels had invariably been translated and published in large editions in Germany within a year or two of their publication in England, whereas Raabe was untranslated and, indeed, unknown in England in Dickens's lifetime.)

A severe puritanism in sexual matters was as characteristic of the German as it was of the English middle classes in Victorian times. The attempted seduction of an innocent girl by a man of the world, without 'honourable intentions', figures as the most loathsome of imaginable crimes in the works of both authors. While Raabe provides almost identical versions of this situation and the characters involved in it, from the early historical novels through *Der Hungerpastor* and *Abu Telfan* down to works of his old age like *Fabian und Sebastian* and *Im alten Eisen*, there is in Dickens a distinct development from the Victorian clichés of *Nicholas Nickleby* (the pursuit of innocent Kate Nickleby by the cardboard aristocratic rake, Lord Frederick Verisopht) to the more complex, not wholly unsympathetic portrayal of Steerforth, the seducer of Emily in *David Copperfield*. A closely related theme which seems to have had a particular fascination for Dickens is that of the innocent, beautiful young girl whom an ageing ogre of a man inveigles or attempts to inveigle into matrimony: there is Madeline whom Nicholas Nickleby loves, bullied into marriage with old Arthur Gride by her selfish father and Nicholas's uncle Ralph, there is the gentle and beautiful wife of the sadistic dwarf Quilp in *The Old*

Curiosity Shop, the marriage of Louisa Gradgrind to the middle-aged Bounderby in *Hard Times*, and the attempt on Mary Graham by Pecksniff in *Martin Chuzzlewit*, on Agnes Wickfield by Uriah Heep in *David Copperfield*. This theme was occasionally handled by Raabe, too, for instance in *Das Horn von Wanza*, but not as vividly. It is, after all, mainly in his accounts of these relationships that Dickens reveals his strong, if repressed, sensuality, a characteristic which Raabe did not share. Those Dickensian heroines who are dedicated to the care of tyrannical, pathetic, or profligate fathers (in Little Nell's case, a grandfather), from Madeline Bray in *Nicholas Nickleby* to Florence Dombey, Little Dorrit, and Lizzie Hexam in the later fiction, have their counterparts in Raabe, e.g. in Albertine, daughter of Lippoldes in *Pfisters Mühle*. But where Dickens manages to instil some individuality even into these figures, they remain novelettish in Raabe's fiction. And the complicated, unsentimental heroines of Dickens's last novels, Estella in *Great Expectations*, Bella Wilfer in *Our Mutual Friend*, have no equivalents in Raabe's work. Dickens's tolerance of unconventional sexuality is, in any case, greater than Raabe's: Louisa Gradgrind's adultery, in *Hard Times*, is portrayed forbearingly, Dr Strong's chivalrous treatment of his 'erring' wife is endorsed, and Headstone's uncontrolled physical desire for Lizzie Hexam in *Our Mutual Friend* is evoked with remarkable compassion. Raabe's novels are, in this respect, much more deeply committed to Victorian stereotype; the mutual love of hero and heroine is not only invariably idealistic and 'pure', but made to originate in a sentimental childhood friendship, in conformity with a convention obtaining in the romances serialized in the then fashionable *Gartenlaube*. This is the case even in later novels like *Stopfkuchen* and *Die Akten des Vogelsangs*, which are in other respects much more original.

Another feature common to both authors is a predominantly negative attitude to political life and institutions. But here, too, a distinction has to be made. Raabe's earlier novels

113

reveal a strong political concern: there are numerous references to the disillusionment which followed the so-called Wars of Liberation and bitter comments on the Holy Alliance of the post-Napoleonic era, as well as a number of highly sympathetic portraits of Liberals who suffer police persecution and exile after the revolution of 1848. But Dr Wimmer of *Die Chronik der Sperlingsgasse* shows Raabe's subsequent political disengagement: a political idealist on the run from that Prussian police which here as elsewhere (e.g. in *Die Leute aus dem Walde*) is scathingly satirized, he abandons the fight and withdraws into bourgeois domesticity. So does Wassertreter in *Abu Telfan*, who in retrospect identifies the Liberal ideals for which he once fought with other follies and delusions of his youth. In *Unsres Herrgotts Kanzlei* (1861), Raabe reads a contemporary Liberal issue into the struggle of sixteenth-century Magdeburg against princely rule, feudalism, and clericalism, and the Germany of the petty principalities continues to be treated satirically in Raabe's work (particularly in *Abu Telfan*), but like so many of his fellow-countrymen Raabe was increasingly satisfied to leave it to Bismarck to impose German unification from above; admiring references to Bismarck abound in the later novels, down to *Gutmanns Reisen* (1890-1), but references to those who engage in party politics (e.g. in *Der Lar*, 1887-8) or actually seek election to the Reichstag (in *Kloster Lugau*, 1891-3) are uniformly scathing.

Dickens's aversion to organs of government and, indeed, to all organized institutions, including the churches, has often been remarked upon, as has his corresponding emphasis on individual human relationships and the family as the primary sources of good. The values in Dickens's novels are unequivocally Christian as, indeed, were his expressed beliefs – 'when his son left for Australia, Dickens handed him a New Testament and impressed on him the truth and beauty of the Christian religion and "the wholesome practice of private prayer" which he himself "had never abandoned" '[10]. But while there are good parsons in *The Old Curiosity Shop*, in *Our Mutual Friend*, and elsewhere, as well as odious ones like the Rev. Chadband in *Bleak House*, biting asides at organized religion and, in particular, the bishops abound. F.R. Leavis connects Dickens's antipathy towards the trade unions in *Hard Times* and that towards the churches and sees in both a prejudice against organization of any kind.[11] In the same way, Dickens appears averse to parliamentary government as he found it. It could, however, be argued that, just as his indictment of the law and of lawyers, in *Bleak House* and so many other novels, is not a repudiation of law as such but of the maladministration of the law, so his satirical treatment of parliamentary elections, in the *Pickwick Papers*, and of parliamentary candidates – Veneering in *Our Mutual Friend*, Gradgrind and Harthouse in *Hard Times*, etc – is directed against an oligarchical system, hypocritically presented as democratic, not against parliamentary democracy as such. Dickens cleary identifies himself with David Copperfield who is made to say: 'I am sufficiently behind the scenes to know the worth of political life. I am quite an Infidel about it; and shall never be converted.'[12] And yet, those who, like George Orwell, have assumed that Dickens was against government as such[13] fail to take into account episodes like that in *Bleak House* where Dickens acclaims the stand of Rouncewell, the progressive manufacturer, against the decadent feudal interest, represented by Sir Leicester Dedlock; and in *Little Dorrit* foreign governments are specifically commended for encouraging and promoting the inventor Doyce who has been frustrated at home by an administration in which corruption and nepotism go with monumental inefficiency: the Circumlocution Office. It is a characteristic difference that, while individuals with political interests figure frequently in Raabe's work, political institutions, which are depicted by Dickens often with nightmarish intensity, are conspicuously absent; they were outside Raabe's range of experience.

Raabe and Dickens also differ considerably in their attitudes to the rising industrial civilization of their time. The world of the stage-coach, as has often been emphasized, is dominant in Dickens's earlier novels, but the railway age, the iron and coal country (particularly in *Hard Times* and *Bleak House*), and London as the cosmopolitan centre of modern business, industry, and commerce are compellingly present in the later work, and the apotheosis of Doyce, the inventor of genius in *Little Dorrit*, shows Dickens's positive attitude to technical progress. In Raabe, on the other hand, the characteristic features of modern civilization are not fully rendered; we merely have some reflections on the positive and negative aspects of economic progress. Several of Raabe's novels are set in Berlin, but except for allusions to machines and workshops, proletarians and social distress (clearly inspired by a reading of Dickens) in *Die Chronik der Sperlingsgasse*, to slum tenements in *Im alten Eisen*, and approximations to Berlin slang in the dialogue of *Villa Schönow*, these novels and the limited social world which Raabe portrays in them could equally well have been set in the small towns with which Raabe was more familiar. In the novels *Prinzessin Fisch* and *Unruhige Gäste*, Raabe presents the beginnings of a 'tourist industry' in mountain villages as a materialistic phenomenon, destructive of the values of traditional rural communities. In *Die Akten des Vogelsangs*, Raabe deplores the swallowing up of an old township with its spirit of neighbourliness by the anonymous suburban sprawl of a near-by big city, and in *Meister Autor* the destruction of old houses and gardens by new estates and traffic arteries, promoted by ruthless development corporations. Nostalgia for the past and fear of the future predominate in *Horacker*, too, where the old headmaster, representing a humane culture and a liberal individualism, is being elbowed out of the way by Neubauer, representative of a new generation, with his cult of efficiency and standardization. In the novel *Pfisters Mühle* Raabe, however, postulates a situation which allows him to expatiate on the past while at the same time admitting the necessity of change and progress. The past in this novel is represented by Pfister, the proprietor of an old mill whose livelihood is ruined by the effluents of a new sugar-factory near by. These effluents clog the mill-stream and, with their insidious smells, drive away the customers to whom Pfister used to serve refreshments in the mill garden. But the hero of the book is Asche, a student of chemistry and tutor of Pfister's son, who becomes a successful industrialist, but remains loyal to the values typified by the old mill and to humanistic culture – it is emphasized that he seeks relaxation from his arduous daily work in the study of Homer. And his task in the novel is to reconcile old Pfister with the new order. But Asche, like the sympathetic industrial entrepreneurs whom Raabe introduces in *Villa Schönow* and *Fabian und Sebastian*, is, as Georg Lukács has pointed out[14], a typical Raabe eccentric and not a convincing embodiment of his profession.

In their attitudes to nationalism and nationality Dickens and Raabe differ even more profoundly. Both authors write predominantly about their fellow-countrymen, and foreigners and foreign countries figure only marginally in their fiction. But Dickens spent many months at a time in the United States, in Belgium, France, and Italy; he had a fluent command of French and mixed easily in Parisian literary society, and is therefore a cosmopolitan figure in contrast with Raabe, who never set foot outside Germany and Austria, prided himself on being a national writer, interpreted the national character[15], and indicted cosmopolitanism in the figure of Freudenstein, the Jewish villain of *Der Hungerpastor*. Raabe shared the longing of nineteenth-century German intellectuals for national unification. Throughout his novels, from the earliest, *Die Chronik der Sperlingsgasse* (1854-5), to the late *Hastenbeck* (1895-8), he laments German disunity, whether due to denominational division, tribal feuds, and local separatism or to the quarrels of political parties; he even appeals to sentiments of national self-pity and resentment of foreigners who are alleged to have exploited German disunity. In his early historical novels and Novellen, Raabe introduces foreign characters to contrast what are supposed to be German virtues – openness, purity, and loyalty – with foreign, French or Italian, vices, i.e. treachery and sexual immorality, in conformity with time-honoured clichés. In fairness one must add that he occasionally modifies this chauvinistic scheme by introducing 'good' foreigners, e.g. Simone Spada in *Der heilige Born* (1859-60) and the Spaniard Jeronimo in *Die schwarze Galeere* (1860). In some later novels, *Deutscher Adel* (1876-7) and *Kloster Lugau* (1891-3), the Franco-German war of 1870-1 and the German victory are whole-heartedly applauded but, at the same time, Raabe chivalrously reminds the reader of the sufferings of French civilians and the courage of French soldiers in the field. In the late novel *Das Odfeld* (1886-7), set in the Seven Years' War, Raabe indicts, once again, the supposed habit of foreign nations (in this case the English and the French) to fight their wars on German soil, and casts Duke Ferdinand of Brunswick in the role of heroic but impotent defender of German interests, but avoids xenophobia by showing that not only French, but German soldiers, too, are occasionally capable of committing atrocities.

Raabe has been repeatedly accused of fostering anti-Semitism with his portrait of Moses Freudenstein in *Der Hungerpastor*, and has defended himself with the argument that this was not a typical, but a renegade Jew, and that elsewhere he has drawn sympathetic portraits of Jews.[16] This defence is not, perhaps, entirely convincing, for not only is Moses, who admittedly repudiates his religious as well as his family loyalties, a wholly repugnant figure, but so is Moses's father, an orthodox Jew who is shown as training his son from an early age to get the better of his Gentile fellows by trickery and deception. It is undeniable that the Nazis' cliché image of Jewish intellectuals as parasitical cosmopolitans with analytical-destructive minds, bent on undermining and subjugating Gentile society, is identical with the portrait of Moses Freudenstein in this novel. In comparison with this central figure in Raabe's most widely read and influential novel, the more sympathetic representatives of Judaism in *Ein Frühling* (1856-7), *Holunderblüte* (1862-3), *Höxter und Corvey* (1873-4), and *Frau Salome* (1874) are only marginal.

It can, on the other hand, be said of Fagin, the Jewish crook in *Oliver Twist*, that he figures as an embodiment of general villainy rather than specifically as a Jewish type, and Dickens has made ample amends for any harm this portrait may have caused in *Our Mutual Friends* where it is the very English usurer and money-grabber Mr Fledgeby who pretends to his clients that the 'noble Jew', Mr Riah, is the proprietor of the business for exploiting the poor, and thereby confirms them in their anti-Semitic prejudices. Moreover, the Jewish mill-owners who give asylum to Lizzie Hexam figure as ideal employers in the same novel. In his introduction to *Bleak House*, Sir Osbert Sitwell has claimed that in creating the characters of Hortense, the French maid of Lady Dedlock in *Bleak House*, and of Rigaud in *Little Dorrit*, Dickens was playing up to the anti-French tendencies of his time[17], but the account of Mr Peggotty's wanderings in France in *David Copperfield* is not Francophobe, nor are the French scenes in *Little Dorrit* and *A Tale Of Two Cities*, while Italy and Italians (particularly Cavalletto), Belgium, and Switzerland are sympathetically rendered in *Little Dorrit*. It is true that America and Americans are satirized in *Martin Chuzzlewit*, but with a brilliance and vitality which are high-spirited rather than venomous, and that the indictment of British insularity in several of the later novels is far more scathing than that of American life in *Martin Chuzzlewit*. The patriotism of Sir Leicester Dedlock in *Bleak House* is exposed as smugly complacent when he defends the nefarious Court of Chancery on the grounds that it is a traditional British institution and therefore above reproach.

119

The critique of British public life is carried further in *Little Dorrit* where the maladministration of the Marshalsea is given a representative character.[18] In the same novel, the rigidly insular Mrs General reproves Amy Dorrit for 'wondering' at Venice by reminding her 'that the celebrated Mr Eustace, the classical tourist, did not think much of it; and that he compared the Rialto, greatly to its disadvantage, with Westminster and Blackfriars Bridges'[19]. In this novel Dickens also reminds us that insularity and xenophobia are not prerogatives of the middle and upper classes, but characteristics of the working class too: having described the arrival of Cavalletto at Bleeding Heart Yard, Dickens lists all the supposed reasons the inhabitants have for disliking foreign immigrants, and exposes them.[20] And in *Our Mutual Friend* we have the epitome of hypocritical smugness in Mr Podsnap, with his motto: 'No other Country is so Favoured as This Country' which he is given to enlarge upon in the presence of foreigners.[21] All in all, in contrast with the pointed Teutonism of Raabe, the cosmopolitanism of Dickens's work is a sign of sanity and maturity.

Dickens, like Raabe, has often been accused of being antagonistic to high society, and incapable of portraying it realistically, but it is doubtful whether the two novelists are really akin in this respect. Reference has already been made to the extreme limitation of Raabe's social experience in comparison with Dickens's. On his father's side, Dickens was descended from domestic servants in a country house, on his mother's from the lesser gentry who staffed government departments, including the Admiralty. The considerable variety of social strata to which he had access, through his numerous relatives, in childhood and adolescence was widened further by his father's fecklessness which involved the family in frequent changes of residence, from Portsmouth to Rochester and Camden Town.

Raabe, on the other hand, originated in the professional middle class, a milieu he never transcended. It is not surprising, therefore, that his knowledge and understanding of people as revealed in his work should be limited to the members of the professional middle class of German small towns and, to a lesser extent, the trades-people whos served them. The princes and noblemen of Raabe's historical novels are stereotypes of romantic fiction; the world of the fashionable and wealthy portrayed in *Ein Frühling* (1856-7), *Die Leute aus dem Walde* (1861-2), and *Der Hungerpastor* (1862-3) is derived from his reading, not from personal observation, and is, consequently, lifeless cliché, and the corrupt princely courts with their parasitic nobility in some of these novels, and particularly in *Abu Telfan* (1865-7), are described entirely in terms of the satiric convention established in the 'Sturm und Drang' period of the eighteenth century for the treatment of this milieu. The situation of the country nobility of the Lauenhof in *Der Schüdderump* (1867-9) is different in that its principal representatives have the characteristics, the virtues and insights of the outsiders and eccentrics of Raabe's later work who usually belong to the middle classes: as noblemen they are not especially convincing. After Raabe settled in Brunswick in 1870, and came to terms with his limitations, he confined himself almost entirely to depicting members of the classes with which he was familiar and, as was pointed out earlier, the occasional industrialist who is introduced into the later novels, e.g. Schönow of *Villa Schönow*, is, like the noblemen of *Der Schüdderump*, convincing as a Raabe eccentric rather than in his professional role.

While the aristocrats of Dickens's earlier novels are, like Raabe's, stock caricatures (Sir Mulberry Hawk and Lord Frederick Verisopht), the later novels show that the author has acquired a sure grasp of all social milieux including that of high society. In *Bleak House*, a county family is subtly realized: Sir Leicester Dedlock with his narrow-minded, rigid commitment to an outdated social order, his touchy intolerance which does not exclude kindness to subordinates and a rough integrity; Lady Dedlock whose snobbery is deadlier because her doubtful origins and antecedents render her insecure; and their effete poor relations. In *Hard Times* Dickens deals convincingly with the uneasy alliance of the old ruling-class interest, represented by Harthouse, and the *nouveau riche* world of Gradgrind and Bounderby, and the treacherous jockeying for position alongside them of the shabbily genteel Mrs Sparsit. The same phenomenon is evoked in *Little Dorrit*. Central in the story is Little Dorrit herself, whose indestructible humanity makes her immune to the pressure of society on her to conform. But the representatives of society in this novel are just as much observed and rendered from life as are those characters with whom Dickens is in sympathy. The same holds true of *Our Mutual Friend*, in which the Podsnaps, the Veneerings, Lady Tippins and the Lammles are highly differentiated individuals, not one-dimensional as so often in Thackeray's social satires, but complex and even, as in the case of Mrs Lammle and Georgina Podsnap, capable of tragic experience.

Dickens's novels (with very few exceptions, such as *Hard Times* and *A Tale Of Two Cities*) are uniform in length: they run into 350,000 words on the average, and were originally serialized in twenty monthly parts. The 'episodic intensification' which this entailed, the even distribution of the incidents and principal characters of the novel in such a way that tension is maintained, a narrative structure where the main plot is loosely linked to a series of subsidiary plots with minor characters, all this suited Dickens's temperament. His zest for life finds expression in the intensely animated detail in which the characters and incidents of his novels are presented, and in his use of words which has been called Shakespearian because of its combination of energy, of poetic exuberance with perfect appropriateness in giving vocal expression to a multiplicity of human temperaments and situations. This method of writing and publishing was not forced on Dickens as is sometimes thought; on the contrary, he freely adopted it because he knew that it suited his particular talent. In the postscript of *Our Mutual Friend* he states: 'That I hold the advantages of this mode of publication to outweigh its disadvantages, may be easily believed of one who revived it in the Pickwick Papers after long disuse, and has pursued it ever since.'[22] Even where, as in some of the earlier novels, the principal plot (revolving, so often, around the suppression and subsequent discovery of a legacy) is conventional, far-fetched, or contrived, and the narrative almost picaresque in form, it is the life residing in the constituent parts of the novel which gives it verisimilitude. This is true even of his later and, as is now generally agreed, his greatest novels in which the main and subsidiary plots are unified by pervasive symbols, such as the prison in *Little Dorrit*, and much more closely interwoven than those of the earlier novels.

In his life-time, and since, Dickens has been criticized for relying on 'fate' or coincidence to motivate the comings and goings of his characters, and many a climax and denouement. Dickens himself denied that this detracted from the realism of his work – in the words of his friend and biographer John Forster: 'On the coincidences, resemblances, and surprises of life Dickens liked especially to dwell, and few things moved his fancy so pleasantly. The world, he would say, was so much smaller than we thought it; we were all so connected by fate without knowing it and people supposed to be far apart were so constantly elbowing each other; and to-morrow bore so close a resemblance to nothing half so much as yesterday.'[23] In his novels, Dickens is sometimes content to let coincidences be coincidences, at other times he hints at an ulterior, a providential design, whether in earnest, as in *Oliver Twist*, where Mr Brownlow tells Monks that Oliver 'your brother: a feeble, ragged, neglected child: was cast in my way by a stronger hand than chance, and rescued by me from a life of vice and infamy'[24], or facetiously, as in *Nicholas Nickleby* where Smike happens to stumble into Squeers from whom he has fled, in a London street: ' "It's

123

clear that there has been a Providence in it, sir," said Mr Snawley, casting down his eyes with an air of humility, and elevating his fork, with a bit of lobster on the top of it, towards the ceiling. "Providence is again him, no doubt," replied Mr Squeers, scratching his nose. "Of course, that was to be expected. Anybody might have known that." '[25] When Frank Cheeryble arrives in the Saracen's Head at the very moment Nicholas happens to visit it, and proceeds to pick a quarrel with a customer about the very girl Nicholas is endeavouring to trace, Tim Linkinwater comments: 'Why, I don't believe now . . . that there's such a place in all the world for coincidences as London is!'[26] And the mysterious attraction which the rescuer and the rescued feel for each other, though ignorant of the blood-relationship between them – in *Oliver Twist*, and again in *Nicholas Nickleby* – is attributed to some sort of guidance operating in human life, and so are other coincidences in these novels, which the sceptical reader might otherwise have suspected are only a clumsy means of bringing a character the author has lost sight of in contact with one who has remained in the limelight. To mention some of these: in *David Copperfield* Micawber just happens to walk past Uriah Heap's house in Canterbury and is thus reintegrated into the plot, likewise Steerforth who happens to use Charing Cross coffee-rooms as David arrives there on his way to Norfolk, and Miss Murdstone re-enters David's life as Dora Spenlow's companion; in *Great Expectations*, the coach which Pip enters on his journey home happens to be carrying the convict he met years earlier, and in the final denouement, Provis's corrupter Compeyson is revealed as identical with Miss Havisham's destroyer and Provis himself turns out to be Estella's father. Similar coincidences proliferate in *Little Dorrit* and *Our Mutual Friend*, but in no novel to the extent they do in *Bleak House*, where everything and everybody is mysteriously interconnected. But Dickens deliberately dispels an atmosphere of fatalism by endorsing Jarndyce's remark: 'Trust in nothing but Providence and your own efforts. Never separate the two.'[27]

Coincidences abound in Raabe's novels, particularly the earlier ones, at least as much as in any of Dickens's, but all too often in ways which are not substantiated, in the Dickensian manner, by vividly presented physical particulars. The accumulation of coincidences reaches a peak in *Der Hungerpastor* and *Abu Telfan*. After that, Raabe resorts to them far more sparingly and, in keeping with the tenor of his more successful later work, broods upon the meaning of coincidence where it occurs, as upon other problems of life. Already in *Die Leute aus dem Walde*, the moral of the book was pointed in the concluding paragraphs in these words:

> Die Sterne wandeln ihren Weg und achten auf alle Menschen. Wenige der Erdgeborenen kümmern sich darum. Ein Messer wetzet das andere und ein Mensch den anderen; die Sterne aber bringen Messer und Menschen zusammen.[28]

> The stars go their way and heed all men. Few of those born on earth take notice of it. One knife grinds another and one man another, but the stars bring knives and men together.

From *Meister Autor* (1872-3) on, Raabe's reflections on coincidence and fate, touched off by the actions of the novels, grow more complex. In the short story *Zum wilden Mann* (1873) he tilts at too smug a reliance on God's providence. In *Im alten Eisen* (1884-6) Raabe makes his characters trace the hand of Providence in the incidents which bring them together, and the protagonist of *Das Odfeld* (1886-7), Buchius, quotes Cicero's 'Dei providentia mundus administratur' in regard to the coincidences of the narrative. The narrator of *Stopfkuchen* (1888-90) provides, with reference to the philosophers Wolff and Schopenhauer, a rational explication of that 'Zusammenhang der Dinge', the interconnection of all things, so often invoked in Raabe's novels, as a meaningful design in life when he shows how his own emigration to South Africa and return to Germany could not have come about if any of the people who had crossed his path at one time or another had not been the men they were and acted as they had done; even the murder of Kienbaum, the false suspicion which led to the ostracism of Quakatz and to so much suffering, appear in retrospect as unavoidable means of bringing Tinchen and Schaumann together, enabling them to triumph over adversity. In *Kloster Lugau* (1891-3) all the main characters, in turn, brood on Providence and see its workings in their respective lives, and Raabe's last completed novel *Hastenbeck* (1895-8) may be said to have the ways of Providence for its principal theme. Thus both authors make extensive use of coincidences, but while Dickens generally makes them more plausible in the context of his narratives, Raabe is given to profounder reflection on the providential character of coincidences in life.

If in Dickens's work a progression can be traced from the loosely contructed, quasi-picaresque novels of his youth to the last novels, with their more tightly knit plots, the corresponding change which Raabe's work undergoes between the eighteen-fifties and the eighteen-eighties is even more marked. His first novel, *Die Chronik der Sperlingsgasse* (1854-5), is perhaps closest to Dickens, in spite of the nostalgic-pessimistic strain in it which, as Raabe later claimed, anticipated the Schopenhauer fashion by several years.[29] Its technique is that of two intersecting narrative planes, that of the few months during which the narrator keeps his diary, and that, stretching over several decades, which is gradually unfolded to the reader by means of revelatory 'flash-backs'. This technique is used by Raabe in all his later novels, though not in the ones that immediately followed the *Chronik*. Raabe's first novel is closest to Dickens in so far as in it he tries to portray a varied world of ordinary people, warmly and sympathetically, by means of a network of plots and sub-plots – even if these are somewhat pale and shadowy, derived from his reading of other novelists, especially Dickens, rather than from his own observations and experience. A relatively positive and open attitude towards humanity remains in evidence in the novels which immediately followed *Die Chronik*, i.e. *Ein Frühling* (1856-7), *Die Kinder von Finkenrode* (1857-8), and the three historical novels of 1859-61. A new, more ambitious note is struck with the series beginning with *Die Leute aus dem Walde* (1861-2) and continuing with *Der Hungerpastor* (1862-3), *Abu Telfan* (1865-7), and *Der Schüdderump* (1867-9). These are of similar length to Dickens's novels; events are related in chronological order as they are in Dickens; there is, too, a main plot with sub-plots, and Raabe attempts to present a broad panorama of the human scene. Because these works met the normal expectations of the novel-reading public – creating a 'world', however book-derived and unreal, and a straightforward narrative, absorbing the reader's imagination – they have had a popularity denied to Raabe's later, more characteristic works. These four novels, however, differ from the earlier ones in that the human collective now appears in a much less favourable light, and sympathy is reserved in the main for outsiders, for persecuted and afflicted people, struggling towards renunciation and serenity.

In his later work, beginning with *Meister Autor* (1872-3), Raabe achieved the literary form which was best suited to his particular talents and limitations. The novels, from now on, are much shorter – they rarely run into as many as two hundred pages; only two or three characters in them are, as a rule, realized in full, i.e. outsiders and eccentrics whose inner lives Raabe evokes successfully. A narrator bridges the gap between them and the hostile collective which is now no longer depicted in detail but merely sketched in satirically, providing occasions for Raabe's bitter generalizations on human nature. Action is reduced to a minimum, situations are merely established to be reflected upon; the technique used, with the intersecting narrative planes, is that pioneered in *Die Chronik der Sperlingsgasse*. Monologues and dialogues predominate in these later novels, and their tone is always the same, whether it is the outsider-hero who is speaking or one of the older women in sympathy with him. These women are invariably tough, managing, and caustic on the surface but 'good as gold' underneath, rather in the manner of Betsey Trotwood in *David Copperfield* on whom they may be modelled. The narrator, moreover, comments in the very same tone: he is usually a successful professional man who is half ashamed of his compromise with bourgeois convention and appreciates the unyielding stand of the hero, often a friend of his youth. When Raabe himself is commenting, or addressing the reader, he does it in the same tone; his observations are deliberately casual and chatty, ranging from the grimly sardonic to the whimsically humorous, and full of worldly shrewdness and concealed kindliness, of resignation and spiritual wisdom. Raabe's attitude to his readers, whom he so often buttonholes in these later novels, could not be further removed from Dickens's naive approach to his public as a 'popular entertainer'. Raabe was acutely aware that his sales and his fame had declined since he published *Der Hungerpastor*; this accounts for his ambivalent attitude: at one moment he pretends he does not care whether he is read or not, and claims, as in the opening of *Das Odfeld* (1886-7), that he is writing merely to entertain himself. And certainly he does not hesitate to make it very hard for the reader to follow him, teasing him with many breaks in the continuity of the narrative and a multiplicity of obscure quotations and allusions. But at other times, Raabe strenuously solicits the reader's sympathy.

The learned allusions which proliferate in Raabe's work to an extent equalled only in that of Jean Paul are not merely a means of acquainting the reader with the breadth of the author's reading, nor are they merely a sign of his lack of vitality and creative spontaneity. They are often used to place isolated incidents in the context of world history, giving them a representative significance. In *Das Odfeld* (1886-7) the battle described by Raabe, which took place in November

1761, is connected, by means of quotations and allusions, with earlier battles in the same area, and the cave in which Buchius and his protégés take refuge is related by the same means to other, earlier, places of refuge in times of calamity, back to Noah and his ark. Walther Killy has argued that in this respect Raabe differed from other nineteenth-century writers of historical fiction who aimed to reconstruct past epochs naturalistically; Raabe, according to Killy, was not interested in this so much as in a philosophical symbolism which makes him the precursor of twentieth-century novelists[30]. Raabe, however, was very much of his time in holding that the differences which distinguish one age from another are superficial, that human nature and the significant problems of human life are the same in every age; this does not, of course, preclude an interest in historical studies, as not only *Das Odfeld* but Raabe's numerous sixteenth-, seventeenth-, and eighteenth-century settings, from the early *Der heilige Born* (1859-60) to the late *Hastenbeck* (1895-8), show. Dickens reveals no similar bent: his two historical novels, *Barnaby Rudge* and *A Tale Of Two Cities*, are set in the recent past of which he might have heard eye-witness accounts in his youth, and *A Child's History of England* hardly shows signs of a 'sense of history'.

Raabe held that human nature is the same, not only in differing historical epochs, but in all parts of the world, in primitive and advanced civilizations. In *Die Leute aus dem Walde*, Captain von Faber, who has sailed twice round the world, assures the police-commissioner Tröster that the life recorded in the Berlin police files is no different from that he encountered on his travels in distant lands:

Die weite Welt und die Polizeistube bieten ein gleich ergiebiges Feld; der Kampf um das Dasein bleibt überall derselbe, im brasilianischen Urwalde wie in der Wüste Gobi, im ewigen Eis von Boothia Felix wie hier unter der gipsernen Nase Ihres weiland Vorgesetzten, Tröster.[31]

The wide world and the police-office offer an equally

129

productive field; the struggle for existence remains the same everywhere, in the Brazilian jungle as in the desert of Gobi, on the eternal ice of Boothia Felix as here under the plaster nose of your late chief, Tröster.

In *Abu Telfan*, Leonhard Hagebucher, who has spent years of slavery in darkest Africa, does not find the family council which sits in judgment on him after his return to his German home-town very different from the cruel clan of his African proprietor, and Nikola von Einstein compares her circumscribed and convention-ridden existence as a lady-in-waiting at the court of the Prince of Nippenburg with Hagebucher's bondage in the land of Abu Telfan.

Various critics, among them Barker Fairley[32] and Benno von Wiese[33], have divided Raabe's career into three periods, that of the early work in which a relatively sunny mood is prevalent, followed by the middle period, with the Schopenhauerian pessimism of *Der Hungerpastor*, *Abu Telfan*, and *Der Schüdderump* in the eighteen-sixties, and a final period, that of the later novels which they consider to be more positive in tone. While the early novels are distinguished – as has been indicated – by an openness to life and an acceptance of humanity which subsequently vanishes from Raabe's work, it is probably more true to say that occasional expressions of optimism and more frequent expressions of pessimism are found side by side in his work in every period. Reference has been made to the fact that Raabe himself claimed to have anticipated the Schopenhauer fashion in his first novel, *Die Chronik der Sperlingsgasse*.[34] Its narrator, Wachholder, is depicted as collecting material, not only for the diary which the novel purports to be, but for his 'opus magnum' entitled 'De vanitate hominum'. Pessimistic reflections similar to those found in *Die Chronik* occur in the succeeding novels (e.g. *Ein Frühling*, 1856-7: 'So ist die Welt: das Glück oder Vergnügen des einen wurzelt sehr oft in dem Elend, dem Missbehagen des andern'[35] (Such is the world: the good fortune or pleasure of one man is very often rooted in the misery, the discomfort of another). In the first draft of *Der Hungerpastor*, Raabe envisaged a tragic end for its idealistic hero; in the final version, on the other hand, Hans Unwirrsch is preserved, after a series of defeats and set-backs inflicted on him by a callous and cynical world, for an idyllic marriage in a rural parsonage. *Abu Telfan* ends ambiguously with the two women, Claudine and Nikola, who have come to grief in the fashionable world, withdrawing from life and society: 'Sie sitzen still, und still ist es um sie her, sie verlangen nicht mehr'[36] (They sit still and still it is around them, they no longer desire anything) – the first of Raabe's characters to practise a Schopenhauerian 'Verneinung des Willens zum Leben' (denial of the will to life); and yet Hagebucher's remark to Täubrich after their last visit to the ladies in their refuge in the 'Katzenmühle' – 'Jetzt wollen wir wieder zu den Lebendigen gehen'[37] (Let us now go back to the living) – seems to hint at a positive alternative, which makes their total resignation appear defeatist. There is no such ambiguity about the ending of *Der Schüdderump*, where the self-exile of von Glaubigern and Tonie from the world of the living is emphatically endorsed by the author:

> Es war für beide die Zeit vergangen, wo sie auf die Gefühle der Leute um sie her Rücksicht nahmen, den Anstand bewahrten und Furcht hatten, sich lächerlich zu machen. Sie waren ja allein in einer Wüste – allein in der Wüste des Lebens, der Lebendigkeit. Sie fühlten wohl den Boden, den Fels, auf welchem sie standen, unter sich wanken, sie wussten, dass die Wogen um sie her wuchsen, dass das Leben, die Lebendigkeit immer recht behält, sie wussten, dass sie verloren waren, und sie waren doch glücklich und sicher.[38]

For both of them the time was over when they had to pay heed to the feelings of the people around them, to observe the proprieties and to be afraid of appearing ridiculous. For they were alone in a desert – alone in the desert of life, of the living. They felt the ground, the rock on which they stood, tottering beneath them, they knew that the waves around them, were growing larger, that life, the living, are always right in the end; they knew that they were lost, and yet they were happy and safe.

That the pessimism of *Der Schüdderump* is a deviation in Raabe's work, as some critics still suggest, is expressly denied in the 1894 preface to the second edition of the novel in which Raabe reaffirms its darker implications.

Raabe's pessimism never turns into nihilism because it is counterbalanced, from *Die Chronik der Sperlingsgasse* on, by that faith in Providence described earlier, which turns defeat and resignation into aspects of a meaningful totality, a 'Zusammenhang der Dinge'. Raabe liked to describe himself, paradoxically, as someone 'dem Goethe, der Optimist, und Schopenhauer, der Pessimist, zu einer Einheit wurde'[39] (for whom Goethe, the optimist, and Schopenhauer, the pessimist, had become a unity). Yet as Raabe was no systematic thinker, it is now the one, now the other element which is predominant in his work. His vacillation shows in the fact that the most deeply despondent book he ever wrote, *Die Akten des Vogelsangs* (1893-5), was immediately followed by *Hastenbeck* (1895-8), with its pervasive providentialism. *Meister Autor* (1872-3) opens the series of later novels where particular situations give occasion to reflect on the folly of mankind. Sometimes Raabe castigates this folly, at other times he sees it as a blessing because it distracts men's attention from the passing of youth and happiness; if we did notice it, the author observes, we would probably prefer a 'beschleunigtes Verfahren' to the 'langsame Hinquälerei'[40] (accelerated produre (to the) long drawn-out torture (of old age)). Aphorism follows on aphorism, Schopenhauerian in tone, e.g.:

> Es ist eine im Grunde lächerliche und dem denkenden Menschen auffällige Tatsache, dass, je mehr das unbefangene Interesse am Dasein und den Bedingungen desselben wächst, in demselben Grade das Vergnügen und Behagen dran abnimmt.[41]

It is really a ridiculous and – to thinking people – startling fact, that to the degree in which one's impartial interest in existence and its conditions grows, one's pleasure and satisfaction in it diminish.

Reflections on the folly and wickedness of mankind are mitigated by consoling affirmations of providential design, and these lead, in turn, to pleas for compassion and resignation:

Man glaubt alle Augenblicke vor einer Wand zu stehen, und jedesmal zu finden, dass ein Weg um dieselbe herumführe.[42]

One believes oneself every few moments to be up against a wall, only to find that there is a way which leads round it.

In the rather less sombre *Horacker* (1875), resignation, in the case of the Konrektor's wife, Frau Eckerbusch, takes the form of a humorous, almost cheerful serenity, and characters like her relieve the prevailing gloom in other novels. *Deutscher Adel* (1876-7) is remarkable not only because in it Raabe elaborates his defence of illusion as a beneficent power in human life, but because in this novel is to be found, for the first time, the phrase 'Freidurchgehen' (to pass freely through) to describe a resigned detachment which turns those who practise it into towers of strength to their neighbours. And in *Alte Nester* (1877-9) we have, as in later novels like *Stopfkuchen* and *Das Odfeld*, a character who emerges triumphant over a hostile environment, after undergoing extremes of isolation and persecution. Another variant of the successfully 'Freidurchgehende' (those who pass freely through) are those explicitly Christian exponents of renunciation, Phöbe in *Unruhige Gäste* (1884) and Leonie des Beaux in *Die Akten des Vogelsangs* (1893-5). By her example, Phöbe is shown to cure Dorette Kristeller of her bitterness and cynicism.

Raabe's attitude to and use of Schopenhauer is therefore ambiguous, not to say contradictory. As had been mentioned earlier, he claims to have arrived at the pessimistic element in *Die Chronik der Sperlingsgasse* independently of Schopen-

hauer, and elsewhere insists that the pessimism of Schopenhauer and the optimism of Goethe must be integrated[43].
Reference has also been made to the 'Verneinung des
Willens zum Leben', that ceasing to will and desire anything,
which according to Schopenhauer constituted the Buddhist
or Christian saint's dying to the world; Nikola and Claudine
in *Abu Telfan*, Tonie Häusler in *Der Schüdderump* are
shown to end in this manner and, more doubtfully, Velten
Andres in *Die Akten des Vogelsangs*. It is not altogether
clear whether Raabe considers Velten enlightened in the
Schopenhauerian sense, or as suffering from a morbid
paralysis of the will, brought on by frustration in love; and
Wunnigel, in the novel of that name (1876), has often been
taken for a caricature of Schopenhauer, combining, as he
does, professed enlightenment with misanthropy and concealed egotism. Occasionally, Raabe, who admitted to being
sceptical about all systematic philosophizing, was capable of
joking about the theoretical formulations he found in Schopenhauer's *Die Welt als Wille und Vorstellung* (The World as
Will and Idea) – e.g. in *Deutscher Adel*[44]. In *Unruhige
Gäste*, on the other hand, Phöbe's attainment of sanctity is
offered by Raabe in Schopenhauerian terms – 'sich des
eignen Willens entäussern'[45] (to renounce one's own will).

Dickens, it is generally held, subscribed to an 'optimistic'
view of life. 'Men who look on nature, and their fellow-men,
and cry that all is dark and gloomy', he writes in *Oliver Twist*,
'are in the right, but the sombre colours are reflections from
their own jaundiced eyes and hearts. The real issues are
delicate, and need a clearer vision.'[46] Similar assertions are
found in several of Dickens's early novels, and are endorsed
by the fiction in which the good are seen to triumph over the
wicked, in which warmth and generosity and an open,
trusting disposition are upheld – even when, as in the
Swivellers, Steerforths, Micawbers, and in many of the
travelling and acting folk presented, this disposition borders
on fecklessness. The opposing quality of meanness, in all its

forms, is rejected with particular force, especially if it is hypocritically disguised – as life-rejecting 'sin and gloom' puritanism (the conventicle in *The Old Curiosity Shop*, Mrs Clennam in *Little Dorrit*), as religious humbug (Chadband in *Bleak House*), as utilitarian worship of prosaic fact (in *Hard Times*), or as class-conscious snobbery, in so many of the novels.

It was his faith in the possibility of changing and improving the world that inspired Dickens's reforming zeal, his exposure of social evils in his novels. If the world is the devil's to the extent that 'die Canaille Herr ist und Herr bleibt'[47] (scoundrels are masters in it and will remain masters), as Raabe puts it in *Der Schüdderump*, then it cannot, of course, be improved by organized action. The point against Raabe and the stoic-pessimistic tradition – that one is, in fact, all the more likely to leave the world to the devil if one withdraws from it – is made tellingly in *Nicholas Nickleby* where Mrs Squeers 'frequently remarked . . . it would be all the same a hundred years hence; with which axiom of philosophy, indeed, she was in the constant habit of consoling the boys when they laboured under more than ordinary ill usage'.[48] David Copperfield takes Mr Spenlow to task for his fatalistic acceptance of the English legal system – and the world as he found it. In his last novels, in *Little Dorrit* (1857), *Great Expectations* (1860-1), and *Our Mutual Friend* (1865), Dickens's indictment of human failings is more scathing, and his vision of life more sombre as well as more complex – a reason why those who, like G.K. Chesterton, found the warm-hearted optimism of the earlier Dickens particularly congenial, wrote disparagingly of them. That even in these novels Dickens's and Raabe's standpoints are totally dissimilar is evident particularly in their respective attitudes to the issue of moral isolation.

In his preoccupation with the outsiders, Raabe follows a tradition of German writing which stretches back to the eighteenth century. In the 'Sturm und Drang' period and early Romanticism, the outsider figures as the young man of genius, the artist, and is acclaimed in his alienation from a time-serving, materialistic society, the Philistine world. In the later, ethically orientated, Romanticism of Arnim, of Eichendorff, the artist is viewed in a more critical light. There is considerable ambiguity in Stifter's portrayal of outsiders whom he does not always explicitly present as artists, and in Keller's fiction, the outsider can save himself from destruction only by renouncing the Romantic imagination and art, and by seeking integration in society. In Raabe's work, however, the social misfit is vindicated once again, and appears in a variety of rôles, by no means always as an intellectual.

Indeed, Raabe at times adopted an anti-intellectual stance, as in parts of *Der Hungerpastor*, and there is the passage at the end of *Abu Telfan* in which he argues that the German man of genius and the German Philistine are dependent on each other:

> Wohin wir blicken, zieht stets und überall der germanische Genius ein Drittel seiner Kraft aus dem Philistertum und wird von dem alten Riesen dem Gedanken, mit welchem er ringt, in den Lüften schwebend erdrückt, wenn es ihm nicht gelingt, zur rechten Zeit wieder den Boden, aus dem er erwuchs, zu berühren.[49]

> Wherever we look, the Germanic genius always and everywhere draws a third of its strength from the Philistine world and as he hovers in the air, he is crushed by the old giant, thought, with which he wrestles, if he does not manage in good time to touch again the soil from which he sprang.

The ambiguity in Raabe's portrayal of the Philistine world is his peculiar contribution to the concern with the diastole-systole conflict which, we saw, pervades German literature of the eighteenth and nineteenth centuries. In *Die Akten des Vogelsangs*, Raabe wavers in his estimate of Velten Andres, an embodiment of genius, and he shows sympathy for the narrator who – like so many of Raabe's narrators – has a foot in each camp, that of the bourgeoisie and that of the outsider.

More often, however, Raabe is wholly hostile to the 'Philisterium'. He was afflicted by the *esprit de contradiction*; and as he will sometimes spring to the defence of the Philistines whom he usually denounces, and as elsewhere he occasionally questions the existence of a Providence which he normally proclaims, so he occasionally introduces outsiders and eccentrics of whom he disapproves. Fuchs in *Unruhige Gäste* and Quakatz in *Stopfkuchen* are presented merely as disagreeable people, but, one must grant, they are unwilling exiles from the collective, and only too glad to be reconciled with it again. Other eccentrics, Wunnigel, Ferrari in *Deutscher Adel*, Lippoldes in *Pfisters Mühle*, men who seek refuge in a world of fantasy without overcoming their egoism, are critically presented, and so are characters who remain enclosed in attitudes of defiant misanthropy, like Schnarrwergk in *Der Lar*. But in general, the eccentrics in Raabe's work are credited with deeper insight than the socially integrated, and with moral superiority, the collective being generally presented as blindly obeying the herd-instinct, engrossed in material pursuits and callously resentful of nonconformists. The dualistic view which Raabe shared with Schopenhauer confirmed him in his exclusion of normal, ordinary people and of empirical reality from his fiction. What he depicts is not so much the world from which the hero withdraws, but the refuge which he seeks and finds, whether this is purely an inner state or whether it has an external equivalent, like the parsonage which Hans Unwirrsch takes over at the end of *Der Hungerpastor*, an oasis of harmony in a wicked world, or the 'red rampart' where Stopfkuchen settles, or the cave in *Das Odfeld*. In *Die Leute aus dem Walde* and the later novels, the phenomenon of withdrawal is occasionally sentimentalized: the outsiders are shown to overcome their isolation by joining in a clique, a charmed circle, with kindred spirits, like them defeated in the battle of life and now on the threshold of renunciation and peace. The outsiders' sympathy with and understanding of each other are evoked with a relish which is sometimes cloying.

In many of the novels, the persecuted hero, though ostensibly unassertive, manages to get his own back on the collective, at least to the extent of making its representatives feel uneasy or even guilty, but in *Alte Nester*, *Das Odfeld* and *Stopfkuchen*, he actually emerges as stronger, in the end, even in a worldly sense, than the members of the collective who despised him. It could be argued that Raabe, who in *Der Hungerpastor* expressed his pietist inheritance, and in *Unruhige Gäste* and *Die Akten des Vogelsangs* gave his characteristic dualism Christian form, takes his place in a tradition which goes back to the New Testament: ' . . . God hath chosen the weak things of the world to confound the things which are mighty; and base things of the world, and things which are despised, hath God chosen, yea, and things which are not, to bring to nought things that are . . . ' (1 Cor. 1:27-8.). But one cannot help wondering whether lives like that of Heinrich Schaumann in *Stopfkuchen*, the despised and persecuted fat boy who rises to a dominant position in the community which rejected him, of Magister Buchius, the outcast schoolmaster in *Das Odfeld* who, in times of war, is depended on to rescue those who had made a butt of him and turned him out – whether these are not arbitrary and implausible constructions, imaginary wish-fulfilments contrived to give comfort and support to fellow sufferers from the world's harshness. In the case of Tinchen we are told that Heinrich Schaumann has transformed her from a shunned and embittered wild creature into a poised and radiantly happy woman; we are not shown how this was accomplished: there is no real continuity, in the novel, between the earlier and the later Tinchen.

Isolation figures in the works of Dickens, too, but not in the dualistic fashion – the superior outsider in conflict with the corrupt collective – which Raabe inherited from the Romantics and from Schopenhauer. In the early novels of Dickens, isolation is preeminently the lot of the villain. The final loneliness of Fagin, of Sykes, of Ralph Nickleby is their greatest punishment, one which they bring on themselves by their misanthropy, their anti-social lives. The loneliness of Dickens's young heroes and heroines, of Oliver, of Little Nell, of young David Copperfield, of Pip in *Great Expectations*, on the other hand, is imposed on them by circumstances, and left behind, sooner or later, along with other afflictions, such as poverty: it is not the product of their own characters and conduct as it is with Dickens's villains, and, in a totally different sense, of course, with Raabe's heroes. Dickens's earlier heroes are not presented as outsiders – they may possess moral superiority, being just, good, considerate, upright to the point of imprudence, but they have no compunction about claiming their rights in the world; there is nothing eccentric about them. Eccentricity occurs in Dickens, but only marginally and never in the central characters, the heroes and heroines. It testifies to Dickens's psychological curiosity, his delight in the picturesque, his zestful interest in all imaginable varieties of human behaviour; his eccentrics are never, as in Raabe, endowed with a significance of a moral-metaphysical order. There are, of course, persecuted figures in Dickens, too, from Oliver Twist to young Pip in *Great Expectations*; but while in Raabe it is the collective which persecutes and the victim who is 'abnormal', out of step with the collective, in Dickens the situation is reversed: the persecuted are at one with the ordinary, normal humanity and the persecutors are the oddities.

Stoic withdrawal from human contact as a means of self-defence, so often advocated by Raabe, is disparaged by Dickens, as for instance in the case of the ever wary Sampson Brass in *The Old Curiosity Shop*. And when his characters claim self-sufficiency – the inner haven of Raabe's eccentrics – i.e. Dombey, or Mr. Bounderby in *Hard Times* who boasts of having 'arrived' by his own efforts, it is exposed as a denial of human community, as ingratitude towards men and God. In Dickens's vision of life, Grace supersedes Justice. In

Great Expectations, the narrator passes judgment on Miss Havisham: 'But that, in shutting out the light of day, she had secluded herself from a thousand natural and healing influences; that her mind brooding solitary, had grown diseased, as all minds do and must and will, that reversed the appointed order of their Maker, I knew equally well.'[50] It is revealing that when Raabe borrowed the externals of Miss Havisham's situation for that of Thekla Overhaus in *Das Horn von Wanza* he should have departed from his model by presenting the case of the woman who has cut herself off from society because she has lost her fiancé, in a much more favourable light, almost as a triumph of loyalty. His Thekla Overhaus is vindicated in the end, and becomes just another variant of Raabe's eccentrics with superior wisdom. Where vicious collectives are described in Dickens, whether in the form of an isolated, corrupted community like the parish work-house in *Oliver Twist*, the first school which David Copperfield attends, the nouveau riche milieu of the Veneerings and Podsnaps in *Our Mutual Friend*, or Society in *Little Dorrit* as represented by Mrs General in her vain attempt to make the heroine conform, these are seen as deviations from a social norm, and positive idealism (such as Nicholas Nickleby's in Dotheboys Hall) which can overthrow the corrupters and reform the collective is always near at hand. Resignation figures in Dickens, too, and is held up for our admiration, but only in certain circumstances; it is far from being all-pervasive as in Raabe. It is practised above all by those self-sacrificing, devoted daughters of erring and feckless parents who are found in so many of Dickens's novels, from Madeline Bray in *Nicholas Nickleby* and Little Nell in *The Old Curiosity Shop* to Florence Dombey in *Dombey and Son*, Agnes Wickfield in *David Copperfield*, Little Dorrit, and Clara in *Great Expectations*. Dickens and his readers found the submissiveness and resignation of these girls touching and appealing, but in most cases these are temporary phases which the girls pass through, like fairy-tale Cinderellas, before meeting a Prince Charming. When it is a son who is blindly devoted to a selfish and hypocritical parent (Turvey-drop in *Bleak House*), Dickens is, in fact, rather more sceptical about the value of such sacrifice.

In Dickens's last great novels, in *Little Dorrit*, *Great Expectations*, and *Our Mutual Friend*, the principal characters are psychologically more complex than in the earlier works, and resignation appears in a new light. Pip's self-criticism and agony of remorse distinguish him from earlier, more naive heroes of Dickens's fiction. In both *Little Dorrit* and *Our Mutual Friend*, the main characters are returned emigrants as in so many of Raabe's novels, and an aura of sadness, isolation, and mystery surrounds Arthur Clennam in the former, Rokesmith in the latter novel. Both are exiles from life and pining for entry into it. Rokesmith succeeds against heavy odds in winning the hand and heart of the young and beautiful Bella Wilfer. But Arthur Clennam, a much more fully realized figure whom Dickens invested with so many of his own fears and hesitations, his despondency, and his remorse on the threshold of middle age, renounces the hope of recapturing the happiness and insouciance of youth with Pet Meagles whom he loves – at a time when Dickens himself had already opted for the opposite by allowing his marriage to break up and establishing Ellen Ternan as his mistress. But Arthur Clennam, resigned though he may be, is not in any way like Raabe's heroes; his isolation is a moral one, he is not eccentric, but a man of the world, his urbanity and worldly *savoir-faire* as well as his humanity and sympathy are established in the context of his business-dealings with his mother and Doyce, and of his relationships with a variety of 'ordinary' human beings. His renunciation arises naturally from his experiences and circumstances, without necessitating a rejection of everyday life and humanity.

Dickens had, by this time, left the naive psychology, the black-and-white melodrama of his early novels behind him: on the one hand, the villains, the Fagins, and on the other, the paste-board embodiments of virtue, the Maylies, the Brown-lows, and between them the early heroes who, like Oliver Twist and Nicholas Nickleby, are not real characters so much as vehicles for the indulgence of the reader's sympathetic interest. But even in the early novels there is much realistic psychological observation and insight, particularly where minor characters are concerned. Human wickedness and weakness are portrayed without illusion in the later work: when the boys in David Copperfield's first school who have been so cruelly treated by Mr Creakles take it out with equal cruelty on the weak Mr Mell, Dickens does not lament the failings of mankind as Raabe does, he reports without commenting. The pursuit of money and status by the Veneerings and Podsnaps and their circle in *Our Mutual Friend*, the deep duplicity between friends and marriage-partners in that novel, between Venus and Wegg, between the Lammles, the abysmal meanness of Hexam and Rider-hood – these things are as dark as anything in Raabe, if more vividly rendered. Nor are they made occasions for pessimistic reflection, but placed in a wider context in which the saving qualities of the more central characters of the novel shine. In *Little Dorrit*, the goodness of Arthur Clennam, his active benevolence, is held in check but not eclipsed by his unresolved personal problems, the pressure of his sense of guilt, while his inner isolation, his resignation are balanced by an active involvement in business and a variety of social contacts; the other, more 'ordinary' characters of the novel have a reality and seriousness equal to that of Clennam, and are represented in a wide range of types, previously unrecorded by novelists.

It was evident in Raabe's early work, both from the frequent specific echoes of Dickens and from that Dickensian openness to life and humanity in *Die Chronik der Sperlings-gasse*, that he aimed at achievements, in German terms, of the kind of fiction exemplified by Dickens's work in England. He continued, as we have seen, to echo Dickens in a number of ways until the end of his life; but by the middle sixties, when the novel trilogy was written (*Der Hungerpastor*, *Abu Telfan*, *Der Schüdderump*), it was apparent that little of the empirical life, the human experience of Dickens came within Raabe's scope, that Raabe's picture of the ordinary world and the plots in which it is embodied are book-derived, novelettish even, that vitality and originality reside mainly in the portraits of outsiders at odds with society. In his own life, Raabe, who never achieved a fraction of Dickens's social experience, chose to lead a withdrawn life in a provincial town, his social contacts being limited to a small group of professional people with literary interests. The vindication in the novels of a withdrawal of this kind corresponded to a mood prevalent among middle-class intellectuals who had been defeated and left isolated by the failure of the 1848 revolution. One need not go as far as Georg Lukács, who sees in the withdrawal celebrated in Raabe's work a protest against a world dominated by 'feudal-monarchistische Klein-staaterei' (feudal-monarchist particularism) in alliance with rising capitalism. 'Jeder bedeutende, ja schon jeder streng moralische Mensch', writes Lukács, 'wird in dieser Welt zum Paria, zum outcast.'[51] (Every significant, indeed, every strictly moral man becomes a pariah, an outcast, in this world). This interpretation ignores the fact that Raabe held, with Schopenhauer and the historians who, like Jakob Burckhardt, were influenced by Schopenhauer, that not only in contemporary Germany, but in every historical period, the cards are stacked against the man of insight and integrity.

We saw that in his later work, from the early seventies on, Raabe, now aware of his strengths and limitations, developed a novel-structure which enabled him to concentrate on the situations and inner lives of his outsider heroes, humanity at large being presented in shadowy contours only. The plots, the patterns of Raabe's works now seem increasingly contrived to illustrate the problems with which Raabe was wrestling: that of meaninglessness and providentialism, for instance, and, in *Prinzessin Fisch* and *Die Akten des Vogelsangs*, that of the positive and negative effects of illusion in human life. The des Beaux family, Frau Feucht, Helene in *Die Akten des Vogelsangs* are attached to life by a sense of purpose which is now referred to as a dream, and now actually dismissed as a 'Märchen' (fairy-tale) by the narrator; Frau Krumhardt's satisfaction with the bourgeois, social compromise is described with mixed sympathy and irony, while Velten is portrayed as 'seeing through' the illusion of others until he ceases to will and dies a Schopenhauerian death. In other novels, e.g. *Meister Autor*, *Alte Nester*, *Das Odfeld*, *Stopfkuchen*, Raabe resolves this ambiguity by making his inwardly resigned outsiders return, in the end, to achieve authority – exercized forbearingly – in the community which had persecuted and rejected them.

There is a good deal of bitterness and misanthropy but also much shrewd reflection and wisdom to be found in these later novels of Raabe. In eliminating the broader social world which, he realized, he lacked the interest and experience to portray, he abandoned much of the sentimentality, the clichés of his earlier work. Having relinquished the ambition to become a German Dickens, he developed a new variant of the 'Novelle' in the relatively short but elaborately structured prose-narrative of his later years. And it is arguable that in them the lack of 'extensiveness' is compensated by 'inwardness' in ways which point forward to the work of Rilke and Kafka.

V

Fontane and English Realism

Reference has been made to Mme de Staël's view[1], later echoed by Otto Ludwig[2] and others, that the absence, in Germany, of a prose-fiction comparable to that of England and France, was due to political disunity, to the lack of a capital city and a cultural centre, and the fragmentation of a society in which intellectuals lived in relative isolation, without the opportunity of gaining a wide social experience. The accuracy of this diagnosis seems to be confirmed by the fact that the first German novelist whose work reflects a compelling interest in and appreciation of a complex social world, should have arisen in the eighteen-eighties, a decade or two after the establishment of a parliamentary system had given the middle-classes access to the sphere of power and privilege, and after the political unification of Germany had made possible the emergence of a cosmopolitan society in what was now the imperial capital of Berlin. Conversely, the hypothesis that the realistic society-novel was simply not available to any German writer until this point in time, serves to account for the fact that Fontane, who was ideally suited to provide it, should have come to it so late in life, not, indeed, until he was almost sixty years old and had tried his hand for decades at other literary forms. For not only had Fontane, as a journalist on the leading Prussian newspaper, availed himself of every opportunity to observe and explore a rapidly expanding social scene in Berlin and Brandenburg, but he had been able to acquire a deeper insight than any German writer before him into the English novelists on whom he modelled himself.

Fontane had paid his first visit to England in 1844; he had worked as a newspaper correspondent in London in 1852, and again from 1855 to 1859, and there been able to study English fiction in the environment which produced it. Scott and Thackeray are the novelists most frequently invoked in his letters and diaries. Already as an author of ballads Fontane had been decisively influenced by Scott's *Minstrelsy of the Scottish Border*. Fontane's travel-book *Jenseits des Tweed* (Beyond the Tweed) in which contemporary Scotland is interpreted in terms of its past, in the spirit of Scott, culminates aptly in a chapter called 'Abbotsford'. In the preface to the first edition of his *Wanderungen durch die Mark Brandenburg*, Fontane states that he conceived the idea of writing a similar work on Brandenburg while collecting material for his Scottish travel-book: it had suddenly struck him that a German writer could find in Rheinsberg opportunities comparable to those at Lochleven.[3] And as a novelist, Fontane came to social realism by way of historical fiction inspired by Scott.

If Thackeray provided more relevant precedents for Fontane's later 'Gesellschaftsromane' (novels of society), Scott remained for him to the end the most congenial of novelists:

> Seine erstaunlichste Eigenschaft, bewundernswerter fast als sein Talent und seine produktive Kraft, war seine Bescheidenheit. Hierin war er ganz grosse Natur, ausgerüstet mit dem unerschütterlichen Sinn für das Einfache und Wahre. Das ist ja auch was seinen Romanen, neben der humoristischen Durchdringung (die übrigens im innigsten Zusammenhang damit steht), ihren Hauptzauber verleiht.[4]

> His most astonishing characteristic, more admirable almost than his talent and productive power, was his modesty. In this respect he possessed real greatness of character, with an unshakable sense of what is simple and true. And that is, after

all, the quality which gives his novels their chief charm, in addition to his pervasive humour (which, incidentally, is closely connected with his modesty).

In Willibald Alexis, Fontane had a predecessor who applied the methods of Scott to the conditions of Brandenburg; but Fontane preferred Scott's work because of the greater human truth he found in it. Scott's 'Darstellung', he wrote, 'ist künstlerisch freier. Er wusste jeden Augenblick, dass er nicht Historiker, sondern eben Geschichtenerzähler war. Er kannte keine Tendenz . . . '[5] (Scott's description is artistically freer. He was conscious every moment that he wasn't a historian but a story-teller. He knew no tendentiousness . . .)

L.A. Shears has traced in detail various parallels between *Waverley* and *Vor dem Sturm* (Before the Storm), Fontane's first novel, and especially the resemblance of Lewin von Vitzewitz, Kathinka, Marie and Ladalinski in Fontane's novel to Edward Waverley, Flora, Rose and MacIvor in Scott's.[6] In both novels the hero attains maturity when he turns from a brilliant woman of the world who has rejected him, to an inconspicuous but deeply authentic girl of the people. Shears also emphasizes the resemblance of Hoppen-marieken, with her spells and prophetic rhymes, to such figures as Meg Merrilies and Edie Ochiltree in Scott's fiction. In his *Formen des Realismus*[7] (Forms of Realism), Peter Demetz has enlarged interestingly on Shears's points and brought out how both authors adopt the same attitude towards the supposedly preternatural, refraining from comment and leaving it to some character in the novel whose credibility remains in doubt, to describe the phenomenon so that the possibility of a natural explanation is left open.

Fontane himself has pointed to other connections between Scott's work and his own. In a highly critical review of Freytag's *Die Ahnen*[8] (The Ancestors) he argued that historical fiction should deal only with the recent past of which the author had heard eye-witness accounts. Scott himself had expressed a similar view in the opening pages of

147

Waverley, and the novels in which he followed this precept, those set in eighteenth century Scotland, are usually regarded as more successful than those set in more distant times and places. In *Vor dem Sturm* and *Schach von Wuthenow*, Fontane was careful not to go back in time beyond 1800. A more fundamental resemblance between Scott's work and his own, is referred to by Fontane himself in a passage on the themes of *Waverley*:

> Mit jener feinen Fühlung, jenem das Richtige treffenden Instinkt, wie er sich nahezu bei allen grossen Poeten findet, ist hier das Torytum, der alte Stuartstandpunkt glorifiziert, ohne doch dem Hause Hannover oder dem whigistisch-englischen Gefühl zu nah zu treten. Sehr geschickt ist hier poetische und politische Berechtigung getrennt worden und zwischen beiden vermittelt. Die Gestalt des Waverley meist einfach als nichtssagend beiseite gestellt, ist hier für den, der scharf zusieht, ein Meisterstück. Diese hier angeregte Seite des Romans ist deutscherweise selten ausreichend gewürdigt worden, weil den wenigsten Lesern vorschweben könnte, welche heiklen Fragen hier zu berühren waren.[9]

> With that subtle tact, that instinct for what is apt, which characterizes almost all great creative writers, Scott glorifies Toryism, the Jacobite point of view, without, however, giving offense to the House of Hanover, or Whig and English feeling. With great skill he manages to separate what is poetically justified from what is politically justified, and mediates between the conflicting interests. The figure of Waverley which is most often dismissed as insignificant, is, in fact, for the sharp-sighted observer, a master-piece. Unfortunately, this aspect of the novel has been rarely appreciated by Germans; few readers realize how delicate the issues are which Scott is touching on.

Fontane's *Vor dem Sturm*, like Scott's *Waverley*, does scrupulous justice to the protagonists of irreconcilable causes, and exposes at the same time the incommensurability of the individual and the collectives of nation, party or class which, according to ideological cliché, should determine him. Fontane once remarked that in Alexis's novels dealing with the Napoleonic period characters were invariably mere embodiments of one or other of the conflicting parties of their time, whereas in reality, and in the novels of Scott, it was only in rare and exceptional cases that individual people reflected fully the accepted image of the group to which they belonged. Every reader of Alexis, he wrote,

> wird glauben müssen, es sei alles so ernst und düster und fanatisch gewesen. Ich selbst würd es glauben, wenn ich ein Fremder gewesen wäre. Meine Eltern aber und die gesamten Swinemünder Honoratioren (unter denen ich meine Jugendeindrücke empfing) haben mir immer nur erzählt, wie kreuzfidel man damals gewesen sei. Alles entente cordiale mit den lieben kleinen Franzosen, alles verliebt und lüderlich. Was Alexis schildert, existierte auch, aber es war die Ausnahme.[10]

> will have to believe that everything had been as serious and sombre and fanatical. I would believe it myself if I had been a stranger. But my parents and all the people of rank in Swinemünde (among whom I spent my impressionable youth) have always told me how gay people had been then. Everyone entente cordiale with those dear Frenchmen, everyone in love and dissipated. What Alexis describes, did exist, but it was the exception.

One is reminded of the stand taken by Günter Grass, with his emphasis, in the Danzig trilogy, on the human-all-too-human concerns and idiosyncracies of individuals, against the rigid stereotyping in earlier post-war fiction in which noble Jews and resistance-fighters are single-mindedly in conflict with depraved Nazis.

Fontane, like Scott, combines a sense of the uniqueness of the individual with an awareness of the importance of social and ideological factors in shaping the milieu in which he finds himself. Like Scott who is equally fair to the Scots and to the English, Fontane stands above the rivalries of Prussians, French and Poles which he depicts in *Vor dem Sturm*. The contrast in Scott's work between the law-abiding stability of England and the anachronistic but romantic wildness of Scotland has its counterpart in *Vor dem Sturm*, where the dependable but somewhat stolid Prussians are outshone by the flightier but aesthetically more interesting Poles.

The obsessive hatred which Berndt von Vitzewitz has conceived for the French, however understandable in view of the insult and personal injury inflicted on him, must yield to true insight. This finds partial expression through Berndt's son Lewin who is too chivalrous to approve of the meanly treacherous tactics of the guerilla fighters and knows that he is himself of French extraction on his mother's side. It is represented, too, by the circle around Amalie von Pudagla in Schloss Guse where the spirit of the Enlightenment, with its French cultural sympathies, is still alive. When Berndt's unauthorized military action miscarries, he learns to suspect his own motives and comes to feel remorse. Class characteristics are exposed as ephemeral when men of middle-class origin fulfil as officers and leaders the functions of the old nobility, and supposed national differences become doubtful to Berndt himself when he recognizes that the anti-Napoleonic liberation movement is inspired by a humanism of French origin.

In his second historical novel, set in the Napoleonic period, *Schach von Wuthenow* (1882), Fontane presents themes similar to those of *Waverley* and *Vor dem Sturm*, but in place of the loose construction of the earlier novel in which a multiplicity of milieux are presented in detail, in the manner of Scott, we now have that economy and concentration characteristic of Fontane's later work. Here too Fontane describes the pressures making for social change, and portrays the social groups which support change and those which resist it, through representative characters who yet are not mere types but in varying degrees individualized. Schach, with his narrow patriotism, his rigid aristocratic prejudices, his conventional Lutheranism and anxious concern for outward appearances, represents several aspects of the social system that is doomed to go down before the onslaught of Napoleon, but his opponent von Bülow, an arrogant iconoclast, is not really of the future either, being a product of the Enlightenment, its rationalism and cosmopolitanism. Fontane may endorse some of his arguments yet he reserves his human sympathy for Schach. Queen Luise provides continuity between the old and the new, being patriotic but also liberal, and Christian in the spirit of the Romantic movement. The aristocratic permissiveness of the ancien régime as represented by Prince Louis Ferdinand and, at its most cynical and decadent, by some of Schach's fellow-officers, is an aspect of the past from which Schach, a gentleman, dissociates himself. And though his stiffness, his unadaptability may be characteristic of the outmoded régime which he serves, they are given a highly personal note, being linked with his painful difficulties in making contact and sustaining personal relationships. An inner paralysis leads to his final tragedy as much as his concern for externals, his fear that Victoire to whom he had momentarily committed himself, may not be 'gesellschaftsfähig' (socially presentable). In this respect Schach's fate anticipates that of Innstetten in *Effi Briest*, of Christine von Holk in *Unwiederbringlich* (Irretrievable). Victoire who passes beyond defeat and humiliation towards a religiously orientated humanism, represents the noblest element in the new Prussia which, like her, rises phoenix-like (the symbol figures repeatedly in the narrative) from the ashes of military defeat.

But already while he was at work on *Vor dem Sturm*, and for many years afterwards, Fontane's letters and articles show him preoccupied with plans for providing Germany with a realistic novel of contemporary life. Here, he believed, Thackeray was a model to follow. In a notice on Paul Lindau's *Der Zug nach Westen* (1886) he wrote:

Es fehlt uns noch ein grosser Berliner Roman, der die Gesamtheit unseres Lebens schildert, etwa wie Thackeray in dem besten seiner Romane 'Vanity Fair'.[11]

What we lack as yet is a great Berlin novel, which describes the totality of our life, rather as Thackeray does in the best of his novels 'Vanity Fair'.

Previous German attempts at social realism he dismissed as contemptuously as G.H. Lewes had done. In a letter of 1879 he wrote of Gutzkow:

> Er hat die deutsche Nation düpiert. In andern Ländern, die mehr natürlichen Sinn für die Künste haben, und durch Bildungsdrill weniger verdummt sind, hätte er vierzig Jahre lang eine solche Rolle gar nicht spielen können.[12]

> He has duped the German nation. In other countries which have a more natural taste in the arts, and are less stupefied by cultural drill, he would never have been able to play such a rôle for forty years.

Thackeray's name figures in Fontane's correspondence more frequently than that of any other novelist except Scott. At first Fontane took issue with the contemporary public for preferring Dickens to Thackeray. In January 1857 he reported to the *Kreuz-Zeitung* that critics, at least in England, were beginning to endorse his own preference.[13] Fontane found the anti-aristocratic bias of the early Dickens and his seemingly propagandist zeal for social reform uncongenial, and considered that Dickens's characters, unlike those of Thackeray, were too often mere caricatures. Like Thackeray and unlike Dickens, Fontane came to devote far more space to the upper than to the lower classes in his fiction. But from the beginning he was also aware of that quality in Thackeray's work which most obviously differentiates it from his own: a heartless and, at times, cynical tone. Fontane wrote of Thackeray:

> Er sucht nach Wahrheit, aber seinem Suchen und seinem Finden fehlt die Liebe. So fehlt seinen Wahrheiten zuletzt doch die höchste Wahrheit und seine getroffensten Porträts

> frappieren überwiegend durch die hässliche Hälfte des Originals.[14]

> He searches for truth; but in searching and in finding he lacks charity. And therefore his truths ultimately lack the highest truth, and his most successful portraits impress us predominantly with the ugly halves of their originals.

This may be the reason why Fontane who had often gratefully acknowledged his debt to Thackeray, came to reverse his earlier judgment in a letter of 1879, and to claim that Dickens was ultimately the greater writer.[15] However, not only Dickens's reforming zeal, but the poetic intensities of his style and the visionary note in his later works, are alien to Fontane. Only in *Vor dem Sturm* are there specifically Dickensian echoes, at least in the passages in which Marie figures. She who comes to heal Lewin and, in fact, to redeem the entire Vitzewitz family from the strain of anger and bitterness which had characterized it since the time of the Thirty Years' War when an ancestor committed fratricide, is repeatedly referred to as a 'Märchenprinzessin' (fairy-tale princess), and recalls Sissy Jupe, Little Dorrit and other Dickensian heroines. There is no figure like her in Fontane's later work. On the other hand, what Fontane admired in Thackeray was his power of bringing contemporary English society to life in his fiction, through a wide range of representative characters and situations. Fontane dissociated himself, as we saw, from Thackeray's attitude to his world which is so often one of mean and complacent knowingness. The complimentary sentimentality where mother-figures are concerned – Helen in *Pendennis*, Lady Castlewood in *Esmond* – which clearly originated in Thackeray's own life-long mother-fixation, introduces an embarrassing contradiction into Thackeray's novels; for his psychological realism compels him to expose in some measure these figures whom he yet insists on regarding as angelic: for instance, Helen Pendennis whose sexual jealousy of her son is shown to make her cruel towards the women, Blanche Amory, Fanny Bolton, with whom her son falls in love. In *Vanity Fair*, Thackeray simpers over Amelia, yet exposes her at the same time as weak and insipid, while the contrasting figure of Becky Sharp is explicitly denounced yet implicitly admired. The basic constellation in Thackeray's novels – the up-and-coming young man, usually a writer or artist and a self-projection of Thackeray, the idealized mother-figure or the girl with motherly qualities, and the cold but fascinating beauty who comes between them as Blanche Amory does between Pen and Laura in *Pendennis*, or Beatrix between Henry Esmond and Lady Castlewood, or even Becky Sharp – briefly – between George Osborne and Amelia, has only one counterpart in Fontane's work, in *Vor dem Sturm* where Scott's *Waverley* provided the model. In the more genial *Newcomes*, the cold and worldly beauty, Ethel, is allowed to develop and improve until she herself comes to prefer natural and kindly people like the Colonel and Laura to her society associates, while the domestic, maternal Rosey, manipulated by her mother, the brutal Mrs Mackenzie, is more fully exposed in all her inadequacy than even Amelia was. Here Thackeray's own unhappy marriage and disastrous relationship with his mother-in-law inspired the writing. As the 'angelic' women are contrasted by Thackeray with the women of spirit, so his 'good' male characters, Dobbin of *Vanity Fair*, Colonel Newcome, forever duped and cheated, or Henry Esmond, are paired with ego-centric but charming rakes, George Osborne, Arthur Pendennis in his early years, or Frank Castlewood. Fontane was careful to avoid Thackeray's cynicism when describing negative figures and their actions; and he does not sentimentalize his positive characters, though figures, purged by suffering and renunciation, and committed to idealistic humanism, – Victoire as she emerges in the last chapter of *Schach von Wuthenow*, Melusine in *Der Stechlin* – correspond to Thackeray's Laura in *Pendennis*, or to Ethel after her transformation in *The Newcomes*.

Thackeray's most attractive figures, on the other hand, those gentlemen who combine successful worldliness with humanity and a sense of humour – the Major in *Pendennis* is their prototype – have near kinsmen in Fontane's fiction.

Thackeray's *Esmond* has definite links with Scott's *Waverley* and Fontane's *Vor dem Sturm*. The brilliant Beatrix resembles Scott's Flora and Fontane's Kathinka in her role as the devotee of a romantic lost cause, who casts a dangerous spell on the slowly maturing hero. But Thackeray is a good deal less tolerant of Jacobitism, and especially of its clerical protagonists, Roman Catholic and High Anglican, than is Scott. And Fontane is in this respect closer to Scott than to Thackeray. But Berndt von Vitzewitz's foolish assault on Frankfurt as the denouement of *Vor dem Sturm* recalls Henry Esmond's final futile escapade on behalf of the Pretender. Scott's and Fontane's cosmopolitanism contrasts strikingly with Thackeray's insular tendencies, his sneering attitude to most of his French characters and to all his Irish characters, the Costigans, Shandons and O'Dowds who are invariably boastful, shiftless scroungers and figures of fun.

Religiosity, whether of the Evangelical or of the High Church kind, figures almost always in Thackeray's novels as at best a private foible and at worst, in the Bates, the Crawleys and Honeymans, as a façade of monstrous hypocrisy. Only in the case of Thackeray's idealized women-figures is religiosity not ridiculed but presented as an ingredient of their 'angelic' make-up, thus intensifying the unresolved contradiction at the heart of Thackeray's work. Fontane's presentation of religion and of religious characters is subtler as well as more sympathetic than Thackeray's, and akin to Scott's.

Thackeray's frequent tirades against loveless matches, against what he calls the 'marriage-market' and the suffering and humiliation inflicted on women there, appear to have a counterpart in Fontane's compassionate portrayal of women like Lene, Cécile and Effi who are exploited by a society which confines women to passive and dependent positions. But in this respect too there is contradiction in Thackeray's world: for his outcry against a system which prevents Colonel Newcome and Léonore, or Clive and Ethel, from marrying contrasts strangely with his tendency to sneer at naive emotion, especially women's proneness to tears, and his ridiculing, elsewhere, of young love as blind folly. The love-affair of Pen and Fanny Bolton has an idyllic quality reminiscent of that of Botho and Lene in *Irrungen Wirrungen*. But Thackeray, elsewhere the critic of loveless marriages, seems to endorse George Warrington who prevents the match by explaining how his own life has been nearly ruined by a match with someone of 'low degree'. In spite of his protestations to the contrary, Thackeray is in individual instances as critical as Fontane of love-matches if they are entered into by members of different social classes. Where sexual morality is concerned, Thackeray is peculiarly ambiguous. In the Preface of *Pendennis*, he deplores the moral constraint under which the nineteenth century novelist labours; but where his favoured young men and women are concerned, he is always insistent that their virtues include what he terms 'purity'. Although he frequently refers to milliners, actresses and danseuses as featuring in the lives of his worldlier male characters, he is less explicit about the demi-monde than Fontane in *Stine*, *Cécile*, and elsewhere. However, Fontane, too, observes that Victorian convention which allows a writer to hint that an illicit sexual encounter is taking place but not to describe it. The seduction of Victoire by Schach in *Schach von Wuthenow*, that of Holk by Ebba in *Unwiederbringlich*, is handled with as much discretion as, say, that of Hetty Sorrel by Arthur Donnithorne in George Eliot's *Adam Bede*. Fontane's attitude to divorce, however, is far freer than that of Thackeray or any other English novelist of the period. Even so wretched a marriage as that of Sir Barnes Newcome and Lady Clara is described by Thackeray as preferable to the consequences of separation and divorce proceedings.[16] Certainly, Thackeray apportions severe blame to the society which compelled Lady Clara to enter a loveless marriage, but at the same time he condemns her marital infidelity with an explicitness which Fontane eschews in *Effi Briest*.

L.A. Shears has argued that Fontane drew directly on Thackeray's *Pendennis* for the theme, plot and characterization of *Frau Jenny Treibel*.[17] There certainly are some striking resemblances. Blanche, like Jenny, sees herself as a romantic idealist and revels in sentimental verse – indeed, she writes some herself – while she behaves with callous selfishness. Both Blanche and Jenny ensnare a supposedly kindred spirit (Pen, and Willibald Schmidt, respectively), only to jilt him when a coarser but wealthier suitor appears on the scene. Certainly, Fontane's satire, throughout this novel, is close in spirit to Thackeray's. But whether the specific resemblances to which Shears refers, are more than mere coincidences, is hard to determine. One could argue with as much, or as little, plausibility that Corinna's attempt on Leopold Treibel derives from the Lammle-Fledgeby-Georgiana Podsnap conspiracy in Dickens's *Our Mutual Friend* which is foiled in similar fashion. Or that Miss Crawley in *Vanity Fair* who professes egalitarian sentiments and encourages and patronizes Becky Sharp but recoils from her in horror when she finds her treacherously 'ensnaring' her nephew and heir provided the model for Fontane's Jenny in her dealings with Corinna. It is also arguable that Mathilde Möhring, manipulating Hugo and the society at Woldenstein, is at times reminiscent of Becky Sharp. But certain patterns and constellations are bound to recur in novels depicting similar societies. It is Thackeray, the creator of life-like dialogue and repartee, able to render a multiplicity of undertones and nuances in conversations at parties and social gatherings who is specifically Fontane's master. Only once, in the uncompleted *Allerlei Glück* (1878-9), did Fontane attempt Thackeray's 'panoramic' method and even here he sought to avoid Thackeray's tone: 'Zeitroman. Mitte der siebziger Jahre; Berlin und seine Gesellschaft, besonders die Mittelklassen, aber nicht satirisch sondern wohlwollend behandelt'[18] (A novel of the age. The middle seventies; Berlin and its society, especially the middle classes, but treated benevolently, not satirically). After *Vor dem Sturm* and *Allerlei Glück*, he wisely confined himself to shorter novels in which special psychological cases and situations are given a representative significance. Fontane never employs Thackeray's 'reminiscential' technique, with a fictitious narrator, nor does he reintroduce the same characters, or their relatives and descendants, in novel after novel like Thackeray. Ironic self-disparagement which in Thackeray's novels occasionally counteracts the illusion created by the narrative and suggests that the author's attitude to his own art verges on the cynical, is not to be found in Fontane's novels though it occurs in some of his verse. On the other hand, the criticism sometimes made of Thackeray that his characters do not develop, is unfounded. Reference has been made to the fact that Lady Castlewood, in *Esmond*, Ethel in *The Newcomes*, develop in the school of suffering much as Fontane's characters do.

Many of the technical devices on which Fontane relies are to be found not only in Thackeray, but in other Victorian novelists. The function of social gatherings in Thackeray and Fontane has already been alluded to. At the opening of *The Newcomes*, Thackeray assembles leading characters of the novel in an exclusive pub where they reveal themselves and at the same time introduce the reader to other characters who are to feature in the narrative, by discussing them in their absence. Fontane provides a similar set piece in the 'Sala Tarone' chapter near the beginning of *Schach von Wuthenow*. The group-excursion at which it is settled whether or not an expected engagement will take place, occurs in *Schach von Wuthenow* and again in *Frau Jenny Treibel*, as well as in *Vanity Fair* (the Vauxhall outing) and elsewhere in Thackeray.

George Eliot makes similar use of a formal occasion, the Archery Meeting in Brackenshaw Park (*Daniel Deronda*), to stage the fatal engagement of Gwendolen and Grandcourt and bring out all its social implications. The Harvest Festival in *Adam Bede* has a similar climacteric function. A dinner-party as the turning-point in a narrative is as common in Dickens as it is in Thackeray and Fontane.

The use of comical and allegorical names occurs in Fontane but is not nearly as prevalent in his work as it is in that of Dickens, Thackeray or Trollope. It is not found in George Eliot, but in other respects, in her symbolism, and in the prominence given to the religious themes, she is closer to Fontane than is Thackeray. References to George Eliot in Fontane's correspondence are few and brief, but indicate that he knew her novels.[19] Like Fontane, George Eliot did, of course, love and admire Scott, and derived from him, as we saw, her sociological approach to the ideologies and faiths of men. There are incidents in Fontane's work which vividly recall similar ones in George Eliot's. Schach flees from Berlin to Wuthenow, and after a night of sleepless wandering on his estate, stretches out in a boat and experiences its drifting into the lake as an anticipation of his own death. Similarly, Romola, after her second flight from Florence, finds rest in a sailing-boat on the sea-shore; she lets it glide on the water, lies down in it to watch the stars and eventually falls asleep like Schach. George Eliot is more explicit even than Fontane about the allegorical significance of the 'Drifting away' as this chapter, the sixty-first of *Romola*, is called: 'She read no message of love for her in that far-off symbolic writing of the heavens, and with a great sob she wished that she might be gliding into death.'[20] The discovery by Effi Briest of the picture of the Chinaman in the old house in Kessin corresponds closely to the opening by Gwendolen, in *Daniel Deronda*, of the panel 'which disclosed the picture of an upturned dead face, from which an obscure figure seemed to be fleeing with outstretched arms'[21]. The respective incidents mark the end of the carefree adolescence of the two girls, recognition of previously unacknowledged fears concerning their new situation, and forebodings of the guilt they are to incur. Such correspondences may be coincidental and not evidence of either direct borrowings by Fontane from George Eliot, or of unconscious recollections from his readings of her work, but they certainly indicate a kinship between the two novelists in the use of symbolical motifs. Such motifs are, however, far more frequent in Fontane than in George Eliot.

In the works of both authors tragedies of marital incompatibility preponderate. In the earlier novels, *Scenes of Clerical Life* and *Romola*, the husbands are the guilty parties, but the wives find their way, through rebellion and hatred, and deep suffering, to self-knowledge and serenity. In *Middlemarch* and *Daniel Deronda*, Dorothea and Gwendolen, like the wives in the earlier novels resist the temptation to desert, but though they, too, are eventually freed from the presence of a detested partner, they are not mere innocent victims, as Janet and Romola in the earlier novels were, but are shown to be to some extent co-responsible with their husbands for their unhappy marriages: awareness of guilt, remorse and penance are necessary phases in their moral growth. In Fontane's novels, from *L'Adultera* and *Graf Petöfy* to *Unwiederbringlich* and *Effi Briest*, the moral responsibility of the partners is not emphasized as explicitly as it is in George Eliot's, and though guilt is not lacking, other factors, including differences of temperament and age-differences which from the start make real community difficult to achieve, are more to the fore. Nor does Fontane insist, as George Eliot does, that marriage is sacred and indissoluble whatever the circumstances: though when he shows a partner, unfulfilled and frustrated in marriage, yielding to the temptation to become unfaithful, the consequences are fatal in *Graf Petöfy*, *Cécile* and *Unwiederbringlich* the marriages terminate in the suicide of one of the partners, and ruin and an early death are the lot of *Effi Briest*. Only in the early *L'Adultera* where separation leads to remarriage, does Fontane contrive a somewhat implausible happy ending.

Some of the themes found in both Fontane and George Eliot, for instance that of the precariousness of love across class-barriers, are, as we have seen, common to other nineteenth century authors. The match between Arthur Donnithorne and Hetty Sorrel, in *Adam Bede*, is presented as impractical for the same reason as that between Botho and Lene in *Irrungen Wirrungen*. 'I know you can never be happy', (writes Arthur to Hetty), 'except by marrying a man in your own station; and if I were to marry you now, I should only be adding to any wrong I have done, besides offending against my duty in the other relations of life. You know nothing, dear Hetty, of the world in which I must always live, and you would soon begin to dislike me, because there would be so little in which we should be alike'.[22] Hetty would have passed from Arthur to Adam Bede as smoothly as Lene does from Botho to Gideon Franke if it had not been for the birth of an illegitimate child. But in George Eliot's world, unlike Fontane's, a Nemesis operates which rouses the dormant consciences of the guilty and compels them to confront the full implications of their failings. On a few occasions, class-barriers are transcended by lovers in George Eliot's work, as they are, once or twice, in Fontane's, for instance in *Mathilde Möhring*. Esther prefers Felix Holt who is a working-man, but self-educated, to her other suitor, Harold Transome, a 'gentleman':

> She had a native capability for discerning that the sense of ranks and degrees has its repulsions corresponding to the repulsions dependent on differences of race and colour . . . And in her fluctuations on this matter, she found herself mentally protesting that, whatever Harold might think, there was a light in which he was vulgar compared with Felix. Felix had ideas and motives which she did not believe that Harold could understand. More than all, there was this test: she

> herself had no sense of inferiority and just subjection when
> she was with Harold Transome; there were even points in him
> for which she felt a touch, not of angry, but of playful scorn;
> whereas with Felix she had always a sense of dependence and
> possible illumination.[23]

In *Felix Holt*, George Eliot deals with the conflict between the conservative landed gentry, the liberal-progressive interests of commerce and industry, and the rising force of working-class radicalism. The novel revolves around a parliamentary election as Disraeli's and Mrs Gaskell's novels and Dickens's *Bleak House* did. Fontane takes up this theme in *Der Stechlin* where, just as in the English novels, the representatives of the old order are presented as often superior morally and more attractive as human beings than the representatives of the new. In *Felix Holt*, the Rev. Lingon, Harold Transome's uncle, in his humorous detachment and flexibility between the rival factions has points of contact with old Stechlin. And Mr Brooke of *Middlemarch* is another 'Fontanesque' figure, a country-gentleman, good-natured, a little eccentric, but shrewd and independent in all things.

As indicated earlier, both Fontane and George Eliot sometimes endorse as realistic the reluctance of certain characters to marry outside their own social class. But people who are slaves of convention are exposed as inadequate by both authors. In the novel *Effi Briest*, the maintenance of appearances which are 'correct', drive Innstetten, against his better judgment and the human realities of the situation, to kill his wife's former lover in a duel and to ruin her and, eventually, himself by imposing separation and social ostracism on her. In the words of Bülow, towards the end of the story:

> Da haben Sie das Wesen der falschen Ehre. Sie macht uns
> abhängig von dem Schwankendsten und Willkürlichsten, was
> es gibt, von dem auf Triebsand aufgebauten Urteile der
> Gesellschaft, und veranlasst uns, die heiligsten Gebote, die
> schönsten und natürlichsten Regungen eben diesem

Gesellschaftsgötzen zum Opfer zu bringen.[24]

There you have the essence of false honour. It makes us dependent on the most vacillating and arbitrary thing there is, the opinion of society which is built on quicksand, and it causes us to sacrifice the holiest commandments, the fairest and most natural impulses to this very idol of society.

It is his inner independence, on the other hand, which enables Briest to forgive his daughter and take her back into his home, in the teeth of society's and his own family's opposition. In the novel *Der Stechlin* the inwardly free, open and unprejudiced outlook of Dubslav and his friends goes with a detachment from convention. In George Eliot's work the principal characters, Edgar Tryan and Janet in *Scenes of Clerical Life*, Dinah in *Adam Bede*, Felix Holt, Romola, Dorothea in *Middlemarch*, and finally Daniel Deronda, defy society more directly than Fontane's do. Dorothea who vindicates Lydgate, when he is persecuted, and disregards convention by marrying Ladislaw, expresses the standpoint of all George Eliot's principal characters.

'I never called anything by the same name that all the people about me did,' said Dorothea, stoutly. 'But I suppose you have found out your mistake, my dear,' said Mrs Cadwallader, 'and that is a proof of sanity.' Dorothea was aware of the sting, but it did not hurt her. 'No,' she said, 'I still think that the greater part of the world is mistaken about many things. Surely one may be sane and yet think so, since the greater part of the world has often had to come round from its opinion.'[25]

In the works of both authors personal independence is often the concomitant of religious faith. Some of Fontane's characters are wholly emancipated from the pressures of convention because they have suffered personal misfortunes which have led them to renounce their claims to normal success and happiness in life: they have little to hope or fear from society any longer and are free to practise self-effacing charity. Among them is Fräulein von Sawatzki, the deformed woman who alone stands by Melanie after her 'fall' in the novel *L'Adultera*. 'Ein halbes Stiftsfräulein,' says Melanie of her, 'und jeden Sonntag in Sankt Matthäi! Aber die Frommen, wenn sie's wirklich sind, sind immer noch die Besten.'[26] (Half-way to being a nun, and every Sunday in St Matthew's Church! But religious people, when they really are so, are always the best.) Roswitha, the servant who saves Effi's life when she is ostracized, is not physically handicapped; but the misfortunes she has suffered – banishment from her native village and environment because she had an illegitimate child, and subsequent maltreatment in various wealthy houses in which she served, in part because her devout Catholicism is anathema to her employers – these have estranged her from the respectable and their conventions. Other characters undergo a process of religious conversion as they mature. Even Melanie does so, temporarily at least, when she goes to church in a moment of crisis, and Effi, when she prays after the disastrous encounter with her child. Victoire, in *Schach von Wuthenow*, disfigured by smallpox while still an adolescent and betrayed by Schach, recovers the courage to live and love in Rome where she prays daily in a Catholic church. Franziska, in *Graf Petöfi*, finds peace in Catholicism, and Cécile returns to it before dying. It is noteworthy that Fontane, perhaps in conscious or unconscious reaction against the prevailing anti-Catholic fashion of the 'Kulturkampf'-period, presents Catholics and Catholicism always in a particularly sympathetic light.

The serenity and humanity which Melusine, in *Der Stechlin*, attains after suffering in an unhappy marriage, is not specifically Christian as was that of her predecessors in the earlier novels, yet she is close to Pastor Lorenzen who professes an open and socially aware Lutheranism. In George Eliot's work the religious commitment of most of her leading characters is even more explicit than in Fontane's. Both authors show a great interest in various sects and present these predominantly as positive forces. The Mennonite community in *Quitt* is the outstanding example in Fontane.

The glowing endorsement of Methodist and Evangelical revivalist movements in George Eliot's fiction does not, however, preclude an occasional unfavourable portrait of their representatives: there is the Lantern Yard community from which Silas Marner is unfairly expelled, and the ambiguous Bulstrode in *Middlemarch*. Similarly, the long series of wise and kindly clergymen in the works of the two authors, admits of an occasional exception such as the careerist Koseleger in *Der Stechlin* and the Rev. Mr Tyke in *Middlemarch*. Mere conventional orthodoxy is presented by Fontane in the case of the Glasenapps in *Effi Briest* or of Adelheid in *Der Stechlin*, as part of their self-righteous, snobbish and intolerant attitude to life; it has its equivalent in the insularity and philistinism of county society in George Eliot's fiction which is exposed by outsider figures such as Klesmer and Daniel Deronda, in the novel of that name.

George Eliot and Fontane have therefore a good deal in common; but there are also great differences between them. Wholly alien to George Eliot is Fontane's penchant for 'causerie'; it makes him propound so many clever but often untenable positions in his correspondence – positions he is the first to contradict when the occasion arises – and it enables him to enliven his novels with so many witty and revealing arguments ('Streitgespräche'). George Eliot is far graver and more ponderous in the expression of her opinions: they are of a kind she would and could always stand by. Again, Fontane shows a special partiality for those of his characters who have a light touch and refuse to be solemn about themselves; qualities of rigidity and self-righteousness, on the other hand, are particularly odious to him. The same can by no means be said of George Eliot. From her earliest work, men of easy-going, affable disposition who are popular and value their popularity highly – Anthony Wybrow in *Scenes of Clerical Life*, Arthur Donnithorne in *Adam Bede*, Tito in *Romola* – are presented by her as selfish: they are shown to bring ruin to others and, eventually, to themselves also. Conventional feminine charm, also, poses a temptation to those who possess it as well as to those they encounter. Nothing like the earnest and ruthless psychological analysis which George Eliot engages in as a prelude to passing judgment on her characters, is found in Fontane who shows a far greater tolerance of compromisers and 'worldly' people. Only in *Quitt* where Lehnert is pursued to his death by a mysterious Nemesis, does Fontane come close to the ethos of George Eliot's work. Reference has been made to occasional 'Fontanesque' characters in George Eliot's fiction, but these are exceptions, just as Holk in *Unwiederbringlich* is an exception in Fontane. In that novel the pattern of human relationships is such that an easy-going, tolerant disposition which is as a rule endorsed by Fontane, becomes a source of weakness as so often in George Eliot. Holk shirks his responsibilities; and it is the escapism, the self-deception of this unsuccessful – mere would-be – bon-vivant which brings about the tragic break-down of his marriage.

It was Peter Demetz who first suggested that of all the English novelists it is Trollope who is closest to Fontane.[27] Demetz makes this point two or three times, without expatiating on it; and it may strike some readers as paradoxical. For there is in fact no allusion to Trollope in Fontane's published work, his correspondence, his essays and reviews, nor is there any internal evidence in Fontane's fiction that he had ever read Trollope or been influenced by him. Moreover, while Fontane's work is relatively sparse and remarkable for its concentration, Trollope produced over forty novels, most of them very long, and several volumes of short stories. For this reason, Trollope has sometimes been regarded as a commercial hack, and many readers are likely to consider Demetz's comparison damaging to Fontane. The general reading public, however, is acquainted mainly with Trollope's Barchester novels – or, at least, was, until the Palliser series was televised – and Barchester is a somewhat idyllic place, unlike Trollope's London, the sphere of metropolitan commerce, politics and government, and of an increasingly disturbed upper-class society. Trollope has sometimes been described as a lesser Thackeray; but as a novelist he possesses virtues which Thackeray lacked. He is free from personal obsessions, his irony is gentle, and he manages to be worldly-wise without being cynical. Like Fontane, he portrays with subtlety and tact a wide range of normal and abnormal characters, but has tended to be underestimated because he favours an unemphatic, at times almost chatty, approach to issues that turn out to be problematic, even tragic. Both authors had conscientiously followed humdrum careers for many years, Fontane as a pharmacist, Trollope as a civil servant, and they came to favour a disciplined, business-like approach to the writing of fiction; indeed, they disparaged inspiration and spoke of literature as a means of earning a livelihood. Trollope's somewhat provocative statements to this effect in his *Autobiography*, appearing as they did in the eighteen-eighties when aestheticism was coming into vogue, proved a factor in the decline of his reputation. But a profound personal modesty, rare among writers, is the essential condition of the particular human sympathy and insight communicated in their respective fictions.

Trollope and Fontane shared other crucial experiences. Both of them had fathers who failed in all their business-ventures and were at loggerheads with their wives though for different reasons. Trollope's father was a highly scrupulous but very difficult man while his mother was a warm-hearted and optimistic woman, proficient both as a housewife and as a popular writer. Fontane's mother was competent too, but of a harsh, critical disposition, his father an amiable idler. Children whose parents are incompatible are forced into an ambivalent attitude towards them: both Trollope and Fontane became detached observers of human behaviour early in life, and the tendency towards objectivity bordering on ambivalence which we saw as characterizing the realistic novel since Scott, is reinforced in their fictions by a disposition originating

167

in a particular childhood predicament. Moreover, the two authors inherited their respective parents' contradictory qualities, and therefore endured personal tensions which were to impart to their art its peculiar vitality. Again and again, Fontane creates marriage-partners who relive the parental conflict, the one rigid, conscientious, correct, and worthy of high respect, the other amiable, weak but sympathetic. Innstetten and Effi Briest, Christine and Holk in *Unwiederbringlich*, Mathilde Möhring and her husband, come to mind. Trollope, too, is partial to scamps and idlers: men like Burgo Fitzgerald, Lord Chiltern, Mountjoy Scarborough, have a charm and human warmth lacking in the respectable. His women are, to their cost, often attracted to such men rather than to their duller, if more dependable, suitors. In *The small House at Allington*, Alice Vavasor deserts John Grey for her cousin George, and in *Can You Forgive Her?* Lady Glencora turns from her husband much as Effi does from Innstetten:

> She wanted the little daily assurance of her supremacy in the man's feelings, the constant touch of love, half accidental half contrived, the passing glance of the eye telling perhaps of some little joke understood only between them two rather than of love, the softness of an occasional kiss given here and there when chance might bring them together, some half-pretended interest in her little doings, a nod, a wink, a shake of the head, or even a pout. It should have been given to her to feed upon such food as this daily, and then she would have forgotten Burgo Fitzgerald. But Mr Palliser understood none of these things; and therefore the image of Burgo Fitzgerald in all his beauty was ever before her eyes.[28]

Like Effi, Lady Glencora 'did not count herself for much'[29], but in Trollope's work tragedy is averted because Platagenet Palliser shows a forbearance of which Innstetten is not capable. Both authors have understanding for those characters who because of inner inhibitions are unable to show and demonstrate the affection they actually feel. Fontane portrayed this – his mother's – predicament in Schach von Wuthenow, in Innstetten (*Effi Briest*) and, most consummately perhaps, in Christine (*Unwiederbringlich*).

The phenomenon is presented in Trollope's novels also, for instance in *John Caldigate*: 'To his wife he had been inwardly affectionate, but outwardly almost stern. To his daughters he had been the same, – always anxious for every good thing on their behalf, but never able to make the children conscious of this anxiety.'[30] In Plantagenet Palliser emotional inhibition of this kind goes with modesty and self-abnegation, and he is in these respects akin to Mr Harding in *The Warden*. Trollope is very partial to both characters as he indicates in his *Autobiography*. But Mr Crawley (*The Last Chronicle of Barset*) in whom Trollope portrayed his father, is not merely conscientious as they are, but pathologically scrupulous and ego-centric. And Kennedy in *Phineas Finn* who appears at first merely aloof and plodding like Palliser, and a little tyrannical, like Innstetten, in his attempts to instruct and mould his wife, gradually reveals those streaks of suspicion and jealous possessiveness which bring about the destruction of his marriage. Louis Trevelyan, in *He Knew He Was Right*, is a yet more extreme variant of the type: he actually becomes paranoiac. Trollope is fascinated by the phenomenon of self-righteousness in women also. His Mrs Proudie is a subtler presentation of the domineering female than Thackeray's harridans because he shows that she and those like her see their despotism as essentially benevolent: the only safeguard of proper order in a world inhabited by weak and incompetent people.

In his portrayal of the conflict of old and new, Trollope's sympathies are divided like those of Fontane and, indeed, of every contributor to the tradition of fiction stemming from Scott. Trollope made his first major impact with *The Warden* in which the reformer John Bold confronts the traditionalist Dr Grantly, the positive and negative elements in the position of each being evenly balanced. For in Trollope's as

169

in Fontane's novels, the merits and the demerits of every cause are complicated by the personalities who choose to identify with it. And in the Barchester novels as in the later political ones, Trollope has a keen eye for the human-all-too-human considerations which motivate characters to adopt this or that partisan position.

Though he acknowledges the need for change, Trollope sympathizes with the ultra-conservative Thornes of Ullathorne who pride themselves on having been in the same place since pre-Norman times, rather like those proudly independent nobles in Fontane who insist that they had been established in Brandenburg before the arrival of the Hohenzollern dynasty. John H. Hagan has spoken of 'the divided mind of Anthony Trollope'[31]. Fontane's mind is divided too. This is a strength rather than a weakness, for it enables him to achieve objectivity, non-partisanship, towards the world he portrays. It could, indeed, be argued that he adopts a dialectical approach which manifests itself in seemingly contradictory attitudes, not merely towards the old and the new, but towards many of the phenomena and issues of his time. In his correspondence, negative generalizations about the society of his time, about the Prussian nobility, or the Jews, alternate with positive generalizations. Attractive representatives of Judaism figure in *L'Adultera*, *Die Poggenpuhls* and *Mathilde Möhring*; but in *Der Stechlin* the negative note predominates. Criticisms that foreigners could and did bring against Prussia are occasionally endorsed by Fontane (as in the case of Bülow's pronouncements in *Schach von Wuthenow*) while elsewhere he registers satisfaction in Prussian virtues and achievements, and his very presentation of Prussian characters and circumstances serves to refute anti-Prussian prejudices. Fontane was himself acutely conscious of his ambivalence where individuals and whole nations, for instance the English, are concerned:

> Es geht einem auch im Leben mit Einzelindividuen so und dann wieder mit ganzen Nationen. Die Engländer habe ich

mit meiner Liebe verfolgt und sie dann doch wieder für egoistische und heuchlerische Bande erklärt.[32]

This has been one's experience both with individuals and with entire nations. I have pursued the English with my love, and then declared them to be an egoistic and hypocritical gang.

With reference to the people of his native region he writes: '. . . mir, dem Verherrlicher des Märkischen, ist alles Märkische so schrecklich'[33] (to me, the glorifier of Brandenburg, everything about it seems so frightful).

Reference has been made to Fontane's chivalrous tendency to present Catholics in a favourable light, countering the prevailing Protestant prejudice of the 'Kulturkampf' era. Similarly, he engages the reader's sympathetic interest on behalf of Prussia's 'enemies', Austrians (in *Graf Petöfy* and *Irrungen Wirrungen*), Poles (in *Vor dem Sturm, Schach von Wuthenow* and *Unterm Birnbaum*), Danes (in *Unwiederbringlich* and *Effi Briest*), and the French in many of his novels. Fontane's own French Huguenot ancestry which he occasionally emphasizes, is clearly a complicating factor where his attitudes to France and Frenchmen is concerned. Trollope cultivates a similar fairness towards his non-English characters. Henry James has complimented him on his Americans: 'His American portraits, by the way, are always friendly: they hit it off more happily than the attempt to depict American character from the European point of view is accustomed to do . . . '[34] Trollope had first found himself a success, as civil servant and novelist, during his sojourn in Ireland, and his novels set in Ireland and the portraits of Irishmen in his other novels, are, quite unlike Thackeray's and other English novelists' of the time, respectful and understanding. Indeed, readers seem to have regretted that Trollope didn't deal in the stage-Irish stereotypes to which they were accustomed. Shane Leslie complains that Trollope's Phineas Finn doesn't seem Irish: 'One thing is clear and that is that Lord Chiltern (his rival for the hand of

Violet Effingham) with his red hair and blackguardly dare-devilry was much more Hibernian than Phineas. He races and gambles and kills a ruffian at Newmarket with his fists.'[35] Where Dickens in *Our Mutual Friend* and George Eliot in *Daniel Deronda* polemicized against anti-Semitic prejudice, Trollope, like Fontane, is content to present Jews now in a favourable and now in an unfavourable light. There are many Jewish crooks and adventurers in his novels, the most conspicuous being Ferdinand Lopez in *The Prime Minister*, Joseph Emilius in *The Eustace Diamonds*, and Auguste Melmotte in *The Way We Live Now*. But then the Jew Breghert in *The Way We Live Now* is one of the few honest people in it, and Madame Max Goesler, courageously establishing her independence from the conventions of a hypocritical society, is fully endorsed in the Palliser novels. She takes her place with Eleanor Harding and Mary Thorne in the Barchester novels, with Lady Glencora, Laura Kennedy and Violet Effingham in the Palliser novels, women of spirit and integrity who defy their own families to acknowledge the love they feel. They enjoy Trollope's deepest sympathy even though their obstinacy may lead them – Alice Vavasor in *Can You Forigve Her?* Emily Wharton in *The Prime Minister*, Emily Hotspur in *Sir Harry Hotspur of Humble-thwaite* – into guilt and tragedy. And Trollope, like Fontane, has repeatedly been considered to show a sympathy for his women heroines, bordering on love.

If it is true – as is often alleged – that Fontane is primarily interested in the upper classes, he yet portrays lower middle-class milieux, in *Irrungen Wirrungen*, in *Stine*, *Mathilde Möhring*, and elsewhere, with warm sympathy. The central figures in Fontane's fiction are in fact almost always portrayed sympathetically, whether they belong to the higher or the lower nobility, the upper middle or the lower middle class. Contrary to what Marxist critics have alleged, the representatives of the newly rich bourgeoisie are also presented in a favourable light at times, especially in *L'Adultera*. And

172

even in *Frau Jenny Treibel* where the satirical note is more to the fore than elsewhere in Fontane, the industrialist Treibel himself is endowed with a bonhommie, an ironic detachment which assimilate him to favoured aristocrats such as Herr von Briest and old Stechlin. These are men who refuse to be solemn about themselves and their concerns, but preserve a measure of serenity in the conflicts of everyday life and a sense of humour which leaves them free to exercize a humanity, conspicuously lacking in those who take themselves and their petty material concerns wholly seriously, or attach decisive importance to social conventions. These may be of any class: the bigoted and title-crazy noblewomen of *Effi Briest* and *Der Stechlin* are at fault in this respect, and so are the commercial bourgeoises of *Frau Jenny Treibel*, being brazenly self-assured in their money-snobbery. (Among Fontane's lower-class figures, on the other hand, there are some who, like the widow Pittelkow in *Stine*, take themselves so seriously that they appear comical, but are redeemed in the author's and readers' eyes because they are, at any rate, capable of taking other people seriously too.)

In characters like Schach von Wuthenow, or Innstetten in *Effi Briest,* conformism is symptomatic of a general human deficiency: Schach, we learn is 'abhängig bis zur Schwäche von dem Urteile der Menschen, speziell seiner Standes-genossen'[36] (dependent to the point of weakness on the opinion of people, especially that of his compeers). This makes him representative, in the story, of a whole society, the Prussia ruled by outmoded convention and blind to the realities of the present in its concern for appearances which suffers defeat at the hands of Napoleon in 1806. In Schach as in Innstetten and, for that matter, in Trollope's Palliser, conventionality goes with a careerism which is an attempt to compensate for an inaptitude in intimate personal relationships. Both Schach and Innstetten are dedicated to a false concept of 'honour' – it is called a 'Gesellschaftsgötze' (idol of society) by von Bülow in *Schach von Wuthenow*[37] and

'Götzendienst' (idol-worship) by Wüllersdorff in *Effi Briest*[38].
It drives Innstetten, against his better judgment and the
human realities of his situation, to kill his wife's former lover
in a duel and to ruin her and, eventually, himself by imposing
separation and social ostracism on her. But, as was indicated
earlier, Fontane does not endorse a defiance of convention
either, if it is blatantly imprudent, particularly where marriage
between members of different social classes is concerned. In
Irrungen Wirrungen the young officer and nobleman, Botho
von Rienäcker, finds a genuineness and humanity in the
seamstress Lene, lacking in the status- and money-conscious
circles in which he moves. But it is precisely his and Lene's
clear sense of realities, their recognition that Botho, at any
rate, is temperamentally incapable of defying convention and
paying for it by suffering disinheritance, poverty and social
ostracism that makes them terminate their liaison and resign
themselves to entering loveless marriages with members of
their own respective classes instead. In the story *Stine* the
young nobleman Waldemar's decision to offer marriage to a
girl of the working-class is, on the other hand, seen not as
evidence of strength of character, but rather of weakness: his
plan to renounce his title, emigrate to America and opt for the
simple life as a pioneer in the West is shown up as a mere
escapist fantasy in one so poor in health that he has had to
resign his army-commission; and his suicide merely confirms
our impression of him as a rootless, isolated figure. In the
novel *Frau Jenny Treibel*, however, the gradual erosion of
the engagement between Leopold Treibel and Corinna
Schmidt through hostile social pressures is treated satirically
by Fontane. The difference between their respective families,
both of them middle-class, is one of income; and society, in
its opposition to the match, is represented primarily by
Leopold's mother, a social climber, who wants him to marry
into an even wealthier and, if possible, an aristocratic family;
and Leopold's failure to resist this pressure and stand by
Corinna, is therefore indicative of his weakness of character.

Trollope's preference for independent women was referred to earlier; these resist the pressures of conventions which stifle integrity and vitality. But a contempt for any and every convention is a mark of the cad in Trollope. Of George Vavasor we are told: 'There had come upon him of late a hard ferocity which made him unendurable. And then he carried to such a pitch that hatred, as he called it, of conventional rules, that he allowed himself to be controlled by none of the ordinary bonds of society.'[39] The antithesis of the cad is the gentleman in Trollope's fiction; he combines observation of the code of manners of his class with delicacy of feeling and consideration for others, and is therefore a rarity. Members of the higher nobility are often anything but gentlemanly, and even the 'nouveau riche' Miss Dunstable is inwardly superior to the noble fortune-hunters who pursue her. In the world of Barset, the de Courcys, in particular, are heartless snobs and unscrupulously selfish, but, in contrast with them, the de Guests, equally aristocratic, are gentlemenly. Trollope is partial, as a rule to the rural gentry but it, too, produces cads, like George Hotspur, as well as gentlemen. Mr Crawley remains a gentleman and is acknowledged as such by all who encounter him though outwardly he is 'déclassé' to an extent which does not occur in Fontane. Not even the Poggenpuhls endured such deprivation and loss of dignity consequent upon the taking – indeed, the soliciting – of charity. Marriages across class-barriers occur in Trollope, but only under exceptional circumstances. Frank Gresham who is in love with the illegitimate Mary Thorne, is prepared to be disinherited and to go as a settler to the colonies, rather like Count Waldemar in *Stine*; but disaster is averted when the girl turns out to be an heiress. A similar deus ex machina, plausible, perhaps, under the circumstances, breaks down family-resistance to the match between an earl's daughter and a journeyman tailor in *Lady Anna*.

It has sometimes been stated that Trollope evades tragedy altogether. This is no more true than the claim that he is unable to show development of character. His John Eames, in *The Small House at Allington*, grows from a nervous youth, unrealistic in his view of life and socially awkward, into a mature man of the world. And in the Palliser novels, Lady Glencora develops from a high-spirited but unstable young girl into a woman of depth and considerable moral stature. The convention of the happy ending is observed in the Barchester novels but not in the later ones. In *Sir Harry Hotspur of Humblethwaite,* Emily's suffering when she is betrayed by her fiancé, is intensified by the guilt she feels at having made her father unhappy; for it was in opposition to him that she encouraged her unworthy lover for so long. Unavoidable conflicts between fathers and children are the theme of the last of the Palliser novels, *The Duke's Children*, of *John Caldigate*, and of *Mr Scarborough's Family*, where an aging man struggles to avert the fate of King Lear which threatens him. And the story of Louis Trevelyan's marriage and its breakdown in *He Knew He Was Right*, is one of unrelieved misery.

Remorse and resignation characterize the experience of tragedy in Fontane's novels. When Effi encounters her daughter after years of separation and finds that Innstetten has turned her into an automaton, she rails against his cruelty, but later she exonerates him and blames herself, her own instability and craving for excitement, for the breakdown of her marriage. Fontane's ambivalence enables him to balance conflicting principles, in this case those of law and of spontaneity, embodied in Innstetten and Effi respectively, and to show the inadequacy of each when asserted in isolation from the other. The conflict between old and new, in so many of the novels, leads to tragedy because the contradiction of the two principles proves unresolvable in particular situations. But different characters respond in different ways to the suffering which is imposed on them. Some, Victoire in *Schach von Wuthenow*, Melusine in *Der Stechlin*, undergo, as we saw, a quasi-religious process of transformation which frees them for serenity and humanity. Others commit suicide. And some characters achieve a compromise, renouncing their high hopes and accepting gratefully the dimished happiness that is still available to them: Effi, in the end, and her father, Botho and Lene in *Irrungen Wirrungen*, Vitzewitz in *Vor dem Sturm*, and Corinna in *Frau Jenny Treibel*. Tragedy occurs in the work of both authors, but it is certainly more prevalent in that of Fontane than that of Trollope.

The two novelists also differ in their attitudes to certain ethical problems. Where sexual morality is concerned, Trollope, unlike Fontane, takes his stand with Dickens, Thackeray and George Eliot. Illegitimacy features frequently in his work, and there are kept women in many of the later novels, for instance in *The Way We Live Now*, in *Sir Harry Hotspur of Humblethwaite* and in *John Caldigate*, but their circumstances and background are merely hinted at, and not fully realized as in Fontane's *Cécile* and *Stine*. The novel *The Vicar of Bullhampton* deals sympathetically with the rescue of a fallen woman, but we are shown only her misery after she has been deserted, and the heroic efforts of the Vicar to rehabilitate her in the eyes of the world, not her earlier way of life. Trollope has none of Fontane's tolerance of divorce but endorses Alice in *Can You Forgive Her?* when she argues that Lady Glencora 'should be true to her marriage-vow, whether that vow when made were true or false'[40]. Trollope's attitude to suicide is also the conventional one of his time. He presents it consistently as 'the last refuge of the scoundrel'. Characters in predicaments brought about by their wrong-doing, like Crosbie in *The Small House at Allington*, George Vavasor in *Can You Forgive Her?* and Burgo Fitzgerald in the Palliser novels, contemplate suicide. Fraudulent characters, facing financial ruin, Lopez in *The Prime Minister*, Melmotte in *The Way We Live Now*, die by their own hand, shamefully, as Merdle does in Dickens's *Little Dorrit*. Fontane, on the other hand, accords not only sympathy but considerable respect to his suicides though he

177

does not vindicate them: Schach von Wuthenow, Graf Petöfy, Christine von Holk in *Unwiederbringlich* and Waldemar in *Stine*, are all shown to be at fault in their life-styles, but, as Fontane states in *Graf Petöfy*, suicides have gone through hard struggles ('schwere Kämpfe') and therefore deserve, at least, respect for their suffering.[41]

While it is impossible to establish the precise nature of Fontane's religious beliefs because of his contradictory utterances about them, Trollope's commitment to a liberal Christianity is unambiguous; yet Trollope's insight into religious phenomena probably doesn't equal Fontane's or George Eliot's. In the Barchester novels he is content to present the conflicts of rival parties, High, Broad and Low Anglican, in terms of competing personalities. He shares Thackeray's anti-Evangelical bias and defends the worldliness of many of his clerics, rejecting 'efforts to reach that which is not the condition of humanity . . . Is not modern stoicism, built though it be on Christianity, as great an outrage on human nature as the stoicism of the ancients?'[42] Yet in the highly sensitive, sincere, humble and charitable Rev. Mr Harding (*The Warden*), Trollope has created the portrait of a Christian which has commanded the admiration of Ronald Knox, a theological critic[43]. And there are studies of Roman Catholic priests in Trollope's Irish stories, especially in *The Macdermots* and *An Eye for an Eye*, which are as sympathetic as Fontane's in *Graf Petöfy*. On the other hand, Trollope's presentation, in the Barchester novels, of the machinery of ecclesiastical power in all its complexity, is, like that of the parliamentary and governmental machinery in the Palliser novels, without equivalent in Fontane's fiction.

In their later work Trollope and Fontane are at one in substituting for Thackeray's panoramic rendering of society portraits of special cases which yet have a representative significance. But while Trollope, like his Victorian predecessors, cultivated the three-volume novel which publishers and readers were accustomed to, Fontane was free to let his fictions vary in length according to their themes. In comparison with Fontane's novels, Trollope's are therefore diffuse and repetitive. There is a multiplicity of sub-plots which are sometimes perhaps too trivial to need the detailed treatment they get. The fact that much of Trollope's fiction constitutes a continuous whole, with the same characters reappearing in sequel after sequel, means that the reader must be put in possession of facts already related in works he may not have read or has forgotten. This Trollope does with great skill, usually by letting some newly introduced character ponder in an internal dialogue some earlier incident with which he has just become acquainted, thereby revealing his psychological make-up which will be new to every reader whether or not he has read the antecedent fiction. Yet the fact that Fontane's narratives are relatively brief and succinct means that they possess greater local intensity than Trollope's; this intensity is heightened, as we saw, by means of an elaborate symbolism which is not to be found to the same extent even in Dickens and George Eliot. Trollope eschews symbolism altogether as he does the building-up of poetic atmospheres, so pervasive in Fontane. Some critics have considered that Fontane's practice in these respects imparts an element of contrivance to his work to which the modern reader is allergic. Brinkmann has criticized, in particular, Fontane's habit of letting his speakers' words carry a double meaning, one intended by the speaker, and another, prophetic in character, which is meant to alert the reader to a wider context of which the speaker is unaware.[44] Peter Demetz, too, has deplored the all-too-obtrusive symbol in Fontane: the fire in *Unwiederbringlich*, for instance, which sweeps through the old castle as Holk succumbs to his illicit passion for Ebba, and the lake in *Der Stechlin*, hidden in the forests of a remote corner of Brandenburg, yet registering sensitively seismic changes in distant parts of the world as the old nobleman in the seclusion of his estate responds to significant social and political developments everywhere. The analogy

179

is not left to be inferred, but is repeatedly pointed out, not only by the author but by characters in the novel, by Armgard, and again at length by Lorenzen when he speaks at Stechlin's funeral, and finally by Melusine who in her person also links periphery and centre, being at home in the salons of Berlin as well as on the remote shores of the lake. Critical opinion is sharply divided about this last novel of Fontane's. W. Müller-Seidel sees it as a forerunner of the modern novel in which exploration of consciousness replaces plot and action.[45] Demetz, on the other hand, sees in the proliferation of symbolism and discursive dialogue evidence of Fontane's declining power as a novelist.[46]

In spite of idiosyncrasies which are particularly apparent in *Der Stechlin*, Fontane's work approximates with remarkable closeness to the genre created by the English novelists of the nineteenth century. Yet there is no consensus among critics as to whether it possesses 'European stature'. It is evident, at any rate, that Fontane's novels have failed to gain a substantial measure of recognition in English-speaking countries at least in his life-time, and various explanations of this fact have been advanced in recent years. Roy Pascal has suggested that the absence of passionate feeling, and of characters capable of it, from the novels of Fontane may be indicative of a deficiency of sensibility which renders even *Effi Briest* inferior to the master-pieces of Flaubert and Tolstoy.[47] What Roy Pascal clearly has in mind here is not the violent feeling and pathos which are the stock-in-trade of romantic writing and are to be found in a fiction like that of Theodor Storm which is contemporary with Fontane's but markedly inferior to it – but rather an adult experience of passion, enacted in a realistically depicted social context. And yet a reader might hesitate to endorse Pascal's reservations about Fontane if he remembers that Jane Austen, too, has been censured for her lack of passion – by Charlotte Brontë, for instance – while few critics to-day would consider that Jane Austen's exclusion of the extremes of human

180

temperament and situation from her work, her interest in the typical and representative, argue a lack of sensibility and vitality in her. A more crucial stricture on Fontane has been voiced by J.P. Stern in a study which places the novelist, in one important respect at least, with the tradition of German inwardness rather than with that of European realism. 'The suggestion is never absent from his novels', writes Stern, 'that private life and morality are one thing and social and political life another, and that the relation of the one to the other is a passive one. The particular narrative energy that would show both the social world and also the way its ethos is actively determined by personal decisions and acts, is not to be found in that tradition or in his novels.'[48] We saw that resignation is indeed pervasive in Fontane's fiction. But although this may take the form of a withdrawal into death as, for instance, in the case of Cécile, or even of Effi Briest, or into a life of religious devotion and self-effacing charity as in the case of Fräulein von Sawatzki (L'Adultera), we saw that elsewhere, in the case of Victoire in Schach von Wuthenow, for instance, it is the prelude to a renewed committal to life and humanity. And while Fontane exposes those who, like Count Woldemar in Stine, defy convention from weakness, in ignorance of realities, he is most critical of those who become slaves of convention but endorses characters who achieve inner independence from it. This is never of an altogether passive kind. When Herr von Briest takes his daughter back into his home, we are made aware of positive consequences: a successful defiance of an inhumane convention by a man of authority and influence inevitably modifies and weakens that convention and thereby furthers civilization.

The Barby family in the novel Der Stechlin is independent of the world but active in it. Count von Barby is, like Dubslav von Stechlin, emancipated from the tyranny both of self-interest and of social convention, but unlike him he is an urbane figure, with experience of affairs of state. Dubslav von Stechlin is sceptical when he hears that his son Woldemar

wants to marry a daughter of Count von Barby; he argues that
for a member of the lower nobility like himself to marry into
the higher nobility to which von Barby belongs, is to ask for
trouble. For the members of the higher nobility who move in
court circles, have social aspirations which a Stechlin could
never satisfy. Woldemar feels that as a generalization about
the class in question, his father's remark may be apt, but like
all generalizations, it does not apply to every case – not to
that of the Barbys, at any rate.[49] The elder daughter of Count
von Barby, Melusine, has indeed passed through the school
of suffering – in an unhappy marriage which ended in divorce
– and emerged with a visionary quality which makes her the
most impressive figure in the book. She is not in conflict with
society, though the hide-bound are exasperated by her
lightness of touch, her liveliness and charm, her free tone;
others realize that beneath the exterior of an amiable and
amusing society-lady, she conceals a radical humility,
humanity and courage which make her just and positive in her
attitude to everyone she encounters. She inspires Lorenzen
to become the conscience of her brother-in-law Woldemar
when he takes over the estate, for she realizes that he hasn't
inherited from his father the judgment and independence
necessary to resist the pressure of social convention, of
collective error. She, too, is shown – as is Dubslav von
Stechlin – to influence others by her attitudes and acts and so
to affect the ethos of the world. Admittedly, there is never any
suggestion that Fontane's characters who are liberated for
humanity, engage in political action to transform society as a
whole. But neither do the heroes and heroines of Dickens, of
George Eliot, or of any major nineteenth century novelist.
Dickens's transformed characters, Pip at the end of *Great
Expectations* and Arthur Clennam at the end of *Little
Dorrit*, have also passed through a phase of resignation; this
has not made them passive in relation to society any more
than Fontane's characters, but the sphere of their action is a
limited one. In these two novels prison and graveyard figure

as symbols of the ineluctable limitations of fallen humanity. In spite of what J.P. Stern has claimed, there is therefore nothing peculiarly German, accounting for the lack of appreciation of his work in English-speaking countries, in the moral and political ethos of Fontane's work.

A more likely explanation of the absence of English interest in Fontane is to be found in the fact that he extended to a Brandenburg-Prussian milieu a literary genre which had been perfected in England more than a generation earlier. His work has, of course, great importance and value for the German reader as the one adequate German attempt to contribute to the fiction of social realism, and it had taken a peculiar combination of circumstances, public and private, to make it possible at all: the political unification of Germany and the growth of Berlin as a cosmopolitan centre, but also the ambivalent temperament of Fontane which impelled him to observe and record with conflicting feelings crucial aspects of the complex society to which he was exposed in his years as a journalist; his apprenticeship in London where he had been able to relate the English fiction which fascinated him, to the life which it reflected, was an indispensable condition for his achievement also. However, when Fontane's three major novels, *Unwiederbringlich* (1891), *Effi Briest* (1894), and *Der Stechlin* (1897), were published, the potentialities of social realism had long been exhausted in England, and literary taste had significantly changed. The original local colour in his work did not suffice to draw an English-speaking public to a fiction that explored in the eighteen-nineties the same social and psychological problems which had been the subject-matter of the English novel in an earlier period. However, in the course of the last two decades a number of his novels have appeared in English translation; and it is no longer unusual to find respectful references to Fontane in English and American writings on realism in fiction.

VI

Into the Twentieth Century

1

In the closing decades of the nineteenth century, Britain was beginning to decline economically and politically, although this was not apparent to most contemporary observers because of the advantages which the country continued to enjoy as a result of its lead in the industrial revolution and the colonial expansion that had followed it. After 1880, however, the economies of the United States and of Germany were growing at a faster rate than that of Britain which had ceased to be the world's first steel-producer: 'As world competition in manufactures increased . . . Britain's share of the world market fell from over 40 per cent in 1880 to 30 per cent in 1913. At the same time Germany's share rose from 19 to 26.5 . . . '[1] The social and cultural changes which accompanied the incipient decline of British power found reflection in the fiction of the period. Where the great English novelists of the mid-century had written as members of the society which they portrayed, accepting it, however defective they found it, as the sphere of human self-realization, such confidence is no longer characteristic of the novelists who came to the fore in the eighteen-eighties and nineties. These abandoned their predecessors' ambition to survey society as a whole and to comprehend it, and confined themselves to depicting limited areas of it. It is ironic that the most eminent English novelist of the fin-de-siècle, Thomas Hardy, should invoke Schopenhauer[2] in support of a fatalistic presentation of rural and small-town life, as localized and archaic as that in any mid-nineteenth century German novel. George Gissing did indeed attempt to render a modern urban scene, but his evocations, under French Naturalist influence, of the grimmer aspects of London working-class life, are devoid of Dickens's hope of change through ameliorative action; and the projection of himself into resentful artist-outsider figures – in *New Grub Street* (1891) and *The Private Papers of Henry Ryecroft* (1903) – is reminiscent of German, rather than English, precedent. However, the *Deutsches Bücherverzeichnis*, the German publishers' cumulative trade-catalogue, shows that over a period of three decades no novel by Gissing and only two by Thomas Hardy found their way into German translation; on the other hand, Oscar Wilde, with some half dozen German versions of *The Picture of Dorian Grey* (1891), scored a success in Germany unequalled by any English novelist since the arrival of Dickens half a century earlier.

Wilde's novel marks the zenith, in England, of the aestheticist movement which gave international currency to certain attitudes which had been firmly established in Germany since the eighteenth century: the aesthetes, like many German Romantics, looked on the external world as mysterious and untransparent; like them, they rejected the realms of business, industry and politics as the preserve of the philistines, and believed it was for the artist to give significance to life by the cultivation of aesthetic sensibility and the creation of beauty. Aestheticism had begun to permeate mid-Victorian poetry, particularly that of the Pre-Raphaelites, though the major novelists of the period were inimical to it: Dickens had portrayed aesthetes as irresponsible and self-indulgent parasites in *Bleak House* (Skimpole) and *Little Dorrit* (Henry Gowan), and George Eliot had indicted aestheticism in *Romola*, in *Middlemarch*, and elsewhere. However, it found an eloquent champion in Walter Pater whose book *The Renaissance* first appeared in 1873; he wrote:

Every moment some form grows perfect in hand or face; some tone on the hills or the sea is choicer than the rest; some mood of passion or insight or intellectual excitement is irresistibly real and attractive for us, – for that moment only. Not the fruit of experience, but experience itself, is the end. A counted number of pulses only is given to us of a variegated, dramatic life. How may we see in them all that is to be seen in them by the finest senses? How shall we pass most swiftly from point to point, and be present always at the focus where the greatest number of vital forces unite in their purest energy? To burn always with this hard, gemlike flame, to maintain this ecstasy, is success in life . . . What we have to do is to be for ever . . . courting new impressions . . . For our chance lies in expanding that interval (between the present moment and death), in getting as many pulsations as possible into the given time . . . Of this wisdom, the poetic passion, the desire of beauty, the love of art for art's sake, has most; for art comes to you professing frankly to give nothing but the highest quality to your moments as they pass, and simply for those moments' sake.[3]

Dorian Grey's self-destructive pursuit of aesthetic experience recalls that of the heroes of early German Romantic fiction, Tieck's *William Lovell* (1795-6), Brentano's *Godwi* (1801). And a systolic recoil from aesthetic abandon, such as that foreshadowed in the closing chapters of *The Picture of Dorian Grey*, was to lead Oscar Wilde, Ernest Dowson, Lionel Johnson and other aesthetes to the same goal as Brentano and Zacharias Werner eighty years earlier: submission to the authority of the Catholic Church. Indeed, in much literature of the Nineties, Christianity emerges as a higher synthesis from the conflict of aesthetic disorder with bourgeois conventionality, as it had done, for all the differences of style and genres, in the fiction of German Romantic writers. If the work of the leading German representative of the aestheticism of the Nineties, Hugo von Hofmannsthal, possesses greater weight and subtlety than that of the English aesthetes, this would appear to be due in part to the fact that, in formulating his mystical vision of a transcendent world unity, accessible to the artist, and a conflict of art and life leading to a religious resolution, he is consciously the heir of Novalis, of Eichendorff, as well as the contemporary of Oscar Wilde; indeed, in German literary histories, Hugo von Hofmannsthal is usually classified as a 'Neuromantiker', a Neo-Romantic.

It is apparent, therefore, that when the Germans acquired a unified state like that of the English, who were now economically in decline, such earlier cultural differences between the two nations as had been reflected in their respective literatures, gradually diminished. On the one hand, the new German Empire failed to win the allegiance of its intellectuals while on the other hand the advent of aestheticism in England was an indication that English artists, too, now experienced that sense of isolation which had long been characteristic of their German counterparts. The withdrawal into inwardness of the aesthetes was, indeed, as clear a symptom of the decay of the social and moral order of Victorian England, as was the demand for radical social change in the writings of Bernard Shaw and H.G. Wells. The defence of the official loyalties now became the concern of strident minority voices like those of Rudyard Kipling and W.E. Henley. In this intellectual climate, it was possible for a German writer to command the interest of an English readership for the first time since Goethe's *Werther* had appeared. In 1900, as briefly during the so-called Age of Sensibility in the eighteenth century, international literary fashion favoured the presentation of traditional German themes and predicaments; and Thomas Mann was acclaimed as an outstanding European novelist by German and non-German critics alike when he adapted the realistic techniques, as cultivated in Germany by Fontane, to treat the problems which were most widely discussed in the aestheticist era.

Thomas Mann was writing for a middle-class public, which was predisposed to look to the creative writer for that interpretation of life that had formerly been provided by the churches; and from the start his fiction was characterized by large philosphical pretensions: it was the era in which Stefan George, Rainer Maria Rilke, and many lesser writers tolerated, or actually encouraged, the formation of 'Gemeinden', congregations of admirers who looked to the poet of their choice for a quasi-Messianic revelation of truth. In his first major novel, *Buddenbrooks* (1900), Thomas Mann made selective use of Schopenhauer and Nietzsche, the fashionable literary philosophers of the period in which the term 'aesthete' was synonymous with that of 'decadent', and he drew on the history of his own family, the observations and experiences of his childhood and youth in Lübeck, to present the decline of vitality and efficiency in the Buddenbrook family as the condition of the emergence of artistic sensibility and aspiration. The ambivalence of Thomas Mann finds expression in a pervasive irony which is directed at the aesthetic as well as at the bourgeois sphere, and his technique of expressing disdain for the commonplace by writing of it in a complicated, somewhat mannered, prose-style, is reminiscent of Flaubert rather than Fontane.

The conflict of bourgeois and artist figures also in many of Thomas Mann's 'Novellen'. In *Tonio Krö*ger (1903), a story to which Thomas Mann always attached particular importance – it is more directly autobiographical, even, than *Buddenbrooks* – the conflict is pondered in a series of essayistic monologues and elaborated by means of symbolism and by the adaptation, to literary purposes, of the technique of the musical 'Leitmotif' in Wagner's operas: certain combinations of terms are reintroduced whenever the particular figures and themes which they characterize, occur in the story. Bourgeois respectability and competence in business are equated here not only, as in *Buddenbrooks*, with 'Leben' (life), but also with a supposed North European racial strain, surprising as this may seem to present-day readers; and the artist's rejection of convention is made to correspond with the

South European temperament as well as with 'Geist' (mind, spirit). The mixed racial descent of Tonio, rather similar to that of Thomas Mann himself, is offered as an explanation of the inner dichotomy which makes him opt for the isolated stance and detachment of the artist while longing at the same time for a rapport with those non-artistic representatives of life whom he despises, but also envies, for being 'ordinary'. Here, as elsewhere in Thomas Mann, a synthesis is attempted; and in a final statement, Tonio accepts, indeed welcomes, his inner division as the source of the characteristic ethos of his work.

Thomas Mann's European reputation reached a peak in the years immediately prior to the First World War, but it is interesting to note that among the discordant voices raised at the time was that of D.H. Lawrence who had gone further than most contemporaries in the rejection of aestheticist attitudes. In 1913, he used the appearance of *Der Tod in Venedig* (Death in Venice) as an occasion for reviewing the achievement of Thomas Mann. D.H. Lawrence was not unimpressed by *Der Tod in Venedig*: the psychological predicament of the artist who succumbs to the fascination of beauty to find that after a lifetime of laboriously cultivated self-discipline there is no way out of his isolation, except in death, is better integrated here, in all its ambiguity, with the characteristic pattern of antitheses, of symbolism and mythological allegory, than elsewhere in Thomas Mann. But Lawrence concludes:

> Already I find Thomas Mann who, as he says, fights so hard against the banal in his work, somewhat banal. His expression may be very fine. But by now what he expresses is stale. And even while he has a rhythm in style, yet his work has none of the rhythm of a living thing . . . There is an unexpectedness in this such as does not come from their carefully plotted and arranged developments. Even *Madame Bovary* seems to me dead in respect to the living rhythm of the whole work. While it is there in Macbeth like life itself.[4]

189

The misgiving of the young Lawrence did not, however, carry weight with the public. The fame of Thomas Mann continued to grow, and along with it, his philosophical pretensions: after the outbreak of the First World War, he extended the range of his polarities to include politics. In *Betrachtungen eines Unpolitischen* (1918), he associates the sphere of art, the irrationalism and pessimism of the Romantic tradition, with German culture as such and with the inwardness of the German intellectual which, he claims, thrives best under the protection of the authoritarian state. The legacy of the Enlightenment, on the other hand, liberal democracy, rationalism and the cult of progress are identified with the Western powers, and presented as a threat to those 'deeper' German values. These antitheses are reiterated by Thomas Mann in his book *Von deutscher Republik* (1922); but he now has reservations about the backward-looking attitudes of the heirs of Romanticism, and argues that the future belongs to democracy, while he also expresses a hope that the Germans as the nation of the middle may attain a synthesis between positive elements in the conflicting traditions. An intellectual synthesis of this kind is what Thomas Mann himself sets out to construct in his 'Bildungsroman' of 1924, *Der Zauberberg* (The Magic Mountain). In what is in some respects a parody of the Goethean genre, Thomas Mann evokes the world of a sanatorium with meticulous realism and comic gusto while ascribing symbolical significance to it as the sphere of illness and death. This sphere is linked, as always in Mann's fiction, with that of art and 'Geist', but even more ambiguously now than formerly. Hans Castorp is made to realize that his stay in the sanatorium is the condition of his inner growth, but that disease and stupidity are not always mutually exclusive. As in *Tonio Kröger* and elsewhere, attitudes to life and the world are correlated with racial and national stereotypes. An Italian patient, Settembrini, and a German-Jewish Jesuit, Naphta, are the protagonists, respectively, of Western liberal enlightenment and of Eastern neo-Romantic authoritarianism, and Hans Castorp who is the target of their proselytizing efforts, learns to recognize the inadequacy of each standpoint, and also the limits of the anti-cerebral vitalism of the Dutchman Peeperkorn who is driven to suicide by fears of old age and death. The moral of the novel is spelt out by Hans Castorp in the chapter entitled 'Schnee' (snow):

> Ich will dem Tode Treue halten in meinem Herzen, doch mich hell erinnern, dass Treue zum Tode und Gewesenen nur Bosheit und finstere Wollust und Menschenfeindlichkeit ist, bestimmt sie unser Denken and Regieren. Der Mensch soll um der Güte and Liebe willen dem Tode keine Herrschaft einräumen über seine Gedanken.[5]

> In my heart, I shall remain loyal to death, but clearly remember that loyalty to death and the past is only malice and sombre voluptuousness and misanthropy if it determines our thought and conduct. For the sake of kindness and love, man must not grant death dominion over his thoughts.

And the novel concludes with an expression of the wish that from the riot of death and destruction of the First World War in which Hans Castorp has become a participant, love would emerge as it did from his snow-dream in the world of the sanatorium.

The publication of this novel led to the award of the Nobel-prize to Thomas Mann, but many critics and readers to-day regard the polarities in *Der Zauberberg*, and the proposed synthesis between them, as an elaboration of the clichés of the period. Thomas Mann was indeed highly sensitive to the fluctuating tastes of the public, and continued to modify the presentation of his basic antinomies in response to them. In the nineteen-thirties when it was the fashion in Germany to deal with contemporary issues allegorically, in mythologizing historical novels, Mann transformed the Biblical legend of Joseph into that of the artist who becomes an outcast before finding acceptance as a leader and prophet in his community. As an exile in the United States, Thomas Mann continued to contribute to the mythologizing trend of the period in *Doktor Faustus* (1947). Here art and illness are as closely linked as in the earlier fiction: the contraction of syphilis which stimulates the genius of Leverkühn, becomes a constituent of the pact with the devil in this version of the Faust-legend. In exchange for his capacity to love and to sustain reciprocal human relationships, Leverkühn acquires the power to create original musical compositions. Music is presented by Mann as an irrational and, therefore, a peculiarly German art, and the career of Leverkühn which culminates in madness, is made to correspond to different phases in the history of Nazism. Writing in the decade in which Christian Existentialism was in vogue, Mann invokes Kierkegaard, and now gives as serious consideration to theology as he had done to other branches of learning in previous novels. The ambiguity in the presentation of Nazism as a 'daemonic' and quasi-artistic phenomenon is heightened by the fact that the imaginary narrator who is both fascinated and morally repelled by the events which he describes, is ironically distanced by Mann as well-meaning but philistine. The novel did not, in fact, meet with as favourable a reception as *Buddenbrooks* and *Der Zauberberg* had done; for German readers were still too close to the events portrayed by Mann not to feel embarrassed by his interpretation of them. By the early fifties, literary taste had changed once again. Younger German writers were now adopting a soberly deflating attitude towards Nazism, resisting the tendency to daemonize it which the Nazis themselves had encouraged. And the mythicization of national character, history and art, practised by Thomas Mann as by so many German intellectuals of the earlier twentieth century, was now regarded with suspicion. By the time of his death in 1955, a reaction against Thomas Mann had set in. The fact remains, however, that in the aftermath of the aestheticist era when the problems of the isolated artist commanded general interest outside as well as inside Germany, Thomas Mann was acclaimed as one of the major practitioners of modern fiction – and this despite the fact that he did not cultivate distinctively modern techniques, apart from marginal experiments with the stream of consciousness method in *Lotte in Weimar* (1939), and the attempt, in *Der Zauberberg*, to render an experience of the relativity of time.

The modern fictional techniques which Thomas Mann by and large eschewed, were being pioneered simultaneously in England and Germany after nineteen-hundred. However, in England too, there were novelists at work in the early twentieth century who were accepted as characteristically modern although they clung to traditional narrative methods. It is perhaps significant that the most distinguished of these, who was to revive the normative ethos which had characterized English fiction prior to the aestheticist era, Joseph Conrad, should have come to it from the outside. For he was born a Pole and did not learn English until he joined the English merchant marine as a young man of twenty. In *A Personal Record* (1916), he describes how service in it had confirmed him in his own values, and how he had found himself as a novelist in adherence to the language and the civilization that had produced the English literary tradition. His unique experience, however, provided the subject-matter of his own fiction. The process of moral isolation is his principal theme; yet unlike most of his contemporaries, he does not glorify it, but follows Dickens and George Eliot in presenting it as impoverishing and destructive. A social realism such as theirs is not, of course, within his reach; on the other hand, he is able to analyze the psychology of loneliness with a particularity that is not to be found in any Victorian novel. When Conrad attempts to evoke the life of a community – as in *Nostromo* (1904) – it is a cosmopolitan one, composed of foreign immigrants, of the English and American representatives of capitalist enterprise, of Italian refugees, displaced native peasants and native adventurers, all of them rootless as he was. A keen sense of isolation afflicts the conscious and

193

sensitive in the South American republic of Costaguana, and also in the colonial societies of Malaysia and Africa which provide the setting of other fictions by Conrad, – and on board those ships where captains have to struggle not only with the vagaries of the weather, but with recalcitrant crews and, ultimately, with their own weakness and confusion. In characters like *Lord Jim* (1900), Marlow in *The Heart of Darkness* (1902), Razumov in *Under Western Eyes* (1911), the sea-captain in *The Shadow-Line* (1917), we encounter the very fear, guilt, and anguish in loneliness that Rilke and Kafka were to articulate:

> Who knows what true loneliness is – not the conventional word, but the naked terror? To the lonely themselves it wears a mask. The most miserable outcast hugs some memory or some illusion. Now and then a fatal conjunction of events may lift the veil for an instant. For an instant only. No human being could bear a steady view of moral solitude without going mad – Razumov had reached that point of vision.[6]

Such characters, like the disillusioned Decoud who 'caught himself entertaining doubt of his own individuality'[7], go under, or else break out of the prison of their solitude as Razumov does; he has been compelled by police terror to lead a life of total duplicity, but the confession which brings him physical mutilation as punishment for his supposed treason, restores him to human fellowship. The isolation of Heyst in *Victory* (1915), is the result of an early training in a stance of aloof self-sufficiency which was to protect him from the delusions and follies to which men are subject. But when he does contract a social tie, he discovers that it 'gave him a greater sense of his own reality than he had ever known in all his life'[8]. His involvement, provoked by an appeal for help which is addressed to him by a victim of bandits, leads to a tragic denouement, but is nevertheless the victory heralded in the title – a victory over the isolationism which appears to Heyst in retrospect as a living death. In *The Secret Agent*

(1907), Conrad deals ironically with the misconceptions which isolated people entertain about each other. When Thomas Mann chose to write about this novel, he emphasized the conflict in it between Russian-inspired terrorism and the humane values of English society as the dominant theme of Conrad. Writing in 1925, Mann related this to the East-West antinomies in his own work of this period, and suggested that the Germans had refused to Conrad the recognition which had been accorded him in England, America and France, because until recently they had sided ideologically with the East against the West.[9] It seems more likely, however, that German intellectuals found the work of Conrad uncongenial because he strips isolation of the glamour with which it had been invested in the German literary tradition.

2

The cult of isolation flourished with a renewed vigour in Germany after the turn of the century. Those German writers who now evolved modern experimental techniques in fiction, were dedicated to it. The most eminent of them, Rilke and Kafka, were natives of Prague; for it was in the multi-national Austro-Hungarian empire where various languages were in competition with German, that the crisis of identity which led to the rejection of traditional literary forms, of conventional language as no longer adequate for the rendering of valid perception, was first experienced. In Vienna, where Sigmund Freud had developed psycho analysis as a means of bringing to light the repressed content of the subconscious of his patients, Hofmannsthal wrote the letter (*Ein Brief*, 1901) in which the imaginary Elizabethan, Lord Chandos, explains to Francis Bacon the reasons which had led him to abandon the writing of books: the language at his disposal compels him to write 'mit dem vereinfachenden Blick der Gewohnheit'[10] (with the simplifying view of habit) which is at variance with his new insights; he would never write again weil die Sprache, in welcher nicht nur zu schreiben, sondern auch zu denken mir vielleicht gegeben wäre, weder die lateinische noch die englische noch die italienische und spanische ist, sondern eine Sprache, von deren Worten mir auch nicht eines bekannt ist, eine Sprache, in welcher die stummen Dinge zu mir sprechen, und in welcher ich vielleicht einst im Grabe vor einem unbekannten Richter mich verantworten werde.[11]

because the language in which it might perhaps be granted to me, not only to write, but to think, is neither Latin nor English nor Italian nor Spanish but a language of which I do not know a single word, a language in which mute objects speak to me, and in which I shall perhaps justify myself one day in my grave, before an unknown judge.

Five years later Robert Musil, another Austrian, published *Die Verwirrungen des Zöglings Törless* (Confusions of the Pupil Törless), an account of the crisis in the life of a schoolboy, occasioned by his incapacity to relate certain emotional and sexual promptings that alter his experience of existence to the consciousness which alone he finds communicable in conventional language; and he comes to doubt the continuity of his own personality. In Rilke's *Die Aufzeichnungen des Malte Laurids Brigge* (1910) (The Note Books of Malte Laurids Brigge), the dissatisfaction with traditional modes of verbalizing experiences and perceptions is, as in Hofmannsthal's *Chandos-Brief* and in Musil's *Törless* the result of a process of isolation. But Rilke goes further than his predecessors in developing an original prose-style and a new narrative form for the adequate rendering of the insights, attributed to Malte. The young Dane who has lost all his relatives and finds himself destitute in Paris, without friends or acquaintances, develops a nervous sensitivity in which the sights, sounds, smells of the city, and the trivial manifestations of human proximity that normally pass unnoticed, acquire a strange, menacing significance. He sees his changed awareness, along with the overwhelming fear, the anguish that characterize his sense of loneliness, as signs of inner growth: 'Ich lerne sehen. Ich weiss nicht, woran es liegt, es geht alles tiefer in mich ein und bleibt nicht an der Stelle stehen, wo es sonst immer zu Ende war. Ich habe ein Inneres, von dem ich nicht wusste. Alles geht jetzt dorthin.'[12] (I learn to see. I don't know how it comes about but everything enters into me more deeply and doesn't stop short at the point where it always used to end. I have an interior of which I did not know. Everything goes in there now.)

> Eine vollkommen andere Auffassung aller Dinge hat sich unter diesen Einflüssen in mir herausgebildet, es sind gewisse Unterschiede da, die mich von den Menschen mehr als alles Bisherige abtrennen. Eine veränderte Welt. Ein neues Leben voll neuer Bedeutungen. Ich habe es augenblicklich etwas schwer, weil alles zu neu ist. Ich bin ein Anfänger in meinen eigenen Verhältnissen.[13]

> A completely different conception of all things has formed in me under these influences, certain differences are there which separate me from people more than everything that has happened so far. A changed world. A new life full of new significances. I find it rather hard at present because everything is so new. I am a beginner in my own circumstances.

Pathos frequently gives way to irony, expressed in para-doxical metaphors and images; and the prose in which Rilke records novel sensations is poetically charged in such a way that the reader will recognize them as his own though he would hardly have heard them put into words before. Rilke's Malte is sustained by the belief that the changes he observes taking place in himself, are historically significant as reflecting the emergence of a new sensibility in a world in which traditional social structures and systems of belief have collapsed. When he is on the verge of a nervous breakdown and falls gravely ill, Malte undertakes to relive certain childhood experiences in order to recover a sense of continuity; but this experiment fails to provide him with the accession of strength and confidence he had expected from it: 'Ich habe um meine Kindheit gebeten, und sie ist wiedergekommen, und ich fühle, dass sie immer noch so schwer ist wie damals und dass es nichts genützt hat, älter zu werden'[14] (I have prayed for my childhood, and it has returned, and I feel that it is still as hard as it was then and that growing older hasn't helped). Readers familiar with Freud's writings will recognize in the childhood predicament of Malte the constituents of the process which leads to inversion: he describes himself as an only child, strongly attached to his mother who partially rejects him in that she makes him feel guilty because he is a boy and not the girl she had lost in infancy; at the same time she prevents him from learning to identify with his father who is disparaged and kept at a distance. Rilke, however, did not favour the psychoanalytic approach to literature, and his own attempt to interpret the phenomena he presents through Malte, a self-projection, are metaphysical. A high regard for the thought of Kierkegaard which Rilke shared with the exponents of Existentialism, had been a factor in the choice of a Dane for the hero of the novel. Malte's commitment to a Kierkegaardian pursuit of authentic existence is made to originate in his resistance, as a child, to the attempts of adults to make him conform to the image they have of him, and it is this commitment which makes him welcome his isolation in Paris, and the chronic anxiety and fear of death consequent upon it, as the conditions of the vision which he seeks to articulate in creative writing. This writing is exemplified in the novel by a series of portraits of historic figures who, in Malte's view, underwent a process of transformation on coming to terms with their suffering. Medieval rulers, artists such as Beethoven and the contemporary Italian actress Eleonora Duse, are assimilated by Malte to certain figures in the streets of Paris, cripples, beggars, and that blind newspaper-vendor who is marked by 'die durch keine Vorsicht oder Verstellung eingeschränkte Hingegebenheit seines Elends'[15] (self-surrender in misery, not restricted by any caution or pretence): they came to resemble each other in their abandonment of all concern for human respect, in their achievement of a total sincerity. This, however, is considered a provocation by society which is hostile to the isolated: Malte is reminded of old paintings, such as those by Hieronymus Bosch, which depict men, daemons, and inanimate objects as conspiring to distract the saint and so prevent him from persevering in his task. Malte attaches special significance to certain collections of verse, diaries, and other documents in which a process of inner change in the course of an unhappy love-relationship is recorded by women 'die, während sie ihn riefen, den Mann überstanden; die über ihn hinauswuchsen, wenn er nicht wiederkam, bis ihre Qual umschlug in eine herbe, eisige Herrlichkeit, die nicht mehr zu halten war'[16] (who while they called him, outlasted man; who grew beyond him when he did not come back . . . until their agony suddenly changed into an austere, icy glory which could not be held back). That Rilke offers a therapeutic technique, if of a different kind from that of the psychoanalysts, is borne out by various letters of thanks which he received from lonely people who had learned from his writings to see their painful, humiliating experiences in a positive light. A key-concept in *Malte Laurids Brigge* as in many of Rilke's poems, is that of 'Umschlag', a reversal of mood which is said to occur in those who accept and 'überstehen' (outlast) their predicament. In the poem 'Requiem' in *Neue Gedichte*, for instance, the suicide of Wolf Graf von Kalckreuth is presented as an act of impatience:

Was hast du nicht gewartet, dass die Schwere
ganz unerträglich wird: da schlägt sie um
und ist so schwer, weil sie so echt ist.

(Why did you not wait until the heaviness became quite unbearable: then it suddenly changes and is so heavy because it is so authentic.) The authenticity which Malte's models achieve through suffering, is its own reward; what in the case of the 'great lovers' he called an 'eisige Herrlichkeit' (icy glory)[17], he describes elsewhere as an entry into nature, and into the dimension of a life beyond death[18]. Indeed, all the historic figures whom Malte invokes, are credited with having attained an extra-temporal stature: and in this sense, there is to be found in Rilke, as in Thomas Mann and many other contemporaries, a 'mythicization' of artists and great men which present-day readers are likely to find distateful. But at least Malte does not mythicize himself. In the version of the parable of the Prodigal Son with which the novel closes, union with God is envisaged as the ultimate goal of human endeavour. But the phenomenon of 'Umschlag' as it figures in the lives of Malte's historical models, is not, as a rule, akin to mystic union but rather to that sense of enhanced significance experienced in defeat which characterizes the heroes of classical tragedy; and the serenity which is the effect of 'Umschlag', is clearly akin also to the peace which is achieved through resignation to suffering in the Stoic tradition and in Christian devotional literature.

The novel has never enjoyed wide appeal: its esoteric message, the private nature of Malte's childhood reminiscences, the obscurity of many historical and literary allusions, and the difficulty of translating its highly idiosyncratic prose-style, are among the factors which have militated against the recognition of Rilke as a pioneer of new narrative devices for articulating a twentieth century awareness. In two important respects, Rilke, indeed, anticipated Kafka whose fiction was to receive the world-wide attention denied to *Die Aufzeichnungen des Malte Laurids Brigge*. In the interest of total veracity, Rilke had refused to follow his nineteenth century German predecessors, down to Raabe, who sentimentalized their lonely heroes: instead, he recorded the abject misery, the nervous irritability and paranoiac obsessions which are the morbid side-effects of prolonged isolation. It is significant that the experience of 'Umschlag' ascribed to his historic models, should elude Malte though he aspires to it: 'Nur ein Schritt', he writes, 'und mein tiefes Elend würde Seligkeit sein. Aber ich kann diesen Schritt nicht tun, ich bin gefallen und kann mich nicht mehr aufheben, weil ich zerbrochen bin'[19] (Only one step, and my deep misery would become bliss. But I cannot take this step, I have fallen and cannot raise myself up again, for I am broken). Writing in the period in which the Expressionists were to demand that the artist should use external objects only as signs to communicate inward states, Malte eulogizes Ibsen who created a theatre 'das immer ungeduldiger, immer verzweifelter unter dem Sichtbaren nach dem Äquivalenten suchte für das innen Gesehene'[20] (which attempted, with ever greater impatience, greater desperation, to find an equivalent among visible objects for what had been seen inwardly). Indeed, specific Expressionist techniques are inaugurated in Malte's attempts to make his new insights comprehensible by expressing them in ways which involve paradoxical distortions of so-called reality. For instance, he says of a woman who has no time to resume her customary facial expression when, startled by Malte's approaching footsteps, she suddenly lifts her head out of her hands, that she 'hob sich aus sich ab, zu schnell, zu heftig, so dass das Gesicht in den zwei Händen blieb . . . ' (she lifted herself out of herself, too fast, too impetuously, so that her face stayed in her two hands), revealing a 'blossen wunden Kopf ohne Gesicht'[21] (naked sore head without a face). And Malte remarks of the noise of a tin-lid rolling on the floor in the room next-door to his – it is inhabited by a Russian student – that 'was diesen Lärm auslöste, jene kleine, langsame, lautlose Bewegung war, mit der sein Augenlid sich eigenmächtig über sein rechtes Auge senkte und schloss'[22] (what set off this noise was that small, slow, soundless motion with which an eyelid dropped arbitrarily over his right eye and closed): the reader must assume that what in fact happens is that a nervous tic, an involuntary closing of his eye-lid, prompts the student to throw a tin-lid on the floor where it continues to roll: a recurrent event which drives Malte frantic. A similar paradoxical effect is achieved by Malte's speaking of apparitions and other psychic phenomena as if they were natural, everyday incidents, occasioning no more surprise to him than they would if they occurred in his dreams at night.

In his fiction, Kafka avoided the explicit philosophizing and the obscure erudition which had restricted the appeal of *Die Aufzeichnungen des Malte Laurids Brigge*, but developed single-mindedly the theme of the solitary for whom an accurately observed empirical setting and everyday circumstances take on a nightmare quality as if in response to his mood of guilt and dread. Kafka repeatedly emphasized that the verisimilitude he sought to achieve was akin to that experienced in dreams: 'Von der Literatur aus gesehen ist mein Schicksal sehr einfach. Der Sinn für die Darstellung meines traumhaften innern Lebens hat alles andre ins Nebensächliche gerückt . . . '[23] (Seen from the angle of literature, my fate is very simple. Concern with the presentation of my dream-like inner life has made everything else unimportant.) In his aphorisms, Kafka, too, referred to a point, resembling the 'Umschlag' in Rilke, where suffering would turn into bliss. Aphorism 5 reads: 'Von einem gewissen Punkt an, gibt es keine Rückkehr mehr. Dieser Punkt ist zu erreichen.'[24] (From a certain point there is no return. This point is to be reached.) And Aphorism 97:

> Nur hier ist Leiden Leiden. Nicht so, als ob die, welche hier leiden, anderswo wegen dieses Leidens erhöht werden sollen, sondern so, dass das, was in dieser Welt leiden heisst, in einer andern Welt, unverändert und nur befreit von seinem Gegensatz, Seligkeit ist.[25]

> Only here, suffering is suffering. Not as if those who suffer here were to be exalted elsewhere on account of this suffering, but in such a way that, what is called suffering in this world is, unaltered and only freed from its opposite, bliss in another world.

Max Brod who was responsible for the posthumous publication of Kafka's major novels, *Der Prozess* (The Trial) and *Das Schloss* (The Castle), in 1925 and 1926, claimed that the sphere of transcendence, the absolute, was represented by the unapproachable courts and authorities which figure in them: the heroes succeed in gaining access only to subordinate organs of power which prove to be corrupt. Brod claimed that Kafka expressed in this way the incommensurability of God. Other critics came to different conclusions. Some, for instance, who were versed in psychoanalytic theory drew attention to what they called the infantilism of Kafka. It is true that, like Rilke before him, Kafka cultivated a child's vision in so far as a sense of wonder at occurrences which the adult takes for granted, goes together, in his characters, with a ready acceptance of phenomena which the adult world regards as abnormal, or as outside the natural order. But Kafka, like Rilke, was inimical to psychoanalysis, and for the same reason: he feared that by exposing himself to it, he might allay the inner conflict which he found conducive to creativity. Yet Rilke laid bare the sources of his neurosis in the childhood section of *Die Aufzeichnungen des Malte Laurids Brigge* in a way that bore out psychoanalytic theory, and so did Kafka in stories such as *Das Urteil* (The Judgment), as well as in autobiographical writings. In the 100-page long *Brief an den Vater* (Letter to his Father) of 1919, he claimed that his work represented a life-long fight for the approval of his tyrannical father which, he knew, he would never obtain. 'Ich hatte vor dir das Selbstvertrauen verloren, dafür ein grenzenloses Schuldbewusstsein ein-getauscht'[26] (I had lost my self-confidence before you, and exchanged it for a boundless sense of guilt), he wrote in this letter in which he justified, accused and condemned himself in turn, vacillating between hope and despair, between rebellion against a seemingly unjust authority and submission so complete as to suggest that by siding with his supposed persecutor against himself he had adopted a form of self-assertion, the only one left open to him.

However, the international Kafka-cult of the forties and fifties was not due to Brod's celebration of the novels as religious allegories nor to psychoanalytic interest in them, but rather to the new mental climate which was reflected also in the Existentialist vogue. Kafka was now read as an exponent of man's perplexity in the era of totalitarianism. In the nineteen-twenties Kafka's writings had made only a limited impression in Germany, and from 1933 onwards his work was prohibited as Jewish and decadent. However, it was introduced to the English-speaking countries by Edwin and Willa Muir in the nineteen-thirties, and Kafka's matter-of-fact language which was, unlike Rilke's, free of poetic metaphors and neologisms, proved eminently translatable. In 1943, Sartre acclaimed Kafka in *L'Être et le Néant*[27], and in the same year Camus published a study of Kafka which was reprinted in *Le Mythe de Sisyphe*[28]. For Camus, the failure of Kafka's heroes to detect any meaning in the activities in which the men around them were engaged, expressed man's sense of alienation in an absurd world. It was in the wake of the Allied occupation in 1945, that the Kafka-vogue reached Germany. And yet, as in the case of the reception of Thomas Mann in the early years of the twentieth century, it was a German tradition that gained international currency with Kafka. For a preoccupation with dreams and dream-like states as giving access to a deeper layer of experience than that available in conscious, waking life, had been characteristic of German Romantic writers. In the fiction of E.T.A. Hoffmann, in particular, an accurately rendered commonplace, domestic world interacted with a sphere of nightmare terror. And Kleist whom Kafka repeatedly acknowledged, had, like him, cultivated a precise, rational, but at the same time tense and convoluted prose-style to describe irrational experience. A reconsideration, not only by Germanists, of the work of Kleist and some other previously neglected German writers was a by-product of the Kafka-fashion which was far more pervasive than the Mann-fashion a generation earlier. While Thomas Mann never exercized any significant influence on non-German writers, techniques regarded as 'Kafkaesque' were adopted by novelists and playwrights in many countries in the post-war decade.

3

Neither Rilke nor Kafka, for all their innovating modernity, had cultivated the stream of consciousness technique which Virginia Woolf in an essay on 'Modern Fiction' of 1919 referred to as the 'quality which distinguishes the work of several young writers, among whom Mr James Joyce is the most notable, from that of their predecessors'[29]. The stream of consciousness technique, she claimed, enabled writers to 'come closer to life, and to preserve more sincerely and exactly what interested and moved them'[30] than more conventional narrative methods. Where the interior monologue in earlier fiction had, like the soliloquy in drama, rendered the thoughts of characters as direct or indirect speech, the stream of consciousness monologue was now to articulate not merely the thoughts but the unverbalized sensations and images which rise up in the mind. In *Ulysses*, Joyce operated with sequences of exclamations and uncompleted sentences, often cryptic in their allusiveness, to suggest the rapid flow of thoughts and sense-perceptions, recollections and imagined incidents, through the minds of his principal characters. The monologues of each are, of course, individualized by Joyce: those of the intellectual Stephen Dedalus, for instance, draw on a somewhat rarefied vocabulary, recording a different sphere of interest and experience from that inhabited by the half-educated Leopold Bloom. In the fifty-page long monologue of Molly with which the novel closes, the stream of consciousness technique is carried furthest, punctuation being abandoned to register her relaxed state of consciousness between waking and sleeping. In this way Joyce succeeded in portraying life as an 'incessant shower of innumerable atoms' in Virginia Woolf's phrase[31], rendering the unconscious as well as the conscious mind with a thoroughness that not even Rilke had approached. But by the time Joyce was at work on *Ulysses*, the method of free association in psychoanalytic treatment had been widely publicized, and modernist poets had experimented with loose concatenations of images to express their sense of a fragmented world. The aesthetes of the nineties had prepared the way for such practices with their emphasis on passing moods, the sensations of the present moment; and that Joyce originated in the aestheticist movement is obvious from the ruminations on art and the preciousness of his prose-style in his earlier fiction. His debt to French Naturalism is apparent in the exhaustive evocation of the physical presence of Dublin in *Ulysses*. And as Flaubert had ironically opposed the perfection of his form and style to the banal, commonplace circumstances which he recounted, so Joyce, in *Ulysses*, placed the trivial, the disreputable and chaotic content of the consciousness of his characters in a network of elaborate literary and historical allusions, of parodies, and paradoxical analogies of which that between the events of one day in the life of Bloom and the episodes of the Odyssey is the most prominent.

Though links between *Tristram Shandy* and *Ulysses* have been traced, Joyce's novel does not fit into any English tradition of fiction. What Joyce most conspicuously lacks is the normative bent of the major practitioners of the English novel. His tendency to deflate and ridicule the conflicting ethnic, religious, and ideological commitments of his Dublin characters by exposing the sexual obsessions which haunt them, might be seen as an attack on hypocrisy and therefore as morally significant. But in spite of this, and in spite of the richly comic vernacular with which various milieux are brought to life, it is a sense of futility which emerges from the accumulation of blasphemy and obscenity, the pervasive note of disparagement in *Ulysses*. If the novel does not seem wholly nihilistic, however, it is because of the compassionate acceptance of the human-all-too-human that is intermittently voiced in it.

Joyce's technical experiments were imitated in varying degrees by a number of German writers, most successfully perhaps by Alfred Döblin in *Berlin Alexanderplatz* (1929); but the novelist whose attempt to record the consciousness of an epoch with monumental exhaustiveness has frequently been regarded as challenging comparison with Joyce, the Austrian Robert Musil, owed nothing to the precedent of *Ulysses*. In fact, Musil had begun to explore the feasibility of articulating the subconscious mind in fiction as early as 1906, in *Die Verwirrungen des Zöglings Törless* (see p. 196 above), and had started to work on *Der Mann ohne Eigenschaften* (The Man without Qualities), the novel to which his posthumous fame is mainly due, before the first World War. In the latter novel, Musil, like Joyce in *Ulysses*, repeatedly abandons the chronological procedure of conventional narration in order to render an experience of the simultaneity of past and present time. 'Der Inhalt (des Romans)', in Musil's words, 'breitet sich auf eine zeitlose Weise aus, es ist eigentlich immer alles auf einmal da'[32] (The content of the novel expands in a timeless fashion; everything, really, is there simultaneously). Yet while Musil attempts to record not only the conscious thought-processes of his characters, but various unconscious promptings and, at times, the images which float through their minds, he does not do so in the manner of Joyce, but in a prose-style which observes the rules of syntax and is always lucid.

Societies in disintegration are evoked in both novels, but Musil focuses attention principally upon upper-class intellectuals as representatives of the conflicting tendencies of the period, and when he analyzes their personalities it is in order to explain how they arrived at the ideas which they propound. Ulrich, the central figure, is described as someone whose intellectual integrity prevents him from accepting any of the current ideologies and from committing himself to any career in which he cannot believe. Because his considerable potential remains, therefore, unrealized in action, he appears as the 'man without qualities' of the title. The scene is Vienna in the year preceding the outbreak of the first World War. The Austro-Hungarian empire is presented as comically antiquated and at the same time characteristically modern in its unresolvable contradictions and lack of faith in itself. The so-called 'Parallelaktion', the Collateral Campaign of leading Viennese circles to launch a project of national importance to mark the seventieth anniversary of the Emperor's accession, is placed in ironical juxtaposition with Ulrich's search for a valid sphere of action. Musil believes that the age is characterized by a dichotomy between the scientific spirit and that quasi-religious counter-movement which manifested itself in Neo-Romanticism, Vitalism and Expressionism. And Musil's Ulrich who has engaged in mathematical research but has also had mystical experiences, is particularly troubled by the seeming incommensurability between his rational and irrational perceptions. He has become disillusioned with the representatives both of science and of mysticism, having found that the average scientist is contemporary only in his scientific work, but 'in allem, was ihm für das Höhere gilt, sich weit altmodischer benimmt, als es seine Maschinen sind'[33] (in everything that he takes to be the higher sphere, he behaves in a way that is far more old-fashioned than his machines), and that the average irrationalist 'nicht aus religiöser Bestimmung eine stark religiöse Neigung neu entwickelt hat, sondern nur wie es scheint, aus einer weiblich reizbaren Auflehnung gegen Geld, Wissen und Rechnen, denen er leidenschaftlich unterliegt'[34] (has not developed a strongly religious tendency as a result of a religious vocation but, as it seems, because of a feminine irritability that has made him rebel against the sphere of money, knowledge, and calculation in which he feels passionately inadequate). Ulrich's friend Walter, for instance, espouses the doctrine that modern civilization is decadent and incapable of creativeness only in order to conceal his own failure as an artist. And the Jew Fischel is prompted by self-interest to uphold an unfashionable liberalism, while his prospective son-in-law,

208

Hans Sepp, is just as dubiously motivated in embracing the opposing view-point, that of anti-Semitic, pan-German chauvinism. Such psychologizing deflation of the representatives of antithetical ideologies is reminiscent of Thomas Mann's procedure in *Der Zauberberg*, but Musil records a wider spectrum of attitudes. He is at his most mordant in his pen-portraits of the leading intellectuals of the period. Ludwig Klages is introduced as Meingast, a seducer of adolescent girls who preaches renunciation of knowledge as the only way to vitality, and the 'Erlösung der Welt durch Gewalt'[35] (redemption of the world through violence), and Rathenau, the Arnheim of the novel, is presented as wholly bogus in his effort to achieve an integration of the spheres of 'soul' and business. Unlike Arnheim, Ulrich is genuinely concerned to find a synthesis between mathematical and mystical perception. He is described also as a 'Möglichkeitsmensch', a potential man, who is in search of a new morality. The contemporary philosopher F.W. Foerster who tried to resuscitate traditional ethics, is caricatured in the figure of Professor Lindner, and the early Werfel, rhapsodizing about human 'Güte' (kindness), is exposed as 'Feuermaul' (Firemouth). In opposition to them, Ulrich advocates a Nietzschean relativism, and argues 'dass es im höchsten Zustand eines Menschen kein Gut and Böse gebe'[36] (that in the highest condition of man there was no good and evil); but the view is also expressed that evil actions require greater imagination and passion than good ones, and that conventionally moral people are 'langweilig'[37] (boring). Ulrich's ability to identify with the murderer Moosbrugger is emphasized, and the temporarily satisfying love-relationship of Ulrich with his sister Agathe, their shared mystical experience, is shown as involving the rejection of traditional standards of behaviour in favour of an experimental morality: Agathe, for instance, commits a forgery, with Ulrich's knowledge, and subsequently engages in incest with him. Clarissa's cult of Moosbrugger as a redeemer-figure is, on the other hand, depicted as unbalanced, and her attempt to set him free, culminates in her mental breakdown. In the completed portions of the novel, Ulrich finds neither a valid sphere of activity nor the synthesis he had sought.

The novel has had a chequered career. The first two parts, published in 1930 and 1932, attracted little attention. A third, posthumous, volume was brought out in 1943 by Musil's widow and an edition of all three parts, together with many previously unpublished sketches and fragments, appeared in 1952. High claims for *Der Mann ohne Eigenschaften* as one of the great novels of the century were first advanced by certain critics in the late forties; other critics expressed reservations which have come to carry increasing weight with the passage of time. Musil himself admitted that Ulrich's one harmonious love-relationship, that with his sister Agathe, possesses an 'autistische Komponente'[38] (autistic component); yet on many occasions, Musil endorses Ulrich's facile assumption of superiority over the characters he encounters, and clearly identifies with him. If this is likely to be found embarrassing by some readers, the pervasive sneering at traditional moral values will seem distasteful to others who have assimilated the records of the survivors of Nazi and Soviet concentration-camps. Moreover, the preoccupation with the discrepancy between man's rational and irrational cognitive powers, which makes Ulrich suggest to the 'Parallelaktion' the setting-up of a 'Sekretariat für Genauigkeit und Seele' (Secretariate for Precision and Soul) as the most pressing need of the age, has lost much of its topicality. And although Musil has stated that a reflective passage, in a novel, 'muss in ein Geschehen münden oder aus einem hervorgehen oder eines begleiten'[39] (must issue in an occurrence or proceed from one or accompany one), he has not acted on this precept. Few critics, however, would dispute that the novel on which Musil worked for more than three decades with such intense cerebral application, occupies a prominent place in the history of modern German experimental fiction.

The conflict between rational consciousness and irrational potencies in human life which preoccupied Musil is a central theme also in the work of the English novelist D.H. Lawrence who was quoted earlier in this chapter as an adverse contemporary critic of Thomas Mann. Lawrence was a fluent German speaker, and it has been suggested that he may have derived his ideas from German sources. Two recent biographers of Frieda von Richthofen, Robert Lucas and Martin Green[40], have claimed that she acted as an intermediary between the eroticist movement in Germany and Lawrence with whom she eloped in 1912; they emphasize that at the time of her marriage with Ernest Weekley she had been in correspondence with Otto Gross, a psychoanalytical thinker who had come under the influence of the 'Kosmiker-runde', the Cosmic Circle in Munich, and that she may have transmitted Gross's ideas to Lawrence. The Munich 'Cosmics' who included Ludwig Klages, the 'Meingast' of *Der Mann ohne Eigenschaften*, had interpreted the familiar antitheses of the period – mind and life, reason and soul, civilization and culture – in terms of masculine and feminine principles in history; and they had advocated sexual liberation as the means to recover that Dionysiac vitality which had, supposedly, characterized pre-historic matriarchal societies. But though Lawrence shared the irrationalism and primitivism of the 'Cosmics', he differed from them, at least in his later work, in the value he attached to monogamous marriage and to male dominance in it. Another critic, Émile Delavenay[41], has argued – as inconclusively – that Lawrence took his ideas from the writings of Edward Carpenter, an English essayist of the Georgian period. But as most of the ideas, scattered through Lawrence's writings, were widely current in his time, and his precise intellectual position shifted a good deal from year to year, under the impact of personal experience rather than as the result of his reading, it is not perhaps very profitable to speculate as to what debt, if any, he may have owed to one or another of the Vitalist theorists of the post-Nietzschean decades.

A rather more useful approach to Lawrence is that which relates him to the English novelists of the nineteenth century. Lawrence's links with George Eliot, the chronicler of a provincial England who found deep significance in seemingly humdrum lives, and with Dickens, the champion of warmth and spontaneity against life-thwarting tendencies in contemporary society, are particularly evident in the earlier fiction: the stories collected in the volumes *The Prussian Officer* (1914) and *England my England* (1920) are remarkable for their sympathetic evocation of working-class life in the Midlands and a poetic intensity in the rendering of the emotions of men and women who transcend their isolation in love-relationships and are healed of inhibiting flaws of personality in the process. The peculiar strengths of the early short stories are found also in the autobiographical novel *Sons and Lovers* (1913) which exposes the personal predicament of Lawrence as man and writer. As a growing boy he had not only been the hyper-sensitive witness of the clash between his parents, his genteel mother's contempt for her miner-husband who defied her, but he had been erotically awakened by his mother, stimulated into a precocious response to her mature emotion and thereby impaired in his capacity to form a stable relationship with a woman in adult life. A mother, Lawrence was later to generalize, who has failed to find fulfilment in her husband, 'throws herself into a great love for her son, a final and fatal devotion, that which would have been the richness and strength of her husband and is poison to the boy', for ' . . . a man never leaves his first love, once the love is established'[42]. The emotional forcing which Lawrence underwent in childhood is, however, the condition of that power to sense fluctuations of mood in slight changes of facial expression, in unconscious gestures and movements of the body, which enables him to record what he terms 'the pulse and flow of attraction and recoil'[43] between

212

people with a sensuous immediacy, unprecedented in fiction. He is akin to the originators of the stream of consciousness technique in his novels *The Rainbow* (1915) and *Women in Love* (1920) where he dispenses with the conventions of plot and characterization to render undercurrents of feeling in a language which remains largely metaphoric and so never rationalizes the phenomena of sympathy and antipathy it presents. And as an attempt to give a cross-section of modern society through characters who embody conflicting tendencies and strive towards a valid synthesis, the two novels are as ambitious as any by Thomas Mann or Musil.

In *The Rainbow*, Lawrence traces the struggle of a family to rise from the 'blood-intimacy'[44] of peasant-life towards a higher awareness, a struggle which shows in the ever more exacting demands which are brought to bear on their marriages by the wives and husbands of each succeeding generation. This evolutionary process which coincides with the irruption of modern industry into a timeless rural world, reaches a climax in the third generation, with Ursula Brangwen who is, like Lawrence, exposed in childhood to a parent's excessive emotional claims and prematurely awakened; like Lawrence, she goes to secondary school and becomes a student at Nottingham University College. Her troubled quest for a balanced love-relationship is the theme of the last chapters of *The Rainbow* and the novel *Women in Love*. By this time, Lawrence had learned to interpret the faulty attitudes of his parents in terms of tendencies inherent in the modern world. Under the impact of marriage with Frieda which he found so difficult because of the adverse conditioning he had undergone in childhood – he has chronicled the difficulties in the cycle of poems 'Look! We have come through!' – Lawrence had come to read a general sociological significance into his mother's contempt for the physical and sensual which had led her to reject her husband and to seek fulfilment in what she regarded as a superior, because purely spiritual, love-relationship with her son: it was symptomatic of the triumph of ideas, of ideals and of mind-directed will-power over human spontaneity and vitality in the economic and political structures of modern society. In *The Rainbow*, the failure of Skrebensky as the lover of Ursula is attributed to his incapacity to find the purpose of his existence intuitively, in response to the impulses which come to man from what Lawrence regards as the supra-personal sources of life; because of his deficiency in vitality, Skrebensky feels compelled to justify his existence in terms of an ideal: that of service in a democratic state which exists to promote prosperity and equality. A more advanced condition of what Lawrence diagnoses as modern degeneracy is represented by Ursula's uncle, the colliery-manager, in *The Rainbow*, and by Gerald Crich in *Women in Love*, men who seek compensation in the perfecting of machinery for their inability to live spontaneously. The world of the coal-mine which had been presented as strangely beautiful in some of Lawrence's early stories, and as providing the miners with an experience of satisfying physical achievement and of comradeship, becomes a symbol of the mechanization of human life in the later fiction.

The same determination to draw a general conclusion from personal childhood experiences and to substantiate it in terms of current Vitalist theory, is evident in Lawrence's polemics against humanitarian ethics and the Christian precept of charity. Mrs Lawrence had disparaged aggression and assertiveness in her sons, and in retrospect Lawrence came to see this also as a damaging interference with natural impulses. In *Women in Love*, Thomas Crich, the father of Gerald, makes his wife ill by his practice of a supposedly perverse Christian philanthropy. And in the tale *The Ladybird*, the humanitarianism of Lady Beveridge produces psychic malaise in her husband and her daughter. Lawrence insisted that marriage-partners should fight out their differences openly, and wrote in *Fantasia of the Unconscious:* 'If you (the husband) hate anything she (the wife) does, turn on her in a fury. Harry her, and make her life a hell, so long as the real hot rage is in you. Don't silently hate her, or silently forbear . . . you should never swallow your bile. It makes you go all wrong inside. Always let fly, tooth and nail, and never repent, no matter what sort of a figure you make.'[45] In *The Rainbow, Women in Love*, and the later novels, the lovers and marriage-partners are not inhibited by any considerations of courtesy or kindness in their conflicts which are at times pursued to the point of physical violence. What Birkin, in particular, claims to be fighting in Ursula is the feminine possessiveness which is concealed in the sentimental and idealistic conception of love; by abandoning it, she is to become capable of sustaining a polarity which would leave both of them intact as individuals but give them access through each other to the deeper sources.

In consequence of his growing tendency to substitute biological for ethical criteria in his fiction, Lawrence exposes his characters to opprobrium because they have physical defects. Already in an early short story, *Daughters of the Vicar*, published in the volume *The Prussian Officer* (1914), Louisa, the younger daughter, is credited with possessing healthy instincts because she 'was unable to regard (the Rev. Mr Massey) save with aversion. When she saw him from behind, thin and bent-shouldered, looking like a sickly lad of thirteen she disliked him exceedingly, and felt a desire to put him out of existence'[46]. When her elder sister becomes engaged to Mr Massey, Louisa is disgusted although the integrity of the clergyman, his altruism and sense of duty, are not in question: for her part, Louisa 'was glad that her blood would rise and exterminate the little man, if he came too near her'[47]. In *Lady Chatterley's Lover*, Sir Clifford is denounced in similar terms because of his impotence which is the result of a war-injury. The misanthropic rantings of later Lawrentian figures against their vitally deficient contemporaries, of Lilly in *Aaron's Rod* and of Mellors in *Lady Chatterley's Lover*, were to culminate, like Louisa's, in calls for extermination –

at a time, admittedly, when the term had not yet been made topical by the Nazis' attempt to rid the world of what they termed 'lebensunwertes Leben' – life that does not deserve to live. It is surprising that F.R. Leavis to whose impassioned advocacy must be attributed the fact that *Women in Love* is now a set book for students of English in many universities, should have been able to express approval of Louisa's revulsion from physical defect.[48] In his essay on *Hard Times*, in *The Great Tradition*, Leavis had upheld the Dickensian world as one in which 'human kindness is very insistently associated with vitality'[49]. But when he comes to Lawrence, Leavis loses sight of the moral values he had previously acknowledged. In discussing *The Fox*, Leavis goes so far as to commend the violence to which Henry, the young soldier, resorts in order to free his fiancée from the influence of Banford. *The Fox* was published in 1923 along with *The Ladybird*, a tale in which Lawrence argues that mankind cannot recover health until the impulse to violence, 'the god of anger who throws down the steeples and the factory chimneys'[50], and the god of sensual love, are accorded places of honour hitherto reserved for the god of spiritual love, and that woman should seek salvation in submission to man, and the 'modern masses' in surrender to a leader 'who is by nature an aristocrat'[51]. The message is reiterated by Lilly in the closing pages of *Aaron's Rod*: in the society of the future, he states, 'there will be profound, profound obedience in place of this love-crying, obedience to the incalculable power-urge. And men must submit to the greater soul in a man, for their guidance: and women must submit to the positive power-soul in man, for their being'[52]. The submission is to leave the man free for 'a great purposive activity' in which woman may have no part[53]. Moreover, from Louisa in *Daughters of the Vicar* to Connie in *Lady Chatterley's Lover* (1928) and Yvette in *The Virgin and the Gypsy* (1930), the Lawrentian heroine is taught the lesson which Lawrence's mother had not been able and willing to learn: that a sophisticated woman can find fulfilment in a union with a man who is socially and in formal education inferior to her, but of spontaneous vitality.

In the virulently aggressive writings of his last years, Lawrence engages in the racial mythicizing of the period. The Lawrentian spokesman in *The Plumed Serpent* (1926) says of his attempt to revive the ancient Mexican religion that 'if I want Mexicans to learn the name of Quetzalcoatl, it is because I want them to speak with the tongues of their own blood . . . the mystery is one mystery, but men must learn to see it differently'[54]. But readers who are conscious that attempts to improve upon the Judaeo-Christian religious and ethical traditions have issued in the Nazi genocides and the Gulag Archipelago, are likely to be wary of the provocative audacities of Lawrence. And yet in fairness to him it needs to be emphasized that even the tendentious fiction of his later years differs in important respects from that which enjoyed official patronage in Germany during the Nazi era. Although Lawrence shares with Nazi novelists a radical antagonism to modern urban, industrial civilization, to democracy and rationalism, he does not claim, as they do, that the 'Nordic race' is superior to other races. Above all, it is the pyschological and social empiricism of Lawrence's earlier fiction, and his innovatory techniques for rendering unconscious impulses which differentiate him from the Nazi men of letters who clung to the literary forms of the nineteenth century. In his stylistic experiments and in the frankness with which he portrayed the sexuality of his characters, Lawrence in fact practised the modernism which was prohibited in Nazi Germany.

4

The Nazi novelists are to-day out of vogue and discredited, but the fiction of some German contemporaries of theirs who were also anti-rationalistic and aesthetically conservative but in other respects antagonistic to Nazism, continues to be read. Franz Werfel, for instance, whom Musil satirized as

Feuermaul in *Der Mann ohne Eigenschaften*, published a series of historical novels, fervently religious in tendency, which have remained in print. And Hermann Hesse, who first made his mark at the turn of the century, in the wake of the Neo-Romantic movement, lived to receive the Nobel prize for literature in 1946 and to become a cult figure for American drop-outs and student rebels in the nineteen-sixties – yet another instance of an international fashion favouring, however briefly, the novelistic exponent of a traditional German malaise. In Hesse's novels and stories, as in those of his Romantic predecessors, it is only the hero, an authorial self-projection, who comes to life, whether he defies bourgeois convention in search of his true self, or alternates between contemplative withdrawal and a pursuit of erotic fulfilment which is equally autistic. Whatever their political affiliations, most German novelists of the thirties and forties abandoned the experimental techniques of the earlier twentieth century. The English novelists of the period, too, were content to cultivate traditional narrative forms again: some of the most distinguished of them, L.P. Hartley, Ivy Compton-Burnett and Elizabeth Bowen, turned once more to the exploration of personal relationships and the moral predicaments of the members of a narrow upper-middle class society. The one English novelist of those decades who reached a world-wide audience, Graham Greene, reverted not only to the plot-structures and methods of characterization which Virginia Woolf had condemned as antiquated; but, with his journalistic flair, he selected highly topical issues and settings for his fiction which, in fact, has affinities with popular genres, such as the crime and espionage thriller. And yet, Greene's novels are pervaded by an intensely personal mood, one of loneliness, boredom and dereliction, a mood which is given an objective correlative in the seedy milieux so compellingly evoked in them. And from *Brighton Rock* (1938) to *The End of the Affair* (1951), Greene provided his fiction with a deeper dimension by means of a theological formula which enjoyed high prestige in those years: the desolate mood and the environment which corresponds to it, are presented as an expression of the state of fallen man whose sense of sin is the condition of his salvation. With the passing of the Christian fashion of the nineteen-forties, Greene came to interpret his visions of human wretchedness in political rather than in theological terms.

A new note of rebellion became audible both in English and in German fiction in the decade after the end of World War II. But where England's Angry Young Men vented a personal frustration by exposing the phoney poses and clichés of an antiquated establishment and often lapsed into a facile cynicism when their resentment was exhausted, their German contemporaries had a far more powerful target in the Nazi tyranny and its legacy and a correspondingly greater sense of mission. The protest of the 'Gruppe 47' had, therefore a vigour that is not to be found in the fiction of a Kingsley Amis or a John Wain. The most notable representative of the 'Gruppe 47', Heinrich Böll, was to be translated into many languages and to become President of the International Pen Club and a recipient of the Nobel Prize for literature. He assimilated various foreign influences, including that of Graham Greene with whom he came to share not only the journalist's interest in topical issues, but a sense of the helplessness of man, isolated in a sordid milieu, and the Catholic motif. His short stories and novels of the later forties which are set in war-time Europe, expose the agony of the individuals caught up in the war-machine whether they are German conscripts or Polish and Hungarian civilians. It is a world of impersonal malice, thinly camouflaged with patriotic and other ideological clichés, in which relief and significance are provided only by occasional manifestations of genuine human emotion and unexpected glimpses of Catholic piety, prayer and self-denial. In his novels and stories of the fifties, Böll deals satirically with aspects of Germany's economic miracle. The frantic struggle now for a 'higher standard of living' is seen as a form of blind self-assertion, not altogether different in quality from the Nazis' fight for living-space. Böll finds true worth, generosity and charity more often in those who are not interested in 'making good', in outsiders and social failures even, who have resisted the pressure of society on them to conform; the successful in these novels, who are often practising Christians, are guilty of smugness, hypocrisy and Pharisaism. In the later fiction, a major threat to the integrity, the innocence and humanity of the individual is seen as coming from the collective which seeks to 'organize' him and conditions him to think of himself and others according to cliché stereotypes of race, class, or political and religious affiliation which contradict the truth of individual experience. Böll points to the consequences of Nazi generalization about the Jews, and he describes the hostility which he encountered as a German soldier in occupied Paris as murderous, too, because it was applied collectively[55].

Though symbolism is extensively deployed in Böll's fiction, his prose-style is unpretentious and keeps close to colloquial usage in order to register faithfully and vividly, with the senses not only of sight and sound, but of touch and smell, the human realities which are relevant to his intention which is avowedly that of a polemical moralist. He claims that he is not greatly concerned with formal qualities which, in his view, can sterilize art and turn it into a 'snobistisches Spiel'[56] (snobbish game). And yet, from *Billard um Halbzehn* (1959) (Billiards at Half-Past-Nine), written when formalistic criticism was once more in the ascendant, Böll resorts, not very relevantly or convincingly, to a variety of experimental techniques, from the stream of consciousness monologue and the collage-method to the form of narration which records the same phenomenon from the perspectives of different characters in turn. In *Entfernung von der Truppe* (1964) (Absent without Leave), Böll states that modern writers are tempted to cultivate experimental devices for no other reason than that the critics expect to find them in a novel. If there is a doubt as to the permanence of his literary reputation, this is not only because of the one-sidedness with which he sometimes mars his salutary messages, but because of the uncertainty about aesthetic means apparent in his adaptation of one currently fashionable technique after another to a subject-matter which is often merely topical.

When the neo-realistic vogue of the post-war era had run its course, a renewal of interest in experimental techniques became apparent not only in the work of established writers like Böll, but in that of younger German novelists who first came to the fore at that time. In England, the multi-perspective narrative had figured in cyclical fictions, such as Joyce Cary's trilogies and the Alexandria Quartet by Lawrence Durrell, where each constituent novel presents the same sequence of events from the standpoint of a different narrator, so communicating a sense of the intransparency of life. In 1959, Böll experimented with this technique within the confines of a single novel, *Billard um Halbzehn*. In the same year, Uwe Johnson had recourse to it also for the purpose of formulating irreconcilable Eastern and Western perspectives on the division of Germany: in his *Mutmassungen über Jakob* (Conjectures about Jacob), the representatives of different political positions focus in turn on the elusive figure of Jakob who is under pressure from the two competing systems to the point where his sense of identity is threatened.

The supreme literary success of the year 1959 was, however, *Die Blechtrommel* (The Tin Drum). Its author, Günter Grass, is also an experimentalist, combining elements of fantasy with a faithful rendering of the concrete actualities of daily life as, for all the differences between them, Kafka had done. The novel abounds in ambiguities, and where the fantasy is concerned, there is no agreement among critics as to whether the numerous quasi-miraculous occurrences in *Die Blechtrommel* and its sequels, *Katz und Maus* (1961) (Cat and Mouse) and *Hundejahre* (1963) (Dog Years), are

221

primarily the products of an exuberant playfulness or are meant to have some deeper symbolical significance. The narrator, Oskar, refers to himself repeatedly as 'zwiespältig', ambivalent; and his claim that the arrest of his growth in early childhood was due to his own effort and, along with the magic power of his drumming and singing, a deliberate means to resist an oppressive environment, could be accepted at its face-value, or taken as mere make-believe on his part, to compensate for the many inadequacies and failures of his life. At times, Oskar presents himself as a sardonically detached observer and cunning tactician in an absurd world, at other times as the agonized victim of a sense of guilt and of his vague fears. In some respects, he resembles Mahlke in *Katz und Maus* who makes a fraudulent adaptation to the world of persecutors which surrounds him, but in other respects he is closer to Amsel in *Hundejahre* who successfully outwits his persecutors with the help of his ironic art, the manufacture of scarecrows, which have an analogous function to that of the tin-drum in the earlier novel. The role of Oskar becomes more confusing still when he emerges from the stance of cynical commentator and amoral practitioner to become a mouth-piece for Grass's well-known views on the phenomenon of Nazism, the ethos of Poland, and other issues.

Böll's campaign against ideologically inspired stereotyping had been anticipated by Grass. The attempt by the hero of Böll's *Entfernung von der Truppe* (1964) to defy the efforts of the collectivists to classify him, by proving to them that he is simultaneously German, Jewish, and Christian, clearly derives from Grass's comic presentation of the identity-problems of his Danzig characters, with their Polish and German, Jewish and Cassubian antecedents. Grass, in turn, had been anticipated by Joyce who placed a man of mixed Irish and Jewish descent in the ethnic context of Edwardian Dublin with similar ironic effect. There are other links with Joyce. The exhaustive physical presence of Danzig in Grass's fiction is reminiscent, at times, of that of Dublin in

Ulysses; and as Joyce uses the obscene to expose the hypocrisies of the dominant orthodoxy, so Grass plays off the human-all-too-human sexual preoccupations of his characters against the phoney idealism which was rampant in the Nazi era. And Oskar's blasphemies in *Die Blechtrommel* function, rather as they do in *Ulysses*, as a reluctant tribute to the hold which Catholic beliefs and practices still have on the speaker. Grass has inherited also, possibly by way of Döblin whom he greatly admires, the skill of Joyce as a parodist of speech-patterns and literary styles. When Grass's novel first appeared, it seems to have had a liberating effect: by reviving not only the buried childhood recollections of a whole generation of readers, but their repressed memories of the Nazi period in a way which enabled them to look at it with ironic detachment, Grass broke powerful taboos and helped his countrymen to come to terms with the past.

There was no resurgence of experimental writing in the England of the late fifties and early sixties. In fact, it was the ambition of leading novelists of that time to restore the panoramic method of Victorian fiction. But C.P. Snow was no more capable of breathing life into his painstaking reconstructions of intrigues in the 'corridors of power', than he was of integrating public and private aspects of the lives of his characters in the manner of Trollope on whom he modelled himself. And Angus Wilson's attempt to resuscitate the elaborate plot and wide range of representative characters of a Dickens novel shows up as contrived and literary in *Anglo-Saxon Attitudes* (1956) and *The Middle Age of Mrs Eliot* (1958): the only passages in those novels which possess vitality are those which deal, as Wilson's short stories do, with nightmare experiences of mental breakdown and the disintegration of family relationships.

Only one thorough-going experimentalist was active in English writing in the post-war era, the Anglo-Irish author Samuel Beckett; but it is significant that he has been more successful as a playwright than as a novelist, and that his

223

novels of the fifties and sixties appeared in French before the English versions were published. His method of rendering the narrowing experience of decrepit and senile characters who are never purged by their suffering, has found imitators in Germany but not in England. Wolfgang Hildesheimer, who had also first made his mark in the theatre of the absurd, traced a similar reductive process in *Tynset* (1965) and *Masante* (1973), though in monologues which are rather more cerebral than Beckett's and more explicit in interpreting the confrontation with 'nothing' as a means of transcendence.

There was no movement in England corresponding to the avant-garde which dominated German fiction in the late sixties and early seventies. Its leading exponent, Peter Handke, managed to hit the headlines with his attacks on the neo-realism of the post-war era as an anachronistic phenomenon: even the stream of consciousness method and the collage-technique had, according to Handke, become mere hackneyed mannerisms in the recent work of German novelists who continued to operate with fixed plots and characters. And yet it is hard to see that the basic arguments of Handke against contemporary realism differ intrinsically from those which Virginia Woolf had employed against Arnold Bennett fifty years earlier. Not even Jürgen Becker, with his programme of recording only what can be apprehended at a given time and in a specific locality, his deployment of documentary material and parodistic exercises in different literary styles, was able to go very far beyond what Joyce had done in *Ulysses*. And Helmut Heissenbüttel merely carries the collage-technique of earlier writers a stage further when, in *D'Alemberts Ende* (1970), he draws the names of his characters from literary history and lets them communicate with each other in quotations taken from a wide range of contemporary writers, with the purpose of relativizing all currently held intellectual positions. Peter Handke's efforts, in *Hornissen* (1966) (Hornets) and *Der Hausierer* (1967) (The Pedlar), of bringing home to the reader the fictitiousness of fiction, by exposing literary clichés, has been anticipated in Lawrence Sterne's *Tristram Shandy* and elsewhere; and his intention of achieving authenticity of expression by transcending the conventions of language which supposedly falsify our experience of reality, echoes Hofmannsthal's in the *Chandos-Brief* and that of the Viennese linguistic philosophers: Handke himself invokes Wittgenstein on several occasions. Handke's undertaking, in *Die Angst des Tormanns beim Elfmeter* (1970) (The Goalie's Fear during the Penalty-Kick), to show how someone's conventional interpretation of the external world collapses as he goes through a process of isolation which reduces him to a near-paranoiac condition, recalls Rilke's in *Die Aufzeichnungen des Malte Laurids Brigge*. A conviction that the neo-experimentalism of the sixties is derivative and a dead end has been articulated by Handke himself. In an interview in *Die Zeit,*[57] Handke disavows the avant-garde view to which he had previously subscribed, that literary progress must manifest itself in increasingly outré stylistic experiments and in ever more radical expressions of disintegration and despair; and in *Die Stunde der wahren Empfindung* (1975) (The Hour of True Sensibility), Handke is at pains to let his fictional characters reestablish communication with each other and rediscover meaning in life.

5

Both the uneasy restoration of conventional narrative methods in the fiction of the thirties, forties, and fifties, and the return, in the sixties, to an experimentalism which was derivative also, are indications, it would seem, of the decline of the novel as a literary form in the twentieth century. A lack of conviction and vitality was more apparent, perhaps, in English fiction of the post-war years than in that of Germany where the traumatic experience of Nazism and its aftermath provided a special challenge and a stimulant to writers. Few critics, however, would claim that even the novels of a Böll or a Grass are comparable in stature to the oeuvres of the major novelists of the nineteenth and early twentieth centuries. And corresponding to the falling-off in the quality of the fiction produced, there has been a discernible shrinking of the market for serious fiction in recent decades. A feature of the publishing-world of the sixties has been the absorption by large financial corporations such as the Springer-group in Germany and the Time-Life complex in the United States, of many of the old family-firms which had grown wealthy and famous through the publication of fiction in the nineteenth century. For the rapid rise in the costs of book-production since World War II had adversely affected the publication of serious fiction. The Swedish publisher Per Gedin has recently presented statistics which show that up to 1950 a sale of 2000 copies made a novel profitable to a publisher but that by 1974 'a printing of 10,000 copies of which 90 per cent must be sold, was necessary to yield a decent profit'.[58] This situation favours the bestseller, and makes it hard for unknown and original authors to find a publisher. Moreover, readership surveys carried out in a number of countries indicate that the time allotted to the reading of books has diminished significantly over a period of forty years.[59] Though more people receive secondary education than formerly and working-hours have been reduced, the coming of the affluent consumer-society has brought a wider range of alternative pastimes within the reach of many. People who possess and use television-sets, record-players, cameras, cars, and other equipment, have correspondingly less time to read novels. Family-reading of fiction, a common leisure-pursuit in the nineteenth century, is no longer practised, and in the mass-society of our time literary culture has lost the social prestige which it enjoyed in the era of bourgeois ascendancy. And not only the television-serial and the television-documentary, but popular psychology and sociology, available in paperback, have usurped some of the informative and critical functions which the novel once performed. It is not surprising, therefore, to find that, according to the statistics, the proportion of fiction in the total book-output has steadily diminished since the war, although cheap popular novels – romances, westerns, crime- and spy-thrillers, war-novels and science fiction –have held their own.[60] It appears that in countries of the Soviet orbit, including East Germany, where publishing-firms are state-owned and not required to make a profit, the percentage share of fiction in the total book-output has not fallen to the same extent as in the West. This, however, may not be evidence of a condition favourable to the creation of literature. The absence of a consumer-orientated system means that there are fewer forms of entertainment available as alternatives to reading. Strict censorship and the imposition of the doctrine of Socialist Realism has meant the promotion of propagandist fiction and discrimination against honest and original work. Uwe Johnson was able to get his *Mutmassungen über Jakob* published only after he had emigrated to the West. A brief spell of liberalization in the mid-sixties made possible the publication of a work as critical and searching as Christa Wolf's *Nachdenken über Christa T.* (1968) (Reflection about Christa T.); but it was soon out of print and hard to come by in East Germany and became widely known only after its publication in the West.

While it is certain, therefore, that fiction of some kind will continue to be published in the foreseeable future, it is unlikely that under present conditions it can again attain the stature, or fulfil the central cultural role, of nineteenth century fiction. It would appear, indeed, that the great era of the novel was coterminous with that of the bourgeoisie: if the pioneering fictions of Daniel Defoe reflected the rise of the English middle-class, its decline was marked by the disintegration of the realistic novel in the experimentalism of the early twentieth century. But then, every great literary form has been the product of a particular culture with a limited life-

227

span, encompassing periods of germination, of blossoming and of decay. The great epic and lyric poetry of ancient Rome was produced within the space of two centuries, and so was the poetry that expressed the courtly culture of the High Middle Ages. The Baroque theatre originated in the sixteenth century when the medieval tradition of the miracle and chronicle play was transformed under the influence of classical Latin drama which had been revived at courts and centres of learning. The greatest achievements of Baroque drama were manifestations of unique cultures, those of the royal courts in the new centralized nation-states of England, Spain and France. And the 'classical' novel, that of social realism, rose and fell with the bourgeois society which it interpreted.

Reference has been made to various critics who, through the ages, have remarked on the paucity of the German as compared with the English contribution to this genre. They have, as a rule, done little more than formulate over-all impressions. The present study, therefore, is an attempt to trace in some detail the development and interaction of the English and the German novel in order to establish with greater precision than has hitherto been done, the respective characteristics, the strengths and weaknesses of the two contrasting traditions. We saw that the novel which sought to portray a contemporary social world objectively, made its first appearance in England, in the early eighteenth century; for the English middle-class had been the first to emancipate itself from feudal restrictions and to achieve affluence and power. Attempts by German writers to contribute to this literary movement, proved problematical. In the eighteenth century, Germany, too, possessed a reading-public avid for the new fiction: translations of Defoe and his English successors headed the German bestseller-list decade after decade. And, as is evident from the numerous German imitations that appeared, there was no lack, either, of German men-of-letters anxious to provide fiction of the new type. But their exclusion from the aristocratic centres of power in a politically fragmented country, their relative isolation in academic surroundings, prevented them from acquiring the experience which they needed if they were to create an empirical fiction on the English model.

However, from a mass of unsuccessful German attempts to portray social life in the manner of Fielding, a type of novel came to stand out in which at least the central figure was plausible, a self-portrait of the author as an isolated artist at loggerheads with a philistine world. So there emerged a specifically German form of prose-fiction, and the poetic utopianism of the 'Bildungsroman' the metaphysical theme and allegorical form of the 'Novelle', compensated to some degree for the deficiency of the empirical content of this fiction. The apotheosis of art and the artist led, in Jean Paul, in Novalis, to a rejection of society and of empirical life, and an abandonment to the imagination which culminated in mystical transcendence. But after writing his *Werther*, Goethe turned away from a 'diastole' which seemed to threaten the artist with psychological disintegration, and proclaimed a 'systolic' submission to the constraints of social reality. The later Romantics favoured a balance between the opposing impulses of diastole and systole – as Jane Austen does in *Sense and Sensibility*; but the Germans expressed by means of poetic allegory what the English writer was able to render in a realistic medium, and this limited their appeal. With the restoration of princely absolutism after the downfall of Napoleon and the defeat of German liberalism in the eighteen-thirties and -forties, the pattern established in the eighteenth century was perpetuated: the German public turned once again to translations from the English, and German writers, whether they tried to imitate Dickens and Thackeray, or like Stifter and Keller, continued to cultivate characteristic German genres and themes, suffered relative neglect. Only towards the end of the century did a writer emerge, Theodor Fontane, who was able to treat, in a realistically rendered German context, the social and psychological issues which had preoccupied his English precursors. And yet he, too, received only limited recognition in Germany and hardly any abroad; for the era of social realism was over by now. The aestheticist movement was in the ascendant. For with the decline of the bourgeois order and the rise of a mass-society, the power-élites in the great Western countries had ceased to command the allegiance of intellectuals and artists, and the expression of alienation became a primary concern of writers everywhere. The panoramic method was no longer at the disposal of novelists, and in the early twentieth century the traditional forms of fiction were abandoned by the experimentalists who aimed at rendering the unconscious as well as the conscious minds of isolated individuals. In this cultural climate, German writers could come into their own: for on the one hand, the age-old German malaise and the perennial theme of German fiction, the conflict between the isolated individual and society, had become universal; on the other hand, German writers had, with Fontane, become skilled at portraying the concrete actualities of daily life. And so it happened that German literature, in the age of Thomas Mann, of Kafka, met with a world-wide response. But the gulf between quality-fiction and popular fiction had widened, and the twentieth century innovators were able to appeal only to a public of sophisticated readers, not to a wide audience as the nineteenth century realists had done. Moreover, authors like Joyce and Musil wrote as lonely outsiders, contemptuously exposing the decadence of contemporary civilization, where the English realists had accepted their society even though they criticized it.

In this respect, the English realists had shared an advantage with the classical authors of Greece and Rome, of the High Middle Ages and the Baroque period, who had regarded themselves as integral members and, indeed, as spokesmen of their respective historical communities; and it is for this

230

reason that one is, perhaps, entitled to refer to the creators of the novel of social realism, the representative art-form of the bourgeois period, as the 'classical' novelists. In 1795, Goethe argued that the political and social circumstances of Germany did not permit the creation of a classical literature: national unity and greatness, conspicuously lacking in the Germany of his era, were among the necessary conditions for the emergence of classical writing.[61] And it is indeed true that 'classical' fiction – the realistic novel – has flourished only in the great nation-states of the eighteenth and nineteenth centuries, first in England and subsequently in France and in Russia. But instead of deploring the fact that there has not been a fourth major contribution, a German one, to the fiction of realism, we should perhaps be thankful to have had another, a complementary narrative tradition in Germany, one which articulated the experience and vision of isolated individuals in the bourgeois era. Not only did this German tradition produce works of instrinsic interest and value, but it pointed the way for the fiction of the twentieth century which everywhere focused on the inner subjective experience of men in a fragmented society – a century, admittedly, in which the novel has forfeited its central role in the cultural life of the West.

Notes

I. The Novel in the Age of Romanticism

1   Henry Remak, in *Comparative Literature: Method and Perspective*, ed. N.P. Stallknecht and H. Franz (Carbondale, 1961), p.3.

2   Otto Ludwig, *Gesammelte Schriften*, vol. 6 (Leipzig, 1891), p.79.

3   Wilhelm Dilthey, *Die grosse Phantasiedichtung* (Göttingen, 1954), p.323.

4   *Briefe die neueste Litteratur betreffend*, Brief 294, XIX (1764), p.159.

5   M. Spiegel, *Der Roman und sein Publikum im früheren 18. Jahrhundert, 1700-1767* (Bonn, 1967).

6   *Teutscher Merkur*, 2 (1773), p.80.

7   G.E. Lessing, *Hamburger Dramaturgie*, 69. Stück, in *Werke* (München, 1969), vol.2, p.564.

8   *Briefe die neueste Litteratur betreffend*, Brief 294, XIX (1764), pp.159-63.

9   J.W. v. Goethe, *Naturwissenschaftliche Schriften*, in *Werke* (Hamburger Ausgabe), 1950-60, vol. XIII, p.27; cf. also 'Ausdehnung und Zusammenziehung', ibid. vol. XIV p.83; also 'Entselbstigen' and 'Verselbsten' in *Dichtung und Wahrheit*, ibid, vol. IX, p.353.

10 J.W. v. Goethe, *Wilhelm Meisters Lehrjahre*, 5. Buch, 7. Kapitel, in *Werke* (Hamburger Ausgabe), vol. 7, pp.307-8.

11 Friedrich von Müller, *Unterhaltungen mit Goethe*, Ausgabe von R. Fischer-Lamberg (Weimar, 1959), p.66.

12   G.H. Lewes, *The Life of Goethe*, 3. edition (London, 1875), p.403.

13   J.P. Eckermann, *Gespräche mit Goethe* . . . hrsg. von H.H. Houben (Wiesbaden, 1959), p.171.

14   Stefan George, *Werke* (Düsseldorf, 1968), vol. 1, p.512.

15   Hugo von Hofmannsthal, *Prosa IV* (Frankfurt, 1955), p.208.

16   Jean Paul, 'Vorrede zu Quintus Fixlein', in *Werke in 60 Bänden* (Berlin, n.d.), vol. 3, p.10.

17   Ibid., vol. 7-10, p.501.

18   Ibid., p.573.

19   Jane Austen, *Love and Freindship* in *Volume the Second*, ed. by B.C. Southam (Oxford, 1963), pp.84-5.

20   Ibid., pp.4-5.

21   Jane Austen, *Northanger Abbey*, in *The Novels*, ed. by R.W. Chapman, 3. edition (London, 1933), p.40.

22   Ibid., p.200.

23   Ibid., p.201.

24   Jane Austen, *Sense and Sensibility*, ed. by C. Lamont (London, 1970), p.303.

25   Jane Austen, *Mansfield Park* (London, 1948), p.17.

26   Ibid., p.259.

27   Jane Austen, *Persuasion*, in *The Novels*, ed. by R.W. Chapman, 3. edition (London, 1933), p.30.

28   Ibid., p.242.

29   Novalis, *Heinrich von Ofterdingen*, in *Schriften*, hrsg. von P. Kluckhohn und R. Samuel (Stuttgart, 1960), vol. 1, p.283.

30   Ibid., p.284.

31   Ibid., p.260.

32   Ibid., p.325.

33   Ibid., p.225.

34   Ibid., p.288.

35   'The Corsair', in Byron's *Poems and Plays* (Everyman's Library) (London, 1910), vol. 2, p.192.

36 Sir Walter Scott, *The Heart of Mid-Lothian* (Everyman's Library) (London, 1906), p.169.

37 Sir Walter Scott, *The Bride of Lammermoor* (Everyman's Library) (London, 1906), p.59.

38 Sir Walter Scott, *Journal* (Edinburgh, 1927), pp.103-4.

39 Sir Walter Scott, *On Novelists and Novels*, ed. by I. Williams (London, 1968), pp.312-53.

40 Ibid., p.335.

41 Ibid., p.348.

42 Sir Walter Scott, *The Antiquary* (Everyman's Library) (London, 1907), p.121.

43 *The Bride of Lammermoor*, p.235.

44 Ibid., pp.35-6.

45 Ibid., p.41.

46 Sir Walter Scott, *Waverley* (Everyman's Library) (London, 1906), p.476.

47 Ibid., p.406.

48 G. Lukács, *The Historical Novel*, trans. by H. and S. Mitchell (Penguin Books) (Harmondsworth, 1969), p.59.

49 Sir Walter Scott, *Old Mortality* (Everyman's Library) (London, 1906), p.62.

50 *The Heart of Mid-Lothian*, p.97.

51 Heinrich Heine, *Sämtliche Schriften* (Darmstadt, 1971), vol. 4, p.162.

52 J.H. Newman, *Apologia pro Vita Sua* (London, 1889), pp.96-7.

53 Sir Walter Scott, *Ivanhoe* (Everyman's Library) (London, 1906), p.447.

54 Ibid., p.12.

55 F.R. Leavis, *The Great Tradition* (Penguin Books) (Harmondsworth, 1962), p.14.

II. Adalbert Stifter and the Reception of his Work

1 E.N. Gummer, *Dickens' Works in Germany, 1837-1937* (Oxford, 1940), p.14.

2   R. Prutz, *Deutsche Literatur der Gegenwart* (Leipzig, 1859), vol.2, p.75.

3   Gustav Freytag, *Erinnerungen* (Leipzig, 1887), p.225.

4   In a letter to Heckenast of 8 June 1861: *Sämtliche Werke* (Prag, 1904-), vol. 19, p. 282.

5   Adalbert Sifter, *Brigitta*, in *Werke* . . . hrsg. von G. Wilhelm (Berlin, 1925), vol. 2, p. 377.

6   Ibid., vol. 7, p. 288.

7   *Stimmen der Zeit*, Oct. 1858, pp. 8-10.

8   *Wiener Zeitung*, 23 Dec. 1857.

9   *Kritische Blätter für Literatur und Kunst*, 2. Jrg., vol. 1, 1858.

10 *Grenzboten*, 17. Jrg., vol. 1, 1858.

11 First published by Fehr of St. Gall and then by Insel-Verlag, Leipzig.

12 *Sämtliche Werke* (Prag, 1904-), vol. XIX, p. 282.

13 *Stimmen der Zeit*, Oct. 1858, pp. 8-10. It is of some interest that the keen concern with current German cultural and literary developments which is in evidence in English periodicals of the mid-Victorian period led to the translation of some stories by Stifter. However, the reviewers (*Athenaeum*, 1848, 1852, 1853; *Westminster Review*, 1852-53) misunderstood them, as did the publishers: when Bentley brought out six 'Novellen' by Stifter in 1850, he gave them the title *Pictures of Rural Life in Austria and Hungary*, and the translator, Mary Norman, states in the preface that the chief interest of these *Studien* consisted in their description of Central European landscapes and customs. A free translation of *Bergkristall* appeared in 1857 (*Mount Gars, or Marie's Christmas Eve*) in a volume with the title *Parker's Illustrated Stories from the Parochial Tracts*.

14 *Sämtliche Werke*, vol. XIX, p. 93.

15 Ibid., vol. XVIII, p. 94.

16 *Werke* . . . hrsg. von G. Wilhelm (Berlin, 1925), vol. 5, p. 226.

17 Ibid., vol. 1, p. 19.

18   Ibid.
20   *Sämtliche Werke*, vol. XVII, p. 239.
21   Ibid., vol. XVIII, p. 29.
22   *Werke* . . . hrsg. von G. Wilhelm (Berlin, 1925), vol. 4, p. 41.
23   In the 1849 volume of the periodical *Europa*, then in the Viennese newspaper *Der Wanderer*, 7 March 1851.
24   *Werke* . . . vol. 4, p. 44.
25   Ibid., p. 45.
26   Ibid., p. 46.
27   *Sämtliche Werke*, vol. XX, p. 273.
28   H.A. Glaser, *Die Restauration des Schönen: Stifters Nachsommer* (Stuttgart, 1965).
29   8. Auflage (Bielefeld, 1880), pp. 644-5.
30   8. Auflage (Freiburg, 1888), pp. 516-7.
31   Hermann Kluge, *Geschichte der deutschen National-Litteratur*, 26. Auflage (Altenburg, 1895).
32   Otto von Leixner, *Geschichte der deutschen Litteratur*, 5. Auflage (Leipzig, 1899).
33   Friedrich Nietzsche, *Gesammelte Werke* (München, 1923), vol. 9, p. 245.
34   It is interesting, however, to find in R. Exner's publications from Hofmannsthal's 'Nachlass' that his response to Stifter was rather more complex than is apparent from the essays, reprinted in his collected *Prosa*. See R. Exner, 'Hugo von Hofmannsthal zu Adalbert Stifter: Notizen und Entwürfe' in *Adalbert Stifter: Studien und Interpretationen*, hrsg. von Lothar Stiehm (Heidelberg, 1968).
35   *Geschichte der deutschen Literatur des neunzehnten Jahrhunderts und der Gegenwart* 4. Auflage (Wien, 1912), p. 145.
36   Adalbert Stifter, *Studien* II, hrsg. von M. Stefl (Darmstadt, 1963), p. 7.
37   *Adalbert Stifter: sein Leben und sein Werk* (Wien, 1928).

38   *Weltanschauung und Pädagogik Adalbert Stifters* (Bonn, 1930).

39   *Das Problem des Schicksals bei Adalbert Stifter* (Berlin, 1941).

40   *Realism and Reality* (Chapel Hill, 1954), p. 58.

41   *Adalbert Stifter in Selbstzeugnissen und Bilddokumenten* (Hamburg, 1965), p. 65.

42   *Adalbert Stifter* (Copenhagen, 1946), p. 1.

43   'Mensch und Schicksal in Adalbert Stifters frühen Studien', *Wirkendes Wort*, 12 (1962), pp. 12-28.

44   *Abdias*, edited with an introduction, notes and an appendix by K. Spalding (Manchester, 1966), p. xxii.

45   *Die deutsche Novelle von Goethe bis Kafka*, (Düsseldorf, 1965), vol. 2, p. 148.

46   *Studien* . . . II . . . p. 26.

47   *Adalbert Stifter: Geschichte seines Lebens*, 2. Auflage (Bern, 1958), p. 171.

48   Adalbert Stifter, *Abdias*: Erzählung, Nachwort von P. Requadt (Stuttgart, 1966).

49   *Diastole und Systole: zum Thema Jean Paul und Adalbert Stifter* (Bern, 1969).

50   'Das antagonistische Naturbild in Stifters *Studien*', in *Adalbert Stifter: Studien und Interpretationen*, hrsg. von L. Stiehm (Heidelberg, 1968), pp. 23-56.

51   *Realism and Reality*, p. 57.

52   *Adalbert Stifter: Studien und Interpretationen*, p. 48.

53   *Studien* . . . II . . . p. 97.

54   Ibid., pp. 25-6.

55   Ibid., p. 99.

56   *Erläuterungen und Dokumente (zu) Abdias*, hrsg. von U. Dittmann (Stuttgart, 1971), pp. 76-8.

57   *Diastole und Systole* . . . (Heidelberg, 1968).

58   *Poems*, edited with notes by R. Bridges, 2. edition (London, 1937), p. 12.

59   Ibid., p. 12.

60   Ibid., p. 18.

61   *Studien* . . . II . . . p. 103.

62 Ibid., p. 66.
63 *Bunte Steine* ... hrsg. von M. Stefl (Darmstadt, p. 220.
64 *Adalbert Sifter: Studien und Interpretationen*, pp. 23-56.
65 Ibid., pp. 171-88.
66 *Briefe, 1937-1947* (Frankfurt, 1963), p. 458.
67 *Adalbert Stifter: Studien und Interpretationen*, pp. 25-56.
68 Ibid., p. 164.
69 Ibid., pp. 57-68.
70 Ibid., pp. 227-44.
71 Ibid., pp. 103-20.
72 See. n. 49 above.

III. George Eliot and Gottfried Keller

1   E.N. Gummer, *Dickens' Works in Germany, 1837-1937* (Oxford, 1940).
2   See p. 41 above.
3   *Westminster Review*, LXX (Oct. 1858), pp. 488-518.
4   *The George Eliot Letters*, ed. by G.S. Haight (New Haven, 1954), vol. 2, p. 486.
5   *Westminster Review*, p. 491.
6   Ibid., p. 492.
7   Ibid., p. 497.
8   Ibid., p. 497.
9   Ibid., pp. 517-8.
10 Gottfried Keller, *Briefe und Tagebücher, 1830-1861*, hrsg. von E. Ermatinger, 3. u. 4. Auflage (Stuttgart, 1919), p. 155.
11 *The George Eliot Letters*, vol. 2, p. 153.
12 *Scenes of Clerical Life* (Everyman's Library) (London, 1910), pp. 250-1.
13 Gottfried Keller, *Sämtliche Werke*, hrsg. von J. Fränkel und C. Helbling (Zürich, 1926-48), vol. 12, p. 293.
14 Ibid., vol. 10, p. 129.

15 Ibid.
16 *The George Eliot Letters*, vol. 5, p. 48.
17 *Felix Holt*, p. 45.
18 *Vossische Zeitung*, 8 April, 1883.
19 See n. 9 above.
20 *Middlemarch*, (Everyman's Library) (London, 1909), vol. 1, p. 186.
21 *Romola* (Everyman's Library) (London, 1907), p. 310.
22 *Middlemarch*, vol. 2, p. 290.
23 *Adam Bede* (Everyman's Library) (London, 1906), p. 173.
24 *Briefe, 1861-1890* . . . (Stuttgart, 1925), p. 397.
25 *Sämtliche Werke*, vol. 7, p. 24.
26 To Barbara Leigh Smith, 12 Feb. 1853. *The George Eliot Letters*, vol. 2, p. 87.
27 *The George Eliot Letters*, vol. 3, pp. 230-1.
28 *Adam Bede*, p. 172.
29 *Sämtliche Werke*, vol. 4, p. 191.
30 Emil Ermatinger, *Gottfried Kellers Leben*, 4. u. 5. Auflage (Stuttgart, 1920), pp. 31-33, 45-50.
31 *Deutsche Literatur im bürgerlichen Realismus. 1848-1898*, 2. Auflage (Stuttgart, 1964), p. 587. See also Wolfgang Kayser, *Das Groteske* . . . (Oldenburg/Hamburg, 1957), p. 117.
32 *The George Eliot Letters*, vol. 2, p. 192.
33 *Felix Holt*, pp. 26-7.
34 *Middlemarch*, vol. 1, p. 71.
35 Ibid., p. 343.
36 *Felix Holt*, p. 205.
37 *Sämtliche Werke*, vol. 7, p. 176.
38 Ibid., vol. 8, p. 48.
39 Ibid., vol. 8, p. 373.
40 Ibid., vol. 7, p. 176.
41 *Gottfried Keller* (Frauenfeld, 1967), p. 70.
42 *Sämtliche Werke*, vol. 6, pp. 321-2.

IV. Charles Dickens and Wilhelm Raabe

1   E.N. Gummer, *Dickens' Works in Germany, 1837-1937* (Oxford, 1940), p. 95.

2   *Little Dorrit*, with . . . an introduction by Lionel Trilling (The New Oxford Illustrated Dickens) (London, 1953), pp. xv-xvi.

3   *Das Odfeld*, in Benno von Wiese, *Der deutsche Roman vom Barock bis zur Gegenwart* (Düsseldorf, 1963), vol. 2, pp. 128-45.

4   *Charles Dickens* (London, 1906), p. 150.

5   *Charles Dickens* in *The Dickens Critics*, edited by G.H. Ford and L. Lane (Ithaca, N.Y., 1961), p. 143.

6   'Charles Dickens und das Genie des erzählenden Dichters' in *Westermanns Jahrbuch der illustrirten deutschen Monatshefte*, vol. 41, Oct. 1876 – Nov. 1877, pp. 482-99, 586-602.

7   *Briefe an Jakob Auerbach* (Frankfurt, 1884), vol. 2, pp. 33-4.

8   *Die Chronik der Sperlingsgasse* in *Sämtliche Werke* (Berlin, 1935), lst ser., vol. 1, p. 39.

9   *Raabe und Dickens* (Magdeburg, 1921).

10 Una Pope-Hennessy, *Charles Dickens, 1812-1870* (London, 1946), p. 446.

11 *The Great Tradition* (London, 1962), p. 246.

12 *David Copperfield* (The New Oxford Illustrated Dickens) (London, 1948), p. 626.

13 Cf. *Collected Essays* (London, 1961), pp. 31-87.

14 *Deutsche Realisten des 19. Jahrhunderts* (Berlin, 1952), pp. 231-61.

15 Cf. his *Gedanken und Einfälle* in *Sämtliche Werke*, 3. ser., vol. 5, p. 438.

16 Hermann Pongs, *Wilhelm Raabe* (Heidelberg, 1958), p. 416.

17 *Bleak House*, with . . . an introduction by Sir Osbert Sitwell (The New Oxford Illustrated Dickens) (London, 1953), p. 57.

18 *Little Dorrit* (The New Oxford Illustrated Dickens) (London, 1953), p. 57.

19 Ibid., p. 475.

20 Ibid., pp. 302-3.

21 *Our Mutual Friend* (The New Oxford Illustrated Dickens) (London, 1952), p. 128.

22 Ibid., p. 821.

23 John Forster, *The Life of Charles Dickens*, ed. by J.W.T. Ley (London, 1928), p. 76.

24 *Oliver Twist* (Clarendon Dickens) (Oxford, 1966), p. 335.

25 *Nicholas Nickleby* (The New Oxford Illustrated Dickens) (London, 1950), p. 499.

26 Ibid., p. 561.

27 *Bleak House* (The New Oxford Illustrated Dickens) (London, 1948), p. 180.

28 *Sämtliche Werke*, i. ser., vol. 4, p. 476.

29 Hermann Pongs, *Wilhelm Raabe* (Heidelberg, 1958), p. 89.

30 See n. 3 above.

31 *Sämtliche Werke*, i. ser., vol. 4, p. 148.

32 *Wilhelm Raabe: an introduction to his novels* (Oxford, 1961).

33 *Die deutsche Novelle* . . . vol. 2, p. 198.

34 See n. 29 above.

35 *Sämtliche Werke*, i. ser., vol. 1, p. 177.

36 Ibid., 2. ser., vol. 1, p. 582.

37 Ibid.

38 Ibid., vol. 2, pp. 285-6.

39 *Gedanken und Einfälle* in *Sämtliche Werke*, 3. ser., vol. 5, p. 433.

40 Ibid., 2. ser., vol. 3, p. 268.

41 Ibid., pp. 276-7.

42 Ibid., p. 325.

43 See n. 39 above.

44 *Sämtliche Werke*, 2. ser., vol. 5, p. 54.

45   Ibid., 3. ser., vol. 2, p. 178.
46   *Oliver Twist* (Clarendon Dickens) (Oxford, 1966), p. 226.
47   *Sämtliche Werke*, 2. ser., vol. 2, p. 199.
48   *Nicholas Nickleby* (The New Oxford Illustrated Dickens) (London, 1950), p. 101.
49   *Sämtliche Werke*, 2. ser., vol. 1, p. 562.
50   *Great Expectations* (The New Oxford Illustrated Dickens) (London, 1953), pp. 377-8.
51   *Deutsche Realisten des 19. Jahrhunderts*, p. 245.
52   *Uber Wilhelm Raabes Stopfkuchen* (Leipzig, 1932).

V. Fontane and English Realism

1   See p. 1. above.
2   See p. 1. above.
3   Preface to the 1. edition of *Wanderungen durch die Mark Brandenburg*, in *Sämtliche Werke*, Abteilung II (München, 1966), vol. 1, p. 9.
4   *Sämtliche Werke*, Abteilung III (München, 1969), vol. 1, pp. 399-400.
5   *Sämtliche Werke*, Abteilung II (München, 1966), vol. 1, p. 459.
6   *The Influence of Walter Scott on the Novels of Fontane* (New York, 1922).
7   *Formen des Realismus* (München, 1964).
8   *Vossische Zeitung*, 21.2.1875.
9   *Sämtliche Werke*, Abteilung III (München, 1969), vol. 1, p. 396.
10   *Briefe* . . . Zweite Sammlung, hrsg. von O. Pniower, P. Schlenther (Berlin, 1910), vol. 2, p. 6.
11   *Sämtliche Werke*, Abteilung III (ünchen, 1969), vol. 1, p. 568.
12   *Briefe an Wilhelm und Hans Hertz, 1859-1898* . . . (Stuttgart, 1972), pp. 210-11.
13   *Sämtliche Werke*, Abteilung III (München, 1969), vol. 1, p. 140.

14 Ibid., p. 157.
15 *Briefe an den Vater, die Mutter und die Frau*, hrsg. von K. Schreinert . . . (Berlin, 1968), p. 100.
16 *The Newcomes* (The Oxford Thackeray) (London, 1908), pp. 775-6.
17 'Thackeray's *Pendennis* as a source of Fontane's *Frau Jenny Treibel*', *P.M.L.A.* 40 (1925), pp. 211-16.
18 *Briefe* . . . Zweite Sammlung . . . vol. 1, p. 413.
19 *Gesammelte Werke* (Jubiläumsausgabe) 2. Reihe: Autobiographische Werke/Briefe (Berlin, 1920), vol. 4, pp. 299-30.
20 *Romola* (Everyman's Library) (London, 1907), p. 491.
21 *Daniel Deronda* (Everyman's Library) (London, 1964), vol. 1, p. 16.
22 *Adam Bede* (Everyman's Library) (London, 1906), p. 320.
23 *Felix Holt the Radical* (Everyman's Library) (London, 1909), pp. 374-5.
24 *Sämtliche Werke*, Abteilung I (München, 1962), vol. 1, pp. 679-80.
25 *Middlemarch* (Everyman's Library) (London, 1930), vol. 2, p. 95.
26 *Sämtliche Werke*, Abteilung I (München, 1962), vol. 2, p. 120.
27 *Formen des Realismus* (München, 1964).
28 *Can You Forgive Her?* (The Oxford Trollope) (London, 1948), vol. 1, pp. 249-50.
29 Ibid., vol. 2, p. 182.
30 *John Caldigate* (The World's Classics) (London, 1946), pp. 1-2.
31 'The divided mind of Anthony Trollope', *Nineteenth Century Fiction*, 13 (June 1959), pp. 1-26.
32 *Briefe an Georg Friedlaender* . . . (Heidelberg, 1954), p. 134.
33 Ibid., p. 105.

34   *Partial Portraits* (London, 1888), p. 120.

35   *Phineas Finn*, Preface by Shane Leslie (The Oxford Trollope) (London 1949), pp. ix-x.

36   *Sämtliche Werke*, Abteilung I (München, 1962), vol. 1, pp. 571-2.

37   See n. 24 above.

38   *Sämtliche Werke*, Abteilung I (München, 1963), vol. 4, p. 237.

39   *Can You Forgive Her?* Vol. 2, pp. 152-3.

40   Ibid., vol. 1, p. 287.

41   *Sämtliche Werke*, Abteilung I (München, 1962), vol. 1, p. 692.

42   *Barchester Towers* (Everyman's Library) (London, 1906), p. 165.

43   *The Warden*, with an introduction by Ronald Knox (The Oxford Trollope) (London, 1952).

44   Richard Brinkmann, *Theodor Fontane* (München, 1967), p. 141.

45   Walter Müller-Seidel, 'Fontane – Der Stechlin' in *Der deutsche Roman* . . . hrsg. von Benno von Wiese (Düsseldorf, 1963), vol. 2, pp. 146-89.

46   *Formen des Realismus* (München, 1946).

47   *The German Novel: Studies* (Manchester, 1956), p. 214.

48   *Re-interpretations* (London, 1964), p. 341.

49   *Sämtliche Weerke*, Abteilung I (München, 1966), vol. 5, p. 247.

VI. Into the Twentieth Century

1   P.S. Bagwell and G.E. Mingay, *Britain and America, 1850-1939: a Study of economic Change* (London, 1970), p. 178.

2   M. Osawa, 'Hardy and the German men-of-letters', *Studies in English Literature*, 19 (1939), pp. 504-44.

3   *The Renaissance* (London, 1888), pp. 249-52.

4   *Phoenix: the Posthumous Papers of D.H. Lawrence*

244

(London, 1936), p. 313.

5   *Der Zauberberg* (Frankfurt, 1966), p. 686.

6   *Under Western Eyes* (Medallion Edition) (London, 1925), p. 39.

7   *Nostromo* (Everyman's Library) (London, 1957), p. 497.

8   *Victory* (Medallion Edition) (London, 1925), p. 200.

9   'Vorwort zu Joseph Conrads Roman "Der Geheimagent" ' in *Altes und Neues* . . . (Frankfurt, 1961), pp. 470-1.

10 *Prosa* II (Frankfurt, 1951), p. 4.

11 Ibid., p. 22.

12 *Die Aufzeichnungen des Malte Laurids Brigge* (Frankfurt, 1963), pp. 8-9.

13 Ibid., p. 67.

14 Ibid., pp. 60-1.

15 Ibid., p. 84.

16 Ibid., pp. 120-1.

17 Ibid., p. 216.

18 Ibid., p. 179

19 Ibid., p. 50.

20 Ibid., p. 76.

21 Ibid., p. 10.

22 Ibid., p. 157.

23 *Tagebücher*, hrsg. von Max Brod (Frankfurt, 1951), p. 420.

24 *Hochzeitsvorbereitungen auf dem Lande und andere Prosa* . . . (New York, 1953), p. 39.

25 Ibid., p. 51.

26 Ibid., p. 196.

27 *L'Être et le Néant* (Paris, 1943), p. 324, p. 635.

28 *Le Mythe de Sisyphe* (Paris, 1948), pp. 189-90.

29 *The Common Reader* (London, 1929), pp. 189-90.

30 Ibid., p. 190

31 Ibid., p. 189.

32 'Brief an G' in *Prosa, Dramen, späte Briefe*, hrsg. von

A Frisé (Hamburg, 1957), p. 724.

33 *Der Mann ohne Eigenschaften*, hrsg. von A. Frisé (Hamburg, 1952), p. 37.
34 Ibid., p. 390.
35 Ibid., p. 834.
36 Ibid., p. 797.

VI. Into the Twentieth Century

1   P.S. Bagwell and G.E. Mingay, *Britain and America, 1850-1939: a Study of economic Change* (London, 1970), p. 178.
2   M. Osawa, 'Hardy and the German men-of-letters', *Studies in English Literature*, 19 (1939), pp. 504-44.
3   *The Renaissance* (London, 1888), pp. 249-52.
4   *Phoenix: the Posthumous Papers of D.H. Lawrence* (London, 1936), p. 313.
5   *Der Zauberberg* (Frankfurt, 1966), p. 686.
6   *Under Western Eyes* (Medallion Edition) (London, 1925), p. 39.
7   *Nostromo* (Everyman's Library) (London, 1957), p. 497.
8   *Victory* (Medallion Edition) (London, 1925), p. 200.
9   'Vorwort zu Joseph Conrads Roman "Der Geheimagent" ' in *Altes und Neues* . . . (Frankfurt, 1961), pp. 470-1.
10 *Prosa* II (Frankfurt, 1951), p. 4.
11 Ibid., p. 22.
12 *Die Aufzeichnungen des Malte Laurids Brigge* (Frankfurt, 1963), pp. 8-9.
13 Ibid., p. 67.
14 Ibid., pp. 60-1.
15 Ibid., p. 84.
16 Ibid., pp. 120-1.
17 Ibid., p. 216.
18 Ibid., p. 179
19 Ibid., p. 50.

20   Ibid., p. 76.
21   Ibid., p. 10.
22   Ibid., p. 157.
23   *Tagebücher*, hrsg. von Max Brod (Frankfurt, 1951), p. 420.
24   *Hochzeitsvorbereitungen auf dem Lande und andere Prosa . . .* (New York, 1953), p. 39.
25   Ibid., p. 51.
26   Ibid., p. 196.
27   *L'Être et le Néant* (Paris, 1943), p. 324, p. 635.
28   *Le Mythe de Sisyphe* (Paris, 1948), pp. 189-90.
29   *The Common Reader* (London, 1929), pp. 189-90.
30   Ibid., p. 190
31   Ibid., p. 189.
32   'Brief an G' in *Prosa, Dramen, späte Briefe*, hrsg. von A Frisé (Hamburg, 1957), p. 724.
33   *Der Mann ohne Eigenschaften*, hrsg. von A. Frisé (Hamburg, 1952), p. 37.
34   Ibid., p. 390.
35   Ibid., p. 834.
36   Ibid., p. 797.
37   Ibid., p. 748.
38   Ibid., p. 1593.
39   Ibid., p. 1589.
40   Robert Lucas, *Frieda Lawrence: the story of Frieda von Richthofen and D.H. Lawrence*, trans. from the German by G. Skelton (London, 1973). Martin Green, *The von Richthofen Sisters* (London, 1974).
41   Émile Delavenay, *D.H. Lawrence and Edward Carpenter* (London, 1971).
42   *Fantasia of the Unconscious, and Psychoanalysis and the Unconscious* (Phoenix Edition) (London, 1961), pp. 122-3.
43   Ibid., p. 183.
44   *The Rainbow* (Phoenix Edition) (London, 1971), p. 3.
45   *Fantasia of the Unconscious*, p. 187.

46   *The Prussian Officer and other Stories* (Penguin Books) (Harmondsworth, 1945), p. 62.
47   Ibid., p. 67.
48   *D.H. Lawrence: Novelist* (Penguin Books) (Harmondsworth, 1964), pp. 75-98.
49   *The Great Tradition* (Penguin Books) (Harmondsworth, 1962), p. 254.
50   *The Ladybird* (London, 1923), p. 93.
51   Ibid., pp. 60-1.
52   *Aaron's Rod* (Penguin Books) (Harmondsworth, 1950), p. 347.
53   *Fantasia of the Unconscious*, p. 106.
54   *The Plumed Serpent* (Phoenix Edition) (London, 1955), p. 245.
55   *Hierzulande* (München, 1963), p. 31.
56   Ibid., pp. 58-9.
57   'Gespräch zwischen Peter Handke und Heinz Ludwig Arnold', *Die Zeit*, March 12, 1976: Feuilleton, p. 17.
58   *Literature in the Marketplace*, trans. by G. Bisset (London, 1977), p. 166.
59   Ibid., pp. 95-6.
60   Ibid.
61   *Werke* (Hamburger Ausgabe) 1950-60, vol. 12, pp. 239-44.

INDEX